P9-CKJ-224

Centennial West

Essays on the Northern Tier States

Centennial West

Essays on the Northern Tier States

Edited by
WILLIAM L. LANG

University of Washington Press
Seattle and London

To Margaret Kingsland and the Montana Committee for the Humanities, for two decades of making things happen on the Northern Tier

Copyright © 1991 by the University of Washington Press
Printed in the United States of America

All rights reserved. No part of this publication may be reproduced or transmitted in any form or by any means, electronic or mechanical, including photocopy, recording, or any information storage or retrieval system, without permission in writing from the publisher.

Library of Congress Cataloging-in-Publication Data
The Centennial West : essays on the Northern Tier states / edited by
   William L. Lang.
        p.   cm.
    Papers from a conference held in Billings, Mont., in June 1989.
    Includes index.
    ISBN 0-295-96965-2 : — ISBN 0-295-96966-9 (pbk.)
        1. Northwestern States—History—Congresses.   I. Lang, William L.
F597.C45   1990
978—dc20   90-6167
                                                                CIP

The paper used in this publication meets the minimum requirements of American National Standard for Information Science—Permanence of Paper for Printed Library Materials, ANSI Z39.48-1984
⊗

Contents

Preface

THIS BOOK, LIKE MANY SUCH COLLECTIONS, HAS A SOMEWHAT CIR-
cuitous history, and its creation is the work of many hands. It began
in mid-1986, when a group of us at the Montana Historical Society
began discussing what kinds of projects we should undertake to com-
memorate the centennial of statehood in 1989. These discussions drew
in many staff members, but in the end the inevitable committee was
formed and given the task of winnowing the ideas. Reference librarian
Dave Walter, oral historian Laurie Mercier, education curator Jennifer
Jeffries Thompson, photo archivist Lory Morrow, and I, at that time
editor of *Montana, the Magazine of Western History*, sifted through the
suggestions and made up a short wish list and hoped we could find
enough money.

Out of the several projects, one stood out as especially ambitious,
very exciting, and decidedly expensive: a major conference that would
explore the histories of *all* the six states that had entered the Union
in 1889–1890, not just Montana. The admission of the Northern Tier
states—Washington, Idaho, Montana, Wyoming, North Dakota, and
South Dakota—had been the largest addition to the Union since the
original molding of the nation. We thought that made each state's centennial all the more important and serious reflection on the region's
heritage all the more desirable, knowing that celebrations in localities
in each state would surely give everyone in the region opportunity to
ballyhoo the century of statehood.

We wanted to ask some serious questions about the history of our
region. We drew up a preliminary plan and first approached the Montana Committee for the Humanities. With their encouragement and
advice, our next stop was the National Endowment for the Humanities, which awarded us a planning grant in 1987. Our charge became
more ambitious as we planned the conference. A call for academic
papers and other presentations brought several dozen proposals that
were evaluated and shaped into a program by a panel of specialists

representing each state and an impressive range of expertise: Arthur Amiotte, Pine Ridge, South Dakota; Judith Austin, Idaho State Historical Society; Robert Carriker, Gonzaga University; Paul Fees, Buffalo Bill Historical Center; H. Duane Hampton, University of Montana; Nancy Koupal, South Dakota Historical Society; William Lang, Montana Historical Society; Michael Massie, South Pass City, Wyoming; Rex Myers, South Dakota State University; David Nicandri, Washington State Historical Society; Charles Peterson, Utah State University; Susan Peterson, University of North Dakota; Paula Petrik, Montana State University; Carlos Schwantes, University of Idaho; Jennifer Jeffries Thompson, Montana Historical Society.

The project soon included far more than the usual academic program. Theatrical presentations, films, demonstrations, literary readings, even an opera, were planned for the three-day meeting, scheduled for June 22–25, 1989, in Billings, Montana. In addition, the planners included educational forums in eleven communities in the six states, to be held during 1989 and 1990 as a means of extending the conference throughout the region. The whole project came under the exceptionally able directorship of Jennifer Jeffries Thompson, who secured the NEH grant for the conference and piloted the whole project to a very successful conclusion.

Apart from the NEH-funded conference, but part of the larger planning from the beginning, was publication of *Centennial West*, a volume that would present the best of the papers submitted for the conference. All authors had the opportunity to submit their essays to an editorial review panel that included Susan Armitage, Washington State University; Judith Austin, Idaho State Historical Society; Herbert T. Hoover, University of South Dakota; Charles Peterson, Utah State University; Carlos Schwantes, University of Idaho. The panel read the submissions with great care and prepared thoughtful critiques that aided authors in revising their essays. Without the superb work by this outstanding panel of reviewers, this book would be much less than it is.

The twelve essays in this volume, while not entirely representative of the range of presentations at the Centennial West conference, are very representative of the quality of papers given at the meeting. In some cases, the essays printed here are expanded or much revised versions, but in all they are true to the general content and point of the original papers. If this book succeeds, it will do more than just document the Centennial West conference. These essays should also alert scholars and students of the region's history to the vitality of current scholarship and stimulate them to pursue questions that are just now being framed.

A book of this sort piles up a lot of debts. The largest is to the authors and to the army of humanist scholars who contribute to our knowledge of the region. To the participants in the Centennial West conference there is also a sizable debt, for without their enthusiasm and effort it would have been a bust. And further, without project director Jennifer Jeffries Thompson and her staff, the whole thing would not have happened. The book is much better because Marianne Keddington put her talented editorial pen to the manuscripts. Finally, the book is attractive and well produced because of the superb work of Julidta Tarver, Naomi Pascal, Pat Soden, and Veronica Seyd at the University of Washington Press.

W.L.

Hood River, Oregon

November 1990

Centennial West

Essays on the Northern Tier States

Introduction
A Region of Regions

WILLIAM L. LANG

UP IN THE GLASSED-IN OBSERVATION CAR ON AMTRAK'S EAST-bound "Empire Builder" passenger train a few years ago, I remember feeling a sense of environmental transit that kept pace with and then overtook my awareness of the time it took to roll across that vast landscape. The deep green of the Pacific Slope and Cascades gave way to the volcanic black and burnt brown of the Columbia scablands, and the next day, after the Glacier National Park massif slowed our travel, we shot out across Montana's Hi-Line wheat country, where Blackfeet and Assiniboine hunters had ruled supreme a century and a half ago. As the diesel locomotives pulled us by abandoned homesteads and the towns that still hold on in Montana and North Dakota, the changes in landscape seemed to dance in rhythm with the changes in culture that two centuries had rendered. The look of the land, the run of the rivers, and the cast of the sky changed so dramatically at moments that it seemed like different countries, not different states. This is not one place, I thought, it is many places, but I knew these many places had a common past.

There is a shared history among the variegated landscape of states that stretch along the northwestern perimeter of the continental United States, which has recently generated a new and celebratory label: The Centennial West. This self-congratulatory title refers to political change—some might say a politically coincidental change—but the title suggests much more than the transformation of territories to states. The six states included under the Centennial West banner—Washington, Montana, North Dakota, South Dakota, Idaho, and Wyoming—entered the Union during the span of nine months, beginning in November 1889, with the inclusion of the Dakotas, and ending in July 1890, with the admission of Idaho and Wyoming. The largest addition to the Union since the transformation of the original thirteen British colonies, the region more than matched its physical size in the economic and cultural enrichment it offered to the nation. It is in the history of those riches that we move well beyond political topics to where we can make out the shape of a region in history.

Thinking of these states as a region, however, raises one of the bugbears of the American historical enterprise: the demarcation of discrete regions and sections. Textbook maps of the nation have colored in a variety of what are presented as historically distinct areas, from New England to the Far West. But there has always been some dissent from these groupings, based sometimes on economic differences, sometimes on cultural distinctions. In that section of the nation labeled as the West, the disputations have been pronounced. Groupings of states have been shuffled like cards. It all depends, it seems, on your purpose. And even to some extent, as recent commentators have underscored, it begins with basic terminology.[1]

In this case, the new map of the West told a story of political deliverance. For the new citizens of the six Northern Tier states, it justified a triumphant chorus of victory and an end to years of discord as victims of federal condescension and neglect. Embedded in the sometimes whining complaints that had been sent east from the territories there was a sense of camaraderie, almost unity, in their pursuit of statehood. Although the new states hardly constituted a political bloc—Washington, Montana, and South Dakota lined up in the Democratic column, while Idaho, Wyoming, and North Dakota fell in with the Republicans—the new political map, inked with the bold lines of permanent statehood in the West, seemed to graphically announce the birth of a new region. But perhaps that just begs the question. Putting aside the importance of the political transformation, can we truly call these new states a region?

Common to definitions of region, whether from historians, geographers, or economists, is the description of place, which may rest itself on a surveyed landscape or be as relatively unformed as a retail market area. The characteristic feature is the idea of boundaries, that this place is in some fundamental way distinguishable from other places.

But does that mean an area apart, an isolated place? In 1938, Howard Odum and Harry Moore addressed that question, emphasizing that regions are the "elemental" components of the national mosaic and regionalism is properly the discovery of unity and cohesiveness in historical change—a distinctive pattern, almost an ethos, that could be attached to place. More recently, Richard Maxwell Brown has described the current emphasis on regionalism as an expression of connection between people and place, of "individual and family identity through identification with the region."[2]

Introducing human perspective and viewpoint into the idea of region and place necessarily diminishes the dominance of the environment. It posits an equity between the influence of our imagination and the power of environment. And it poses a question: Is the idea of region inherently vested in the land, or is it merely how we see that land? Geographers have been evaluating the balance of this proposition for some time and their conclusions offer up intriguing suggestions about the relationship of region and history.

In refining their definitions of region and place, geographers like Donald Meinig and Edward Relph emphasize that people, not the land itself, give places meaning. A region is a congeries of things, forms, and creations that are given pattern and substance by the people who live within it and those who look at it from outside. We create borders that are often physical and graphic, but we are as likely to fabricate invisible ones, which express how we think about the landscape. Yi-fu Tuan describes the construction of place in the human mind as a selective mingling of the functional and the aesthetic elements in a landscape. The creation of home, a place of like-minded people, is mythic, David Sopher emphasizes, and it often identifies and elevates the idiosyncratic to the position of an icon. In San Francisco it is a cable car, but in Butte, Montana, it is a yawning, open-pit copper mine.[3]

This discussion has taken us some distance from the Centennial West, but the idea of region and place is implicitly and explicitly embedded in the essays that appear in this volume. While the authors do not head directly at the subject of regionalism, each contributes to our understanding of some of the main themes in the history of the Centennial West: the discontinuous and continuous in our history; the image of the West as an economic colony; the expectations and realities of settlement; and the creation of new institutions and culture.

The polar forces of continuity and discontinuity in the history of Native Americans in the Northern Tier are addressed in three essays. Frank Pommersheim's exploration of the Indian reservation as place plots the story of calamitous discontinuities and powerfully creative continuities in the saga of South Dakota's reservations. Pommersheim describes the successive batterings of Sioux Indian culture and the steady diminution of their reservation lands, but he focuses more on Indian cultural survival. Carole Barrett, however, finds the discontinuous overwhelming in the Sioux Act of 1889, which made the Standing Rock Sioux tribe disfunctional, split up the Great Sioux Reservation, and cut the Indians off completely from their traditional life. Barrett thinks the conjunction and coincidence of statehood achieved and Sioux tribalism destroyed should not be ignored. In the case of the Muckleshoot Indians of Washington state, there was continuity within a discontinuous history. As Kent Richards explains, the creation of a reservation located on prime agricultural land near Puget Sound during the 1850s wars fed directly into the later effort to transform Native Americans into Christian, family farmers. As with other tribes, reservation life cut off the Muckleshoot Indians from their traditional life, but unlike other tribes they succeeded as agriculturalists well into this century, even as whites purchased their land and diminished the Muckleshoot reservation. In the end, it was the same story as was played out elsewhere in the West: Indian rights were discarded in lieu of the whites' pursuit of the economic main chance.

The Northern Tier as a zone of economic opportunity is a theme of development as old as the first white investments in the region's fur trade. Today, as it was a century and more ago, the region is dominated by a natural resource economy, and to one degree or another that has meant exploitation. William G. Robbins considers the history of natural resource development in the northern West as typical of other colonial economies in the world, where absentee investors wrung great profits from the region by remote control with no consideration for the future or for local economics. In timber and mining industries, the images are plunderous and the methods rapacious.

On the dry-land and irrigated farming frontiers, the images are hucksterish and the methods opportunistic. The resultant economic history of the Northern Tier is colonial, Robbins argues, because it was not the communities but the wealth in the land that drew investment. Remote from the centers of financial and cultural power, the Northern Tier became a colony in America's hinterland.

From the beginning, the region's distance from markets and metropolitan power had incarcerated it in a capital-poor prison. Partial deliverance came with the railroad, the most dynamic machine of economic change to come to the Northern Tier. John Hudson's analysis challenges the common view that the railroads brought urbanization to the northern West. It was the market they pursued, and in that pursuit James J. Hill, the Northern Pacific managers, and the Milwaukie Road planners plopped small agricultural towns along their lines as shipping points to freight out the resource they coveted. In many ways, the railroads were transit lines to the colonial region.

Those lines, extending through the grain fields of the Dakotas and ranches of eastern Montana and Wyoming and to the mines of Montana and Idaho, brought industrialism to the Northern Tier. Railroads employed thousands of workers. Along with miners, loggers, and other wageworkers, the railroad men often were the first to feel the sting of recessions as the railroads lowered wages or laid off workers.[4] W. Thomas White's comparison of the Pullman Boycott of 1894 and the Shopmen's Strike in 1922 reveals a constancy in Northern Tier labor relations. In communities across the region, residents pointed blaming fingers at the railroads and gave strikers support, even during the 1920s when fear of radicalism seemed to put an indelible mark on all dissenters.

Many of the reactions to the railroad companies' tactics, White makes clear, were also expressions of anger at the distant corporations' disdain for the welfare of Northern Tier communities. It was part and parcel of the ongoing drama—economic dependency that afforded people in the region only reactive roles. In many ways, as recent studies of the twentieth century West make clear, the script remains much the same: natural resource economies remain dependent, and relative isolation still plagues the Northern Tier.[5]

A second partial deliverance came with the huge New Deal investments in the Northern Tier during the 1930s. Leonard Arrington and Don Reading assay the importance of those investments during a period of extreme economic deprivation, when Montana's unemployment rate—22 per cent—topped the nation. The Northern Tier states were near the top in per capita expenditures during the New Deal, which serves to point up how dependent they were on a natural resource economy; states with more balanced economies received far less New Deal money. While the New Deal, as Arrington and Reading conclude, established the principle of federal responsibility for aid in the face of national and regional disasters, the realities of Northern Tier economics remained as they had been. As William G. Robbins has commented, the region was still "at the end of the cracked whip" of the national market economy.[6]

People who chose the northern West came to the region in hopes of carving out a more independent existence, presumably with more opportunity. Why settlers came and why they stayed, despite the hardships meted out by an often austere environment and hegemonic forces beyond their control, is the question Paula Nelson poses in her study of the area west of the Missouri River in South Dakota. The country was built on faith, Nelson concludes, a faith in God's benevolence and the work ethic. The country gave up its riches reluctantly, and the settlers struggled against the odds. As happened also in North Dakota and Montana, catastrophic climate changes—first the drought of the twenties and then the seering winds of depression in the thirties—should have demythologized their faith, but they have continued to believe in "next year country." Nelson's west river people have created their own country of hope as a bulwark against some of the harsh realities of the northern West.

The realities of community posed a different set of challenges to settlers in the Northern Tier. Frederick Jackson Turner, seminal historian of the West, argued that, in matters of government and institutional life on the frontier, innovation meant success and conservatism meant failure. When we turn our attention to political institutions, as William Lass does, it is not altogether clear whether innovation or imitation was regnant. Lass describes the first effort to create a Dakota Territory as a blend of political and economic opportunism that tried to transform squatter sovereignty into legitimate government. The use of squatter's rights is old, but the manipulations employed by Minnesotans who stood to gain from a Dakota Territory were creative. As Turner's critics have charged before, frontier political institutions do not prove the case for western exceptionalism.

The case of western exceptionalism in the prosecution of law and in law enforcement is another question. The popular image of the West—especially the mining districts of the Northern Tier—as violent and usually coupled with the advent of western vigilantism underscores western exceptionalism in the application of law. In his investigation of federal law enforcement in the Northern Tier, Roland DeLorme finds little to support the idea that the region was more violent than more settled areas or that law enforcement was exceptionally inept. The differences that existed related to relative isolation, the immense distances between settlements, and a parsimonious federal bureaucracy.

The image of the Northern Tier as a harsh and exceptional environment for law and lawyers is where John Wunder begins, and his findings convince him that the region developed a unique legal culture. His examples are divorce law and Native American competency in court. Wunder finds that at least in part because of frontier conditions, courts in the northern West gave divorce petitioners more liberal tests and easier avenues to break the bonds of marriage. Those courts also allowed Indian testimony, which was at variance with the practice of other western states. This suggests that the region's legal personality was independent and that it created a new identity.

The topic of identity brings us back to the question of region and what that might mean today and in our history. If there is a cultural identity that we can attach to the Northern Tier, what would it look like? Donald Worster's answer recognizes the power of environment and how people have and still view their land. The landscape is part of their reactions to life, to its problems and solutions. More importantly, it has been a subtle part of the experience of living in the Northern Tier, embedded in the mundane. Worster's summation suggests the question posed earlier in this essay—whether it is the land or our vision of it that defines place, that gives it and us identity.

Wallace Stegner offers a partial answer. He finds that it is some of both and a bit more. It takes land, people, *and* time. "A place is not a place," he writes, "until people have been born in it, have grown up in it, lived in it, known it, died in it."[7] Region and a place within it, then, is a piece of living history that continually undergoes revision.

A century of change had altered the Northern Tier landscape I had looked at from the "Empire Builder." The environmental transit I experienced on that Amtrak journey across the Northern Tier disclosed many regions and many historical changes within that larger space. Beyond the region, at the end of that trip in metropolitan Minneapolis-St. Paul, I was struck with how singular the stretched-out landscape to the west looked—much as it may have appeared to James J. Hill a century ago, when the Northern Tier was understood in the first place as a hinterland. Then and now, it nurtures many places that are genuine, surprisingly distinct unto themselves, and indigenously fascinating. If we are to get the picture of this region right, those places must be painted true to their own colors, which have changed with the decades.

Notes

1. Patricia Nelson Limerick, in *Legacy of Conquest: The Unbroken Past of the American West* (New York: Norton, 1987), 21–32, emphasizes that the term "frontier," as used by Frederick Jackson Turner, underscored discontinuity and should be abandoned to embrace continuity as the new guide in exploring western history. William Cronon, in "Revisiting the Vanishing Frontier: The Legacy of Frederick Jackson Turner," *Western Historical Quarterly* 18 (April 1987): 154–76, reviews Turner's normative terms, suggesting that the most important is the idea of "movement," which should lead regional historians to the investigation of the interaction between pioneer and settled societies. Michael P. Malone, "Beyond the Last Frontier: Toward a New Approach to Western American History," *Western Historical Quarterly* 20 (November 1989): 407–27, encourages historians to recognize the limitations of earlier definitions of "frontier" and replace it with "globalization," which more accurately reflects the place of frontier in historical development. In "New West, True West: Interpreting the Region's History," *Western Historical Quarterly* 18 (April 1987): 141–56, Donald Worster calls the "true West" not the advancing frontier but the interface between people and their environment in an essentially arid region.

2. Howard W. Odum and Harry Estill Moore, *American Regionalism: A Cultural-Historical Approach to National Integration* (New York: Henry Holt and Company, 1938), 6, 13, 16, 18, 39; Richard Maxwell Brown, "The New Re-

gionalism in America, 1970–1981," in William G. Robbins, Robert J. Frank, Richard E. Ross, eds., *Regionalism and the Pacific Northwest* (Corvallis: Oregon State University Press, 1983), 61. For works on regionalism and especially regions in the Trans-Mississippi West, see Merrill Jensen, ed., *Regionalism in America* (Madison: University of Wisconsin Press, 1951); Daniel Elazar, *Cities of the Prairie: The Metropolitan Frontier and American Politics* (New York: Basic Books, 1970); Raymond D. Gastil, *Cultural Regions of the United States* (Seattle: University of Washington Press, 1975); Richard Jensen, "On Modernizing Frederick Jackson Turner: The Historiography of Regionalism," *Western Historical Quarterly* 11 (July 1980): 307–22; Clyde F. Kohn, "Regions and Regionalizing," *Journal of Geography* 69 (1970): 134–40; Raymond D. Gastil et al., "A Symposium: The Pacific Northwest as a Cultural Region," *Pacific Northwest Quarterly* 64 (October 1973): 147–62; Spencer C. Olin, Jr., "Toward a Synthesis of the Political and Social History of the American West," *Pacific Historical Review* 55 (November 1986): 599–612; Carl Abbott, "United States Regional History as an Instructional Field: The Practice of College and University History Departments," *Western Historical Quarterly* 21 (May 1990): 197–217.

3. For development of the ideas suggested in this paragraph, see Donald W. Meinig, ed., *The Interpretation of Ordinary Landscapes: Geographical Essays* (New York: Oxford University Press, 1979); Donald W. Meinig, "American Wests, Preface to a Geographical Interpretation," *Annals, Association of American Geographers* 62 (1972): 159–84; Edward Relph, *Rational Landscapes and Humanistic Geography* (London: Croom Helm, 1981); Yi-fu Tuan, *Topophilia: A Study of Environmental Perception, Attitudes, and Values* (Englewood Cliffs, N.J.: Prentice-Hall, 1974); E. V. Walter, *Placeways: A Theory of Human Environment* (Chapel Hill: University of North Carolina Press, 1988); Donald Parkes and Nigel Thrift, *Times, Spaces, and Places: A Chronogeographic Perspective* (New York: John Wiley, 1980).

4. For discussion of the wageworkers' frontier, a region differently defined, see Carlos Schwantes, "The Concept of the Wageworkers' Frontier: A Framework for Future Research," *Western Historical Quarterly* 18 (January 1987): 39–55.

5. Gerald D. Nash, *The American West in the Twentieth Century* (Albuquerque: University of New Mexico Press, 1977); Michael P. Malone and Richard Etulain, *The American West: A Twentieth Century History* (Lincoln: University of Nebraska Press, 1989); Howard R. Lamar, "Persistent Frontier: The West in the Twentieth Century," *Western Historical Quarterly* 4 (January 1973): 5–25.

6. William G. Robbins, "At the End of the Cracked Whip": The Northern West, 1880–1920," *Montana, the Magazine of Western History* 38 (Autumn 1988): 2–11.

7. Wallace Stegner, *The Idea of Place* (Ann Arbor: University of Michigan Press, 1988).

1

Persisting Reality
The Northern Tier States as
"Plundered Provinces," 1900–1940

WILLIAM G. ROBBINS

> The West of my grandparents . . . is the early West, the last home of
> the freeborn American. It is all owned in Boston and Philadelphia and
> New York and London. The freeborn American who works for one of
> those corporations is lucky if he does not have a family, for then he has
> an added option; he can afford to quit if he likes it.
> —Wallace Stegner, *Angle of Repose*

PERHAPS MORE THAN OTHER NATIONAL GROUPS, AMERICANS ARE
prone to believe in a largely mythical past, a belief that their historical traditions have been different from those occurring elsewhere.[1]
That "escape from history" permits descriptions of the subjugation of
native people as the story of unmitigated success, of economic plunder
as the work of the industrial statesmen.[2] Reality in that sense has often
taken a back seat to mythical qualities that better served the national
purpose. The result has been a positivist refrain that describes Americans as standing on the cutting edge of progress, blazing the trail for
the rest of humanity.[3]

Although that exceptionalist view has been repeatedly attacked during the last several decades, it still lives on as a persuasive ideological
argument. That is especially true for interpretive work on the American West, where the haunting figure of Frederick Jackson Turner
has imposed such a commanding framework and design on regional
scholarship.[4] For the southwestern borderlands, David Montejano referred to a "triumphalist literature," a body of writing that enshrines
the story in terms of victory and progress: "Drama, the easy virtue to
fashion for southwestern history," he observed, "has taken the place

of explanation and interpretation." A brief perusal of the more popular chronicles on the northern West, some of them of recent vintage, suggests that the exceptionalist version is vibrant and alive in this region as well.[5]

The persistence of the Turnerian paradigm (which posits the West as exemplar of American exceptionalism) can be attributed in part to the failure of historians to develop convincing alternative models to explain the region's past—although in recent years there have been suggestions for a new direction. Even in Borderlands historiography, where the Turnerian model is most problematic, David Weber noted that no new explanatory framework has emerged to challenge the Turner myth.[6] The intention in this essay is to examine the development of the northern West from the coming of the great transcontinental railroads to the outbreak of World War II, and to place the transformation of the region against the backdrop of the ever-changing and revolutionary order of modern capitalism. Lewis Mumford's explanation, that the stability achieved under the structures of capitalism was akin to the "equilibrium of chaos," fits what is conventionally referred to as economic development from the wheat country of the Dakotas and eastern Washington to the copper mines of Montana and the timbered slopes along the Pacific Coast.[7]

It is critical to recognize that the northern West was one of the great natural resource reservoirs and investment arenas for eastern and European capital. In that sense, the region was part of the wider subordination of colonial sectors to the requirements of metropolitan-based economies. In a variety of ways the great advances in the Atlantic-centered economy depended heavily on western resources. Hence, this is a story in the exercise of power and influence, of decisions made in faraway places, of chicanery and hucksterism, of limited local autonomy, and of grass-roots suffering when the bets were called in banking centers in New York, Boston, London, Paris, and Berlin. Simply put: the transformation of the northern West was always part of a wider arena of activity, where events and circumstances in distant places influenced local conditions. During the first four decades of this century the region was progressively integrated into national and international exchange relationships. In that sense, an understanding of the wide-ranging relationships associated with modern capitalism offers unique insights to the interpretation of historical change in the northern West.[8]

The motive behind most western enterprise during the last half of the nineteenth century, according to Rodman Paul, was "the ruthless pursuit of private gain." For Robert Athearn, the most enduring historical theme for the Intermountain region was one "of exploitation and experimentation carried on by remote control." It was a place with abundant natural resources to exploit with little concern given to "what was left when the stripping was finished." Those assessments are at one with those drawn by Wallace Stegner, Joseph Kinsey Howard, K. Ross Toole, Carl Frederick Kraenzel, and Bernard DeVoto, to name only the more significant writers who have described the colonial character of the region's economic development.[9]

The most enduring historical theme for the northern West, in my view, is external control and perpetual, even revolutionary change. In a recent biographical sketch of Nannie Alderson, an early comer to southeastern Montana, William Bevis underscored the one constant of the mythic West—change: "In Nannie's ten years of ranching, the buffalo disappeared, the Indians starved, the railroad and the barbed wire came, and the market crashed. Her old West was wild and free, but much of the wildness was in the market, and the free were often left alone." [10]

Nannie Alderson was similar to others who came to that vast sweep of territory extending westward from St. Paul to the Pacific. Like so many bees clustered about the honeycomb, most of that recently arrived population hovered within striking distance of the expanding rail network that progressively linked the region to metropolitan centers in the East and on the Pacific Coast. That was a world rife with the energy of venture capitalists, some large, others small, some shrewd, discerning, and artful, others lacking in judgment and easily gulled.

Whatever one's view of the "development" of the northern West, no person looms larger during those years of frenetic activity than Canadian-born James Jerome Hill.[11] From his Summit Avenue command post in St. Paul, high atop a bluff overlooking the Mississippi River, Hill could look westward to an empire of steel rails, timber, farming, and mining enterprises that literally defied the imagination. Like a giant octopus with its head centered in St. Paul, Hill's principal vehicle to power, the Great Northern Railway Company, had extended its financial tentacles to Washington's Puget Sound by 1893. For the next fifteen years, Hill jostled with other railroad barons for strategic positioning in the resource-rich northern West, a struggle the calculating Canadian would not lose.

Hill emerged from the depression of the early 1890s with a greatly enhanced financial reputation. He shrewdly manipulated the advantages of unique geographic and marketing opportunities with ties to impressive eastern and European financiers. A soundly financed and efficiently operating line, Hill's Great Northern was in a position to deal on more than equal terms with its principal rival, the less efficient and financially troubled Northern Pacific Railroad. Finally, Hill and his London associates and J. Pierpont Morgan and the Deutsche Bank (representing a syndicate attempting to reorganize the Northern Pacific) signed the "London Agreement," which, by the turn of the century, would give Hill control of the older company. Like other entrepreneurs of the time, James J. Hill wielded enormous power.[12]

Although the famous Northern Securities case in 1904 denied a formal legal merging of the two properties, the spirit of the London Agreement meant the cessation of competition between the two roads with the intent of "protecting the common interests of both companies." In practice, according to W. Thomas White, Hill and his backers continued to dominate rail transportation in the region. But whether the "friendly and harmonious working of the two systems" would redound to the benefit of the common people of the northern West was another issue. Although Hill is billed as the "Empire Builder" by some, others have described him as the "Empire Wrecker." That acrimony persists to the present day.[13]

The great railroad buccaneer and his financial bagmen in New York, London, and Paris typified the pattern of the investment money trail during those years. John S. Kennedy, the New York-based railroad financier, worked closely with Hill, especially during the 1880s, in piecing together the web of smaller lines that became the Great Northern. Another was George Stephen, Canadian immigrant, president of the Bank of Montreal, a person with established ties to London bankers, subsequently a British baronet, and a life-long business associate of Hill.[14] There were others, some with links to the House of

Morgan, involved with financial decision making that affected even the tiniest of settlements in the northern West.

For his part, Hill kept his New York and overseas backers informed of Great Northern activities, the financial health of the line, business prospects from the Dakotas west to the Pacific, and confidential information regarding competing roads. But Hill was no doubter when it came to the Great Northern's chief competition, the Northern Pacific. When the House of Morgan moved slowly to implement the London Agreement, Hill informed Stephen that if the Great Northern were "forced into a fight with the Northern Pacific, there would be no doubt as to the outcome." Because the properties were "so intimately connected," he told Stephen, either one or the other would "pitch the key and dominate policy, and I do not think there is any room for doubt as to which that one will be." Hill was equally blunt with the Morgan interests, criticizing the expansion plans of the Northern Pacific, enterprises that would "bring about a contest which will not have any doubtful result." [15]

Hill was no less forceful and equally sanguine in his dealings with the powerful Canadian Pacific Railroad. He negotiated with William C. Van Horne, president of the road, a general strategy covering all Canadian Pacific and American matters west of Lake Superior. He suggested to George Stephen, the former head of the Canadian firm, a "permanent and safe settlement on territorial lines" that "would remove all cause for friction in the future." And then he informed Van Horne directly of his desire to "quietly discuss the matter of a territorial arrangement." Hill told the Canadian executive that he wanted an agreement where "both you and ourselves can make the fullest and greatest use of our respective railways in traffic going or coming from either side of the International boundary between Lake Superior and the Pacific." He wrote to T. G. Shaughnessy, Van Horne's successor, that he saw no "reason why we cannot work together for mutual protection . . . so as to give each other the least trouble and expense." [16] Removing the sources of friction with the Canadian Pacific was similar to Hill's effort to gain control of the Northern Pacific—to eliminate the destabilizing influence of competition.

The jurisdictional disputes between Hill's lines and those of Edward H. Harriman's Union Pacific were, if anything, even more volatile. Working with the Morgan interests, Hill outbid Harriman in 1901 for control of the Chicago, Burlington and Quincy Railroad, a line originating in Chicago with a connection extending from Nebraska to Billings, Montana. The road would also provide Hill with the opportunity to extend his influence to the Southwest. In a long and complicated struggle for control that put the stock market in a frenzy, Hill won a victory over the Harriman interests. The two now controlled nearly all of the great rail lines in the trans-Mississippi West. In the midst of those struggles, Charles H. Coster, a Morgan representative, spoke of establishing "an armed truce" between the competing lines. "If we can get matters in shape," he suggested to Hill, "we shall have done a great deal towards insuring that peace and harmony we are all striving to maintain." Putting the best light on the role that he and Hill played in the matter, Coster observed: "I am glad to read in the Good Book that peacemakers will be rewarded in the next world."[17]

Through all those years, Hill paid close attention to the warp and woof of the political world. He used his influence with politicians in the northern West to lower tariff barriers, especially those with Canada where much of his traffic originated. He corresponded frequently with business-oriented presidents, such as McKinley and Taft, and he worked tirelessly with others of his class to finance and direct the political process.[18] But entrepreneurs like Hill who could deal on equal terms with presidents of the United States, J. Pierpont Morgan, Edward H. Harriman, or the Canadian Pacific would be even more arbitrary with those who were less powerful.

At the other end of the geographical and social spectrum, in the small towns and farming communities scattered across the northern West, a different scenario was unfolding, one that was not flattering to the manipulators of capital in St. Paul, New York, and London. It is important to remember that it was the likes of James J. Hill's fellow capitalists—those who followed the rails west to invest in lumbering, mining, shipping, and other lucrative, resource-based enterprises— who were the advance guard in shaping life in the region. By the early twentieth century, the names of Rockefeller, Guggenheim, Weyerhaeuser, and Hearst controlled much of the significant economic activity that took place in the countryside beyond the rail networks. Theirs was a world that had little in common with the people who were making their homes in Montana's mining country or along the timbered slopes of western Washington—except, that is, as an environment and a people who presented opportunity for exploitation and personal gain. In that sense, the northern West was at one with similar developments in the southern Rocky Mountains and in California's great Central Valley.[19]

The two fronts of Everett, Washington—one to the markets of the Pacific Rim through the waters of Puget Sound and the other to the industrial heartland of the United States via the transcontinental rail link—would seem to place that coastal community in a favorable situation. Those natural advantages to the contrary, the community has enjoyed little sustained prosperity since its establishment in the early 1890s. An export terminal for the timber and mining resources in the surrounding hinterland, Everett is a prototype for the extractive manufacturing towns in the northern West. The community's financial history is also sprinkled with the names of some of the great entrepreneurs of the turn of the century: Hill, Rockefeller, Guggenheim, Weyerhaeuser, and the agents who did their bidding. All benefited through their investments in the region, and some, like Rockefeller, pulled out and still cleared several million dollars.[20]

Norman Clark has likened conditions in Everett during the first twenty years of this century to "competitive plunder," a system in which the capitalist class was at war with itself and with the wage earners who made their wealth possible. Although not as glamorous to newspaper editors as Montana's "War of the Copper Kings," conditions in the lumber industry produced a mercurial and destructively competitive economic environment that rivaled the cycles of instability and turbulence that afflicted the copper towns in the Big Sky state.[21] That system, in the case of Everett and other lumber towns, according to Clark, "was constantly at war with rationality and order."[22] But it was also at one with the ever-changing character of capitalism during the twentieth century, swaying oftentimes wildly in concert with cycles of prosperity and depression. In truth, the lumber industry during the twentieth century has functioned as a fully integrated component of the American economic order.

Until the great construction boom following World War II altered competitive conditions, the lumber trade on the Pacific Slope provides the classic example of easy access to timber, an over-built manufacturing capacity, and little concern for the future. That system, in which profit and loss were the major criteria for decision making, both created and impoverished communities in the timbered regions of the northern West. While investors in New York, Chicago, St. Paul, and Tacoma made the decisions to build new mills, to move on to fresh stands of timber, or to close operations when the market was tight, it was the men and women in the small lumber towns who suffered the social costs of those actions.[23]

Even in the best of times before Pearl Harbor, overproduction was the great nemesis to lumber capitalists. Because many of them had overextended their investments in timberland and manufacturing facilities, it was necessary to operate the mills, even under the worst of glutted markets, to defray bonded indebtedness and the costs of taxes and fire protection. Robert Ficken has illustrated how the Weyerhaeuser firm's profit and accounting ledgers forced decisions that further contributed to overproduction. To generate cash to pay the taxes on its great timber estate, the company built several new sawmills—at Longview, Washington, and Klamath Falls, Oregon—and purchased other existing mill sites during the late 1920s. In the year of the stock market crash, the Weyerhaeuser facilities at Longview, Snoqualmie Falls, and Everett produced by far the largest volume of lumber in the region. Even George Long, the shrewd manager who directed the company's timber operations, admitted that the new plants had come on line "at an unfortunate time for market conditions."[24]

The market-related circumstances that drove down the price of lumber wrought havoc in the woods and even rewarded wasteful practices. Those competitive conditions placed a premium on cutting, hauling out only the best logs, and then moving on to the next stand. There was no incentive to conserve, to implement sustained-yield practices, or to reforest the cut-over timberlands. While those circumstances were more pronounced in western Washington because of the industry's early beginnings there and the huge productive capacity in the region, they prevailed elsewhere as well: in the ponderosa pine country of eastern Oregon, in northern Idaho's white pine districts, and along the redwood coast in northern California.[25] The single restraint on private timberland harvests paralleled corporate behavior in market-oriented resource economies elsewhere: the need for profits and the availability of markets, not a social commitment to local communities, guided the liquidation of timber.

It was no accident that western Washington lumbering communities faced their day of reckoning in the 1930s. Two market-related calamities brought distress and misery to the region: the Great Depression and greatly reduced stands of private timber. A Forest Service study of the Grays Harbor area at mid-decade reported "excessive sawmill installations" that had been constructed "with no consideration of permanent timber supplies, but only as to a timber supply adequate to depreciate them." That the industry had lasted for fifty years could not be attributed to "planning on the part of the timber industry but rather to the huge . . . original timber supply and the restrictions on production imposed by general market conditions." [26] In brief, the market system had functioned in classic manner and to the detriment of the communities who were left with the social costs.

As for Everett, it survived through the depression years in the midst of the rusting hulks of empty, aged, and silent mills, the remnants of a period of industrial enterprise. Only the Weyerhaeuser Company with its huge financial resources, Norman Clark pointed out, was able to "thrive on the misfortunes of its competitors." As a harbinger, the firm constructed a state-of-the-art electrically powered mill in 1923, a plant that established precedents for technological efficiency. With streets named to remind its citizens of an earlier age of entrepreneur (including Rockefeller), Everett continued to move—even in the best of times after the post-World War II era—in concert with decisions made in distant places. [27] In recent years, the defense establishment has anointed Everett with a naval shipyard, which some describe as an economic savior for the community. In the larger sense, however, that development may prove as economically risky and turbulent for the town as did its earlier dependence on the lumber industry.

The long arm of the investment capitalist is more apparent in the western mining industry than in any other industrial enterprise. That "notoriously unstable and cyclical industry," Michael Malone observed, has been critically important in shaping the region's social, political, and economic order. To Malone's Montana colleague, William Lang, the story of the great mining enterprises evokes images of power, "the classic stuff of the Gilded Age political economy when corporations manipulated commonwealths at will and justified muck-rakers' vitriol."[28]

Contemplate Montana without Butte, northern Idaho without Wallace and Kellogg, or Colorado without its Telluride district—communities where working-class culture permeates the historical mosaic. The occupation may be less appealing than farming, but it is as American as motherhood and apple pie. Although mining "ran counter to the ideal expectations for the westward movement," Patricia Limerick noted that it "set the pace and direction of Western development."[29] That was especially true for the northern Rockies, where mining has been the bellwether, along with agriculture, for the region's political economy.

And the stakes were high, sufficient to invite collusion early on between Jim Hill's Great Northern and Montana's copper brokers. Marcus Daly, one of Butte's two great mining developers, informed Hill in 1893 that the sizable Anaconda Company and Great Northern property in Montana meant that "there will hardly be a Legislature meeting in the future that we will not be interested in some way." He hoped that Hill would give the subject "the importance that it deserves." He need not have worried, because the astute railroad entrepreneur took care of such matters as he would his daily business activities. Although Hill and the copper magnates differed over monetary policy, on most issues they worked in concert. It can be said that Hill's "agents" were everywhere in the states and territories of the northern West.[30]

Over the course of the twentieth century, what Montanans and others refer to as "The Company" has loomed even larger in the state's affairs than the personage of James J. Hill. The Anaconda Copper Mining Company, which emerged from the entrepreneurial jousting for control of Butte's rich copper lode, casts a greater shadow over the state's history than the Great Northern Railway. At the corporate level, according to Malone, the "battle for Butte" was "a classic instance of raw, unrestrained frontier capitalism." And like the frontier, Butte has held the public's interest: it "was rich, unabashedly exploited, turbulent—and endlessly fascinating."[31]

Butte was even more. Arnon Gutfeld, who studied the influence of the company during World War I, referred to Montana as "the ultimate example of economic colonialism in the American West." Early on in his own professional career, Ross Toole concluded that by World War I Montana "was a one company state." Joseph Kinsey Howard, Montana journalist and crusader for the just cause, was even less restrained (even though more imaginative) in his indictment of Anaconda.[32] One might quibble that his role as "Montana's Conscience" may have colored Howard's assessment of the company, but no one has yet stepped forward to say, "It ain't so, Joe."

Although Anaconda dominated Montana's industrial economy until after World War II, it did not bring stability to the region. Linked through capital ties to world economic fluctuations in metal prices, the industrial work force periodically suffered through pangs of unemployment, especially when new sources of copper entered the scene in the 1920s or when the price of ore plummeted on the international market. Anaconda itself moved heavily into "Third World" copper mining in Chile. "With the passing years," Malone concluded, "the mining industry went through cycles of boom and bust: up during the two world wars, down during the inter-war period, and then into a slow decline after 1945."[33]

That scenario aptly portrays developments in the ore metal industry beyond the Butte copper district. To the east, where the Hearst syndicate first achieved fortune, the great Homestake gold mine was an anomaly: from its beginning in 1877 and lasting until the outbreak of World War II, the Homestake venture generated great profits for its investors and regular paychecks for the miners. From its inception to 1935, the mine produced more than 80 per cent of all the gold bullion taken out of the Black Hills.[34] Homestake has been the backbone of the mining economy of South Dakota and a dominant presence in the politics of the Black Hills and beyond.

According to the company's biographer, Joseph H. Cash, however, Homestake was atypical of the mining districts in the northern West: Lead, South Dakota, the company town, "achieved and maintained a degree of stability unusual if not unique in the West." The nature of the ore being extracted and the size of the mineral body precluded the kind of instability and turbulence that occurred in Butte. But in important respects the differences between Homestake and other mining districts blur into the familiar pattern: the Hearst syndicate crushed a union organizing effort in a winter lockout (1909–1910); adopted a reactionary, antiunion stance in the aftermath; and, like other non-resident corporate owners, directed mining operations from its offices in San Francisco and siphoned great profits from the enterprise even after its control began to erode.[35]

As with other mining regions in the American West, gold also triggered the initial rush to northern Idaho's Coeur d'Alene district. But the building of a transcontinental railroad through there in the early 1880s transformed that early treasure hunt into heavily capitalized operations controlled by distant investors, including Andrew Mellon, the Union Pacific Railroad, Jay Gould, and the Bank of England. If there is continuity in the Coeur d'Alenes between mining activity during the nineteenth century and that of the late twentieth century, it rests in the economic colonialism involved. When the multinational firm, Gulf Resources, Inc., announced the closing of its Bunker Hill mining and smelting facility in Kellogg in late 1981, the event was merely the most recent in a long series of decisions made in distant places that have affected the Coeur d'Alene communities.[36] The action by Gulf Resources, one that echoes back through the years to similar corporate moves, suggests that in the world of modern capitalism extractive economies function in concert with the profit-and-loss figures in the investor's accounting books.

The emergence of the Lewisohn- and Rockefeller-controlled American Smelting and Refining Company (ASARCO) at the turn of the century established monopoly control over much of the lead-silver smelting operations in northern Idaho. The trust proved cumbersome to the Lewisohns, and within a year Meyer Guggenheim and his sons had assumed control. Through their expertise and efficiency in mining enterprises, ASARCO became an exceedingly profitable investment for those who financed its operations. Amidst the various corporate advances and strategic retreats, the largest investors made enormous profits. As for business propriety, Thomas Navin's judgment fits well: "The stakes were high and the ethics low."[37] For resident workers and their families, a different story emerges from the one that took place in the executive boardrooms in New York.

There was little autonomy to industrial activity for most of the mining areas of the northern West. Tied to events and circumstances elsewhere, the viability of life in the ore-producing districts of Idaho and southern British Columbia paralleled that of Butte. During World War I, investors in the lead-silver extractive business made great profits, production in the mines peaked, and employment was steady. But those peaceful labor relations ended with the armistice, when the workers struck. Then, when the bottom dropped out of the metal market, the owners closed the mines. Mine managers subsequently reestablished their own hiring halls, and open-shop conditions prevailed. Operations opened when the price of lead rose and closed when it declined. John Fahey observed that the 1920s passed "in cautious vigilance," and with the stock market crash of 1929 the mines closed one by one "to wait for better days."[38]

At the turn of the century, the open range was closed and new forms of agriculture emerged in the northern West: the expansion of irrigated acreage and the gospel-like spread of dry-land farming. "By 1900," Robert Athearn pointed out, "the Indians were pretty well fenced in, and the cattle kings were fenced out."[39] But while the cattle barons bewailed the passing of their species, enterprisers with innovative scientific and technological ideas were on the scene to make capital out of the new circumstances. With their sizable real estate holdings and investments in rolling stock, the great transcontinental railroads once again played a leading role in promoting those would-be agricultural paradises in areas of marginal precipitation.

At the onset of the twentieth century, agriculturalists had already taken up the best farmland in the northern West. Grain, hay, and row-crops predominated in the Willamette Valley and Puget Sound lowlands, and wheat production already had established itself in Washington's Palouse Hills and in the Dakotas' great Red River Valley. Despite the new acreages put to the plow, an equally impressive increase in cultivable land would take place between 1900 and 1920. In 1920, however, agricultural expansion took place in areas of much less precipitation. As in the earlier period (when settlers moved into the "East River" country in the Dakotas or to Washington's Palouse Hills), railroad officials actively promoted the settlement of marginal lands in the western Dakotas, in eastern Montana, and in the arid valleys between the Cascade Range and the Rocky Mountains.

Although the methods popularized as the "dry-farming system" were approved agricultural practices well before 1900, what had changed was the element of publicity. Developed in the Great Plains and promoted with evangelical fervor, the advocates of dry farming, according to Donald Meinig, viewed it "as the road to agricultural salvation for all those who struggled to wrest a living from the earth."[40] Pitchmen for the railroads and the promotional schemes of land settlement companies lured people to take up land in the arid regions of the West. For those who did, the hardships were many and immediate: summer drought, winter storms, grasshopper plagues, and a political economy that did not function in the interests of small farmers.[41]

Those who attempted dry farming on the high Plains between 1900 and 1920 were seemingly oblivious to the failures of an earlier age of agricultural expansion. Gilbert Fite has observed that although the first boom-and-bust cycle on the Plains occurred between 1878 and 1896, it was not to be the last. During the first two decades of the twentieth century, settlers once again moved beyond what Walter Prescott Webb called the "line of semi-aridity," especially to the arid lands of the northern West. Spurred on by the likes of Hardy Webster Campbell, a dry-farming advocate who found lucrative employment with the railroads, the boosters initiated a series of dry-farming congresses whose successes in promoting settlement were truly impressive.[42]

The railroads, especially James J. Hill's lines, provided most of the financing for the dry-farming congresses, commencing with the first one in 1907. In Montana, where Hill controlled three major roads, he was in an excellent situation to reap the benefits of increased settlement. But dry farming was also promoted for eastern Washington and in the south-central part of Oregon and the Deschutes River Valley. Thomas Shaw, the best known proponent of dry farming in Montana and the Dakotas, began lecturing on the subject in 1907, initiated a demonstration project three years later, and by 1911 was the chief agricultural agent for the Northern Pacific and the Great Northern.[43]

The collective promotional work of the dry-farming congresses and Shaw's tireless lecturing and pamphleteering did attract homesteaders. Many settled in western North Dakota between 1900 and 1920, and the population grew by 220,000 in Montana's eastern counties. The Great Northern Railway alone moved 135,750 new settlers to

Montana and another 64,000 to North Dakota during the ten years following 1909. But this was only a small part of a larger movement of people onto the high Canadian prairies and into Oregon and Washington. In South Dakota's "west river country," 100,000 newcomers arrived between 1900 and 1915.[44]

At first blush this repeopling of "the last frontier" would seem but another chapter in the wonders of the westward movement. And at least until the American entry into the Great War, the financial backers of dry farming—James J. Hill and his son, Louis—might be termed the great industrial and agricultural statesmen of the northern West, empire builders of epic proportions, far-sighted and social-minded with their investments. But the historical record tells a different story, one of abysmal failure everywhere in the submarginal lands. Joseph Kinsey Howard has noted that James J. Hill's grand scheme for settling the high plains with homesteaders "became a witless nightmare" as his rail cars "rattled empty through dying towns."[45]

Although the U.S. Department of Agriculture had warned that the promoters of dry farming were interested chiefly in "exploiting the attractions and resources" of the arid West, a cycle of abnormally wet years put those premonitions of disaster to shame and gave the illusion of success.[46] Bumper crops and wartime demand kept prices high through 1915 and 1916, but that second boom period, Gilbert Fite has noted, like the one that preceded it, "ended in a bust." Recurring drought and blowing soil in parts of the region, faltering prices for crops, and rising production costs (primarily in mechanized equipment) brought ruin to many.[47] In a broader sense, however, the technological shifts that occurred in farming were at one with changes in the larger arena of agriculture: the trend toward eliminating labor as a factor in production, the introduction of ever-more expensive types of mechanized equipment, and the move toward the consolidation of landholdings.

In her able study of efforts at dry farming in the Fort Rock-Christmas Lake Valley area in south-central Oregon, Barbara Allen illustrated the influence of natural and economic circumstances in the population exodus that took place. What had been billed "the promised land" became in the end "a land of bondage," and the area's population, which peaked at 1,200 in 1912, declined to 360 by 1920. Similar conditions on a larger scale prevailed in South Dakota's "west river country" where unpredictable precipitation, extremes in temperature and wind, and problematic farm prices brought a sizable out-migration. Many left, and for the few who remained, Paula Nelson has pointed out, theirs was a life based "on changed assumptions and diminished expectations"—and, she added, one "of dreams and ambitions thwarted."[48]

The drought and hard times immediately following World War I in the Dakotas and Montana were but a harbinger of the future. Depressed agricultural prices through the 1920s, recurring years of marginal precipitation, high interest rates, and the rising cost of manufactured goods brought depressed conditions to the region well before the stock market collapse. The frontier boom had turned to disaster. For Montana, Michael Malone and Richard Roeder observed, "the flood of immigration reversed itself and became an exodus to greener pastures elsewhere; and the dreams of the boosters soured into bitter memories." Carl Kraenzel indicated that the rural population for the Great Plains states was lower in 1950 than it was in 1920 (during the 1920s, the population of Montana actually decreased). The figures for South Dakota indicate even more persuasively the economic stasis in the region: between 1920 and 1985 the population increased less than 8 per cent (637,000 to 687,000).[49] Need we wonder, then, about the popularity in the inter-war period of radical protest movements like the Nonpartisan League.

Natural calamities—searing drought and high, frightening winds— accompanied the Great Depression in the states to the east of the Continental Divide. Known as the "Dirty Thirties" on the Canadian plains, an area whose physical and economic realities are similar to those of its neighboring states, the depression wrought havoc on both sides of the border. In eastern Montana's wheat country, most of the counties applied for Red Cross relief in 1931. In neighboring North Dakota, where half of the population was on relief, the economy was a shambles. In David Danbom's words, the state "had become a ward of the United States."[50]

Only the advent of another world war and a large out-migration of young people have helped maintain a semblance of social and economic stability on the Northern Plains. Occasional forays into petroleum development (in response to rising international prices) in eastern Montana and the western Dakotas have brought the briefest flurries of prosperity to a few towns. There remains, however, what Carl Kraenzel termed the "high cost of space." Public expenses for schools, highways, hospitals, and a myriad of other activities have escalated while the revenue to support those services has declined. A few years ago, before the farm foreclosures of the 1980s, Gilbert Fite warned: "As the population continues to decline on the farms and in the small towns, lack of support for institutions and essential services will bring a crisis in many communities."[51] Those changes, however, are consistent with the continued transformation of the countryside during the twentieth century.

While the high plains region, especially the western Dakotas and eastern Montana, provides the classic boom-and-bust story at the margins of American agriculture, there were more stable components to farming enterprise in the northern West. If the dreamers and investor-promoters committed a cruel hoax in enticing the "honyocker" to the semi-arid lands of the Northern Plains, in truth they had modest successes too: in the expansion of irrigated agriculture along the great sweep of the Snake River and its tributaries in southern Idaho; in Washington's fruit-growing areas in the Yakima and Wenatchee valleys; and, on a lesser scale, in Oregon's Hood River Valley.[52] But diversification of crops, small-scale, intensive-farming practices, large federal subsidies for reclamation projects, and *relatively* more stable markets were the most important factors in those achievements.

With the considerable financial support and publicity work of the Northern Pacific Railroad, private irrigation companies had constructed a series of canals and ditches in the Yakima Valley during the early 1890s. Continued promotional efforts and the construction of additional irrigation waterways tripled the valley's population by 1910. By the middle of that decade, congressman and then senator Wesley L. Jones had worked effectively with lobbyists for the railroads to commit the Reclamation Service to fully developing the Yakima Valley as a federal project; and with the onset of World War I the valley sent forth a huge volume of apples to national and international markets.[53]

Following the Northern Pacific's example in the Yakima Valley, the Great Northern initiated its own private irrigation enterprise in the

Wenatchee Valley to the north. For their part, the railroad companies did not offer the new farmland as a benevolent gift, as an exercise in generosity to would-be orchardists. One source estimated that it required about thirty-five hundred dollars for a beginning orchardist to purchase a forty-acre plot, build a small house and a few outbuildings, put in fruit trees, and pay irrigation fees. To make ends meet, heads of families had to seek seasonal work—as loggers, farmhands, or miners—to defray expenses while their orchards matured.[54]

Beyond that, there were the normal perils confronting small-scale enterprise: uncertain markets, the need to diversity crops, and malefactors lurking behind some of the irrigation schemes. In a few instances, the courts sentenced over-zealous speculators to prison terms for issuing fraudulent bonds and for bank pyramiding schemes related to canal and ditch ventures. And there were more powerful elements to deal with: the Great Northern Railway and the Northern Pacific Railroad, direct beneficiaries of the large volume of fruit and other row-crop produce shipped out of the Yakima Valley and elsewhere. "Beneficent, malignant, fickle," according to John Fahey, the railroads nevertheless provided the route to markets for the people they had lured to those new, would-be gardens. To confront the power of the railroads, growers organized market cooperatives, established warehousing schemes, and lobbied Congress to gain more favorable rate structures. They fought equally hard in state legislatures to regulate the roads.[55] But not until the advent of the motorized truck and improved highways in the late 1920s did farmers have access to alternative means of transportation.

Nowhere in the northern West is the distribution of water more important to the success of agriculture than in Idaho. The beginnings of the state's reclamation projects date from the 1890s and the fledgling farming oasis on the western fringes of the Snake River basin and in the early Mormon cooperative settlements in the southeast. The construction of a transcontinental branch line across the Snake River plain in 1884 gave those agricultural communities access to markets (and sparked the interests of still more investors).[56]

Among those grand ventures, the New York Canal (with the backing of investors from that state) was the most grandiose, but engineering problems and the lack of funds delayed the delivery of water. Not until 1890, and then under different management, did a successor firm complete a segment of ditching to the Nampa area, west of Boise. The New York Canal was not finished until after 1900, and then the new Reclamation Service provided the funds. Even at that, it required the construction of three federally funded dams on the Boise River to provide sufficient water for the canal and its extensive system of ditches.[57] Elsewhere (again with the assistance of federal money), promoters were more successful in bringing water to the Snake River plain.

With the exception of its great water diversion systems in Arizona and California, some of the largest and oldest Bureau of Reclamation operations are in Idaho. The Snake River's Minidoka Dam, which dates from the earliest years of federal reclamation projects, is one of these. Despite the construction of several dams, canals, and ditches, Idaho remained a vicious battleground for its precious water resource (thirty irrigation districts and forty different companies competed for the use of the Snake River water by 1920). The state's tradition of mixing private enterprise with federal largesse contributed to that situation; the result was chaos. After protracted deliberation, Snake River irrigators agreed to cooperate in the delivery of water and, most important, to demonstrate a common front in the quest for even larger storage facilities.[58]

But those engineering successes tell only part of the story about southern Idaho's quest for more water: dam building displaced Indian people from bottomland along the rivers; national economic dislocations drove farm prices down following the end of World War I; and an ensuing agricultural depression that lasted until 1940 put farmers in constant danger of failure. It is grand testimony to the functioning of much economic activity in the northern West that the venture capital and federal intervention that made possible the expansion in agricultural productivity also carried with it the curse of twenty years of overproduction. "Next to Montana," Ross Peterson noted, "Idaho had the highest rate of emigration of any western state during the 'roaring twenties.'"[59] The emergence during the postwar era of agribusiness giants like Simplot and ORIDA on irrigated land in southern Idaho and neighboring Oregon further eroded the agrarian dream of the small farmer.

Norman Best grew up in the small northern Idaho community of

Coeur d'Alene.[60] The famous mining district of that name, the center of protracted industrial warfare and labor radicalism before the turn of the century, lay more than forty miles to the east. Emigrés from the agricultural country around Prairie Farm, Wisconsin, where his paternal grandfather helped form the Farmers' Equity to combat extortionate railroad rates, Best's parents arrived in Coeur d'Alene in 1907 (when Norman was a year old). By that time, lumbering already had surpassed mineral production as the area's key enterprise. Best's father and his older brother worked in the woods at first, using family learned skills in horsemanship to skid heavy logs to a loading site. Two other uncles, engineers for the Great Northern Railway, worked out of Hillyard, a suburb of Spokane.

The sounds of sawmill whistles, stories about the woods, the failures and successes of railroad workers, and the struggles of the Industrial Workers of the World in the mills and logging camps filled Norman Best's growing-up years. Equally significant was the Nonpartisan League campaign in northern Idaho in the 1920 election. His father, Best later recalled, learned that farmers "were having hard times because of the low prices they received for their products and the high cost of everything they had to buy." As a consequence, his father actively supported the League's program and loaned his automobile and his son's services to chauffeur candidates through Idaho's three northern counties. Norman Best worked at several semi-skilled jobs until the early fall of 1926, when he enrolled as a student at the University of Washington. That experience ended abruptly in the spring of 1930 when the family bank in Coeur d'Alene failed. Best returned home to the life of a wage laborer.

Why is Norman Best's story pertinent to this essay? Precisely because his boyhood and youth (indeed, his entire life experience) illustrate the instability and uncertainty of economic life in the northern West. Although those volatile employment conditions existed everywhere in the United States prior to World War II, they were especially pronounced across the Northern Tier because of the extractive and colonial nature of the region's economy. "Walk the sad streets of Butte," the writer William Kittredge said recently, "a town mined and abandoned by Anaconda and ARCO and . . . see if you understand." For the last one hundred years Montana and its neighboring states were exploited as colonies, he pointed out: "The money went East, and we were left with holes in the ground."[61]

Most scholars do not consider Montana the extreme example. K. Ross Toole, a Montana historian beloved for his subjectivity, put the case bluntly for his state and, by extension, the northern West: "It is a 'raw materials' area, not a fabricating area. Its wealth in terms of minerals, timber, grass, and abundant water is enormous. But by the very nature of things the largest percentage of this wealth is not kept at home." Clark Spence, another historian of the state, concurred: together with Idaho and Wyoming, he considered Montana "one of the last strongholds" of colonialism.[62]

But was there a real difference between the "nature of things" in Montana and other extractive centers in the region? The argument presented in this essay suggests not. The northern West from the Dakota farm country west to the timbered slopes of Washington might serve as the exemplary case for exploitation in an advanced industrial nation. With the exception of the two great metropolitan centers at its opposite ends—the Twin Cities and the greater Seattle area—little happened in the region that did not have the sanction of external capital. Moreover, the persisting transformation of modern capitalism—from the corporate mergers of the turn of the century to the leveraged buy-outs and hostile take-overs of the present day—have reverberated all across the northern West. For the people who have lived through those changes—and they include the likes of Nannie Alderson where this story began—the mark of success was simply the ability to endure.

Notes

1. For a few of the best critical sources, see James O. Robertson, *American Myth, American Reality* (New York: Hill & Wang, 1980); David W. Noble, *The End of American History: Democracy, Capitalism, and the Metaphor of Two Worlds in Anglo-American Historical Writing, 1880–1980* (Minneapolis: University of Minnesota Press, 1985); Loren Baritz, *Backfire: A History of How American Culture Led Us into Vietnam and Made Us Fight the Way We Did* (New York: William Morrow, 1985); Alan Trachtenberg, *The Incorporation of America: Culture and Society in the Guilded Age* (New York: Hill & Wang, 1982); William Appleman

Williams, "Thoughts on the Fun and Purpose of Being a Historian," *OAH Newsletter* 16 (February 1988): 2–3.

2. The expression is from Warren I. Susman, *Culture as History: The Transformation of American Society in the Twentieth Century* (New York: Pantheon Books, 1984), 25.

3. Frances FitzGerald, *Fire in the Lake: The Vietnamese and the Americans in Vietnam* (New York: Random House, 1972), 9. Also see Noble, *The End of American History*, 7.

4. For an excellent analytical account of Turner's influence, see William Cronon, "Revisiting the Vanishing Frontier: The Legacy of Frederick Jackson Turner," *Western Historical Quarterly* 18 (April 1987), 157–76.

5. David Montejano, *Anglos and Mexicans in the Making of Texas* (Austin: University of Texas Press, 1987), 1. Some bicentennial state histories are especially prone to delineating the exceptional qualities of people. See Robert P. Wilkins and Wynona Huchette Wilkins, *North Dakota: A Bicentennial History* (New York: W. W. Norton, 1977), 205–8; F. Ross Peterson, *Idaho: A Bicentennial History* (New York: W. W. Norton, 1976), 182–92; Gordon B. Dodds, *Oregon: A Bicentennial History* (New York: W. W. Norton, 1977), 3–4, 229–30; T. A. Larson, *Wyoming: A Bicentennial History* (New York: W. W. Norton, 1977). Also see Gordon Dodds, *The American Northwest: A History of Oregon and Washington* (Arlington Heights, Ill.: The Forum Press, 1986), 352–3.

6. William Cronon, for one, has suggested the study of core and peripheral relations as one way to understand variations in "frontier experience." See Cronon, "Revisiting the Vanishing Frontier," 174–5. Also see David Weber, "Turner, the Boltonians, and the Borderlands," *American Historical Review* 91 (1986): 81*n*. For an excellent historiographical discussion of world-systems theory, see Steve J. Stern, "Feudalism, Capitalism, and the World-System in the Perspective of Latin America and the Caribbean," *American Historical Review* 93 (1988): 829–72.

7. Lewis Mumford, *Technics and Civilization* (New York: Harcourt, Brace and Company, 1934), 431.

8. For a discussion of the influence of capitalism as a transforming influence, see Donald Worster, *Dust Bowl: The Southern Plains in the 1930s* (New York: Oxford University Press, 1979), 5–8; Peter L. Berger, *The Capitalist Revolution: Fifty Propositions About Prosperity, Equality, and Liberty* (New York: Basic Books, 1986), 7–8, 26–27; Fernand Braudel, *Civilization and Capitalism, 15th–18th Century*, vol. 3 of *The Perspective of the World*, trans. Sian Reynolds (New York: Harper & Row, 1984), 619; Braudel, *On History*, trans. Sarah Matthews (Chicago: University of Chicago Press, 1980), 31.

9. Rodman W. Paul, *The Far West and the Great Plains in Transition, 1859–1900* (New York: Harper & Row, 1988), 299; Robert G. Athearn, *High Country Empire: The High Plains and the Rockies* (1960; reprint, Lincoln: University of

Nebraska Press, 1965), vii–viii. For the principal works by these authors that address the colonialism issue, see Wallace Stegner and Page Stegner, "Rocky Mountain Country," *Atlantic Monthly* 241 (April 1978): 45–91; Joseph Kinsey Howard, *Montana: High, Wide, and Handsome* (New Haven, Conn.: Yale University Press, 1943); K. Ross Toole, *Twentieth-Century Montana: A Land of Extremes* (Norman: University of Oklahoma Press, 1972); Carl Frederick Kraenzel, *The Great Plains in Transition* (Norman: University of Oklahoma Press, 1955); Bernard DeVoto, "The West: A Plundered Province," *Harper's Magazine* 169 (August 1934): 355–64, and several other essays in *Harper's*.

10. William Bevis, "Nannie Alderson's Frontier—And Ours," *Montana, the Magazine of Western History* 39 (Spring 1989): 33.

11. The standard biography of Hill is Albro Martin, *James J. Hill and the Opening of the Northwest* (New York: Oxford University Press, 1976). For Hill's influence at the highest levels of government, see W. Thomas White, "A Gilded-Age Businessman in Politics: James J. Hill, the Northwest, and the American Presidency, 1884–1912," *Pacific Historical Review* 57 (1988): 439–56.

12. Martin, *James J. Hill*, 430, 455–9, 464; White, "A Gilded-Age Businessman in Politics," 454. A recent history of the Great Northern argues that the 1896 agreement left real control of the reorganized Northern Pacific with the Morgan interests and the Deutsche Bank. See Ralph W. Hidy, Muriel E. Hidy, and Roy V. Scott, with Don L. Hofsommer, *The Great Northern Railway: A History* (Boston: Harvard Business School Press, 1988), 90–92.

13. Memorandum of a Conference held in London on the [date missing] of April 1896, in General Correspondence, James J. Hill Papers [Hill Papers], James Jerome Hill Reference Library, St. Paul, Minnesota [Hill Library]; White, "Gilded-Age Businessman in Politics," 448. The phrase, "Empire Wrecker," is from Bruce Nelson, *Land of the Dacotahs* (Minneapolis: University of Minnesota Press, 1946), cited in Athearn, *High Country Empire*, 173. For the favorable view of Hill, see Martin, *James J. Hill*, and Hidy et al., *The Great Northern Railway*. More critical assessments are Howard, *Montana*; W. Thomas White, "The War of the Railroad Kings: Great Northern-Northern Pacific Rivalry in Montana, 1881–1896," in *Montana and the West: Essays in Honor of K. Ross Toole*, ed. Rex C. Myers and Harry W. Fritz (Boulder, Colo.: Pruett Publishing Company, 1984), 37–54; John W. Fahey, *The Inland Empire: Unfolding Years, 1879–1929* (Seattle: University of Washington Press, 1986), 36–37.

14. For John S. Kennedy and George Stephen, see biographical sketches in card file, Hill Library. Also see Martin, *James J. Hill*, 135–8, 146–61, 159–61.

15. James J. Hill to George Stephen, September 27, 1898, General Correspondence, Hill Papers.

16. Hill to Stephen, October 9, 1898, Hill to William C. Van Horne, November 27, 1898, Hill to T. G. Shaughnessy, June 24, 1899, Hill Library. Also see Hidy et al., *Great Northern Railway*, 86–87, 92.

17. Dodds, *The American Northwest*, 140; C. H. Coster to James J. Hill,

November 26, 1898, General Correspondence, Hill Papers. For an account of the financial health of the Hill-controlled lines shortly after the turn of the century, see Hill to Charles Ellis, May 19, 1902, General Correspondence, Hill Papers. On the Hill and Harriman fight, see Hidy et al., *Great Northern Railway*, 92–93.

18. For this assessment of Hill's influence, see White, "A Gilded-Age Businessman in Politics," 451–6.

19. For a select few studies that address the various forms of economic exploitation in the northern West, see Norman H. Clark, *Mill Town: A Social History of Everett, Washington* (Seattle: University of Washington Press, 1970); Richard White, *Land Use, Environment, and Social Change: The Shaping of Island County, Washington* (Seattle: University of Washington Press, 1980); Michael P. Malone, *The Battle for Butte: Mining and Politics on the Northern Frontier, 1864–1906* (Seattle: University of Washington Press, 1981); Donald W. Meinig, *The Great Columbia Plain: A Historical Geography, 1805–1910* (Seattle: University of Washington Press, 1968); Arnon Gutfeld, *Montana's Agony: Years of War and Hysteria, 1917–1921* (Gainesville: University Presses of Florida, 1979); Carlos Schwantes, *Radical Heritage: Labor, Socialism, and Reform in Washington and British Columbia, 1885–1917* (Seattle: University of Washington Press, 1979); Brian W. Blouet and Frederick C. Luebke, eds., *The Great Plains: Environment and Culture* (Lincoln: University of Nebraska Press, 1979); Patricia Nelson Limerick, *Legacy of Conquest: The Unbroken Past of the American West* (New York: W. W. Norton, 1987); William G. Robbins, *Hard Times in Paradise: Coos Bay, Oregon, 1850–1986* (Seattle: University of Washington Press, 1988). Also see Fahey, *Inland Empire*, and Howard, *Montana*. For a sampling of similar studies of the Southwest, see Donald Worster, *Rivers of Empire: Water, Aridity, and the Growth of the American West* (New York: Pantheon Books, 1985); Worster, *Dust Bowl*; Marc Simmons, *New Mexico: An Interpretive History* (Albuquerque: University of New Mexico Press, 1988); Carl Abbott, Stephen J. Leonard, and David McComb, *Colorado: A History of the Centennial State*, rev. ed. (Boulder: Colorado Association University Press, 1982); Montejano, *Anglos and Mexicans in the Making of Texas*; Peter Wiley and Robert Gottlieb, *Empires in the Sun: The Rise of the New American West* (New York: G. P. Putnam, 1982); Cletus E. Daniel, *Bitter Harvest: A History of California Farmworkers, 1870–1941* (Berkeley: University of California Press, 1981); Carey McWilliams, *Factories in the Field: The Story of Migratory Farm Labor in California* (1935; reprint, Santa Barbara: Peregrine Publishers, 1971); McWilliams, *California: The Great Exception* (1949; reprint, Santa Barbara: Peregrine Smith, 1976).

20. The suggestion that Everett might serve as a prototype for an extractive industrial town is based on my reading of Norman Clark's classic study, *Mill Town*. See especially pp. 30–33.

21. The phrase is from a book of that title: C. B. Glasscock, *The War of the Copper Kings* (New York: Grosset & Dunlap, 1935).

22. William G. Robbins, "The Social Context of Forestry: The Pacific Northwest in the Twentieth Century," *Western Historical Quarterly* 16 (1985): 414; Clark, *Mill Town*, 233.

23. William G. Robbins, *Lumberjacks and Legislatures: Political Economy of the U.S. Lumber Industry, 1890–1941* (College Station: Texas A&M University Press, 1982), 242–8; Robbins, "Social Context of Forestry," 415–20. Also see Robbins, *Hard Times in Paradise*, 122–37.

24. Robbins, *Lumberjacks and Legislatures*, 133–71; Robert E. Ficken, *The Forested Land: A History of Lumbering in Western Washington* (Seattle: University of Washington Press, 1987), 176. Long is quoted in Ficken.

25. For a summary of the sequence and the most dramatic periods of the timber harvests in the modern West, see William G. Robbins, "Lumber and Forestry in the Modern West," in *Major Issues in Twentieth-Century Western History*, ed. Gerald D. Nash and Richard Etulain (Albuquerque: University of New Mexico Press, 1989), 233–56.

26. I. J. Mason, "Grays Harbor Study," April 4, 1935, in S Plans, Timber Management, Olympic, 1927–35, Box 54139, Federal Records Center, Seattle, Washington; Robbins, "Social Context of Forestry," 417–18.

27. Clark, *Mill Town*, 235–8.

28. Michael Malone, "The Collapse of Western Metal Mining: An Historical Epitaph," *Pacific Historical Review* 55 (1986): 455; William L. Lang, "You Have to Start with the Work," *Northern Lights* 4 (January 1988): 25–26.

29. Stephen Voynick, "The Birth of the New Frontier," *Northern Lights* 4 (January 1988): 9; Limerick, *Legacy of Conquest*, 124.

30. Marcus Daly to James J. Hill, January 29, 1893, General Correspondence, Hill Papers. For a discussion of Hill's "representatives" in Montana and the northern West—Paris Gibson and Martin Maginnis—see Martin, *James J. Hill*, 333–5; Hidy et al., *The Great Northern Railway*, 56–57; W. Thomas White, "Paris Gibson, James J. Hill & the 'New Minneapolis': The Great Falls Water Power and Townsite Company, 1882–1908," *Montana, the Magazine of Western History* 33 (Summer 1983): 60–69.

31. Malone, *Battle for Butte*, 217.

32. Gutfeld, *Montana's Agony*, 1; K. Ross Toole, "When Big Money Came to Butte: The Migration of Eastern Capital to Montana," *Pacific Northwest Quarterly* 44 (1953): 29; Howard, *Montana*, 83. For an appraisal of Howard's career, see Gerald Diettert, "Montana's Conscience," *Northern Lights* 3 (1987): 35.

33. Malone, "Collapse of Western Metal Mining," 459.

34. Herbert S. Schell, *History of South Dakota*, 3d ed. rev. (Lincoln: University of Nebraska Press, 1975), 146–7; John Milton, *South Dakota: A Bicentennial History* (New York: W. W. Norton, 1977), 116–17.

35. Joseph H. Cash, *Working the Homestake* (Ames: Iowa State University Press, 1973), 27, 55, 67; Milton, *South Dakota*, 117.

36. Fahey, *The Inland Empire*, 174–5; William G. Robbins, " 'At the End of

the Cracked Whip': The Northern West, 1880–1920," *Montana, the Magazine of Western History* 38 (Autumn 1988): 10; (Portland) *Oregonian,* November 2, 1981.

37. Fahey, *The Inland Empire,* 181–2; Thomas R. Navin, *Copper Mining and Management* (Tucson: University of Arizona Press, 1978), 117.

38. Fahey, *The Inland Empire,* 185–7.

39. Robert G. Athearn, *The Mythic West in Twentieth-Century America* (Lawrence: University Press of Kansas, 1986), 26.

40. Mary Wilma Hargreaves, *Dry Land Farming in the Northern Great Plains, 1900–1925* (Cambridge, Mass.: Harvard University Press, 1957), 83–84; Meinig, *Great Columbia Plain,* 411.

41. See Kraenzel, *Great Plains in Transition,* 137–40.

42. Gilbert C. Fite, "The Great Plains: Promises, Prospects," in *The Great Plains: Environment and Culture,* 187–8; Walter Prescott Webb, *The Great Plains* (1931; reprint, New York: Grosset and Dunlap, n.d.), 17–26; Hargreaves, *Dry Land Farming,* 85–97.

43. Hargreaves, *Dry Land Farming,* 109, 158, 179. For dry farming in eastern Oregon, see Barbara Allen, *Homesteading the High Desert* (Salt Lake City: University of Utah Press, 1987). Thomas Shaw's pamphlet, *Dry Farming in America* (St. Paul: Great Northern Railway, n.d.), carried the following on its cover: "Some fundamental principles which should be followed by the farmer who is cultivating land where the rainfall runs from 12 to 20 inches a year."

44. Hargreaves, *Dry Land Farming,* 442, 449; Allen, *Homesteading the High Desert,* 116–21, 129–33; Gerald Friesen, *The Canadian Prairies* (Toronto: University of Toronto Press, 1984); Paula M. Nelson, *After the West Was Won: Homesteaders and Town-Builders in Western South Dakota, 1900–1917* (Iowa City: University of Iowa Press, 1986), xiv–xv.

45. Howard, *Montana,* 196.

46. The USDA report is printed in Hargreaves, *Dry Land Farming,* 115.

47. Howard, *Montana,* 183; Hargreaves, *Dry Land Farming,* 442, 447; Fite, "The Great Plains," 189.

48. Allen, *Homesteading the High Desert,* 97–102; Nelson, *After the West Was Won,* xiv–xv.

49. Wilkins and Wilkins, *North Dakota,* 88–89; David B. Danbom, "North Dakota: The Most Midwestern State," in *Heartland: Comparative Histories of the Midwestern States,* ed. James H. Madison (Bloomington: Indiana University Press, 1988), 115–16; Michael P. Malone and Richard B. Roeder, *Montana: A History of Two Centuries* (Seattle: University of Washington Press, 1976), 216; Kraenzel, *Great Plains in Transition,* 160; Herbert T. Hoover, "South Dakota: An Expression of Regional Heritage," in *Heartland,* 199.

50. Howard, *Montana,* 285; Danbom, "North Dakota," 115. For an account that brilliantly captures the essence of the depression on the Canadian plains, see James Gray, *The Winter Years: The Depression on the Prairies* (Toronto: Macmillan, 1966). Also see Friesen, *Canadian Prairies,* 382–417.

51. Kraenzel, *Great Plains in Transition*, 151; Malone and Roeder, *Montana*, 255–8; Danbom, "North Dakota," 116, 123; Fite, "The Great Plains," 200.

52. For a description of "honyockers," see Howard, *Montana*, 180–1.

53. Fahey, *The Inland Empire*, 87–90; W. Thomas White, "Main Street on the Irrigation Frontier: Sub-Urban Community Building in the Yakima Valley, 1900–1910," *Pacific Northwest Quarterly* 77 (1986): 95.

54. Fahey, *The Inland Empire*, 94–96.

55. Ibid., 100–103, 118–20.

56. Hugh T. Lovin, " 'Duty of Water' in Idaho: A 'New West' Irrigation Controversy, 1890–1920," *Arizona and the West* 23 (1981): 6; Peterson, *Idaho*, 123. Wallace Stegner has captured the entrepreneurial spirit of the place and the time in *Angle of Repose*, a novel based on the writings of Mary Hallock Foote.

57. Hugh T. Lovin, "A 'New West' Reclamation Tragedy: The Twin Falls-Oakley Project in Idaho, 1908–1931," *Arizona and the West* 20 (1978): 7; Peterson, *Idaho*, 125–8.

58. Peterson, *Idaho*, 134–8. For an overview of reclamation activity in Arizona and California, see Worster, *Rivers of Empire*; Donald J. Pisani, *From the Family Farm to Agribusiness: The Irrigation Crusade in California and the West, 1850–1931* (Berkeley: University of California Press, 1984).

59. Peterson, *Idaho*, 140.

60. This discussion is from Norman Best's memoir, *A Celebration of Work*, ed. William G. Robbins (Lincoln: University of Nebraska Press, 1990).

61. Kittredge is quoted in the *Oregonian*, April 29, 1984.

62. Toole, *Twentieth-Century Montana*, 281; Clark Spence, *Montana: A Bicentennial History* (New York: W. W. Norton, 1977), 196.

2

Agrarianism, United States Indian Policy, and the Muckleshoot Indian Reservation

KENT D. RICHARDS

THE CIRCUMSTANCES THAT LED TO THE CREATION OF THE MUCKLE-shoot Indian Reservation in western Washington in 1856 seemed to portend anything but success for the reservation and its inhabitants. When Isaac I. Stevens was named the first governor and superintendent of Indian Affairs for Washington Territory in 1853, the pressure of white settlement abetted by the Oregon Donation Land Law dictated that his first priority be the settlement of Indian land claims. For that task, Stevens relied on recently concluded treaties with tribes in Kansas and Nebraska, which provided the basis for the government's reservation system.[1] But Stevens and his team of negotiators made one significant departure from their instructions: in order for the many Puget Sound bands to remain near their traditional sources of sustenance, Stevens provided for a number of small reservations in western Washington rather than one or two large ones.[2]

The treaty process did little to alleviate tensions, however, and to some degree it exacerbated them. War broke out in the Yakima country in the fall of 1855 and soon spread to the Puget Sound bands. Governor Stevens, who rushed back from negotiations on the Judith River to deal with the crisis, adopted a policy designed to keep hostile warriors isolated from the non-warring Indians. He moved peaceful bands to temporary reservations under the watchful eye of Indian Department employees and formed companies of volunteers that patrolled the mountain passes to prevent disaffected warriors from infiltrating the Puget Sound country.[3]

In the Puget Sound region, only a relatively small number of Indi-

39

ans were actively hostile. Many of the warring faction came from the vicinity of the Green and White rivers, east of present-day Tacoma on the south end of the Sound. Ironically, those Indians were disaffected because they had not been included in the treaty process (also a reason that contributed to the hostilities east of the Cascades). As one settler later remembered, the Indians living on the waters of the Pacific Ocean or Puget Sound were reasonably satisfied with the treaties because they could live near their "usual haunts," but

> not so with the Indians living on the upper reaches of the Green, White, Puyallup and Nisqually Rivers, where the occupants lived by the chase and on the natural products of the soil, who were wide-awake Indians and were the tribes that went on the warpath.[4]

For white settlers, the low point of the war came on October 28, 1855, when Indians killed three families living on the White River. The "White River Massacre" created a near panic throughout the region, with one army officer describing the settlers on the Sound as in a "condition of wild alarm." Governor Stevens put several volunteer companies into the field, and by early 1856 an uneasy truce settled over the region. But an estimated two hundred hostile warriors led by Leschi and Nelson continued to pose a threat. In August, Stevens held a conference with Indian leaders on Fox Island, in Puget Sound near Tacoma, where he announced his intention to set up a "special reservation under the surveillance of the military." In a letter to Commissioner of Indian Affairs George Manypenny, the governor elaborated on his plan, "the result of which [conference] was arrangements to modify the [Nisqually and Puyallup] reservations and the establishment of a new reservation at the Muckleshute [sic]."[5]

Stevens's primary reason for setting up the Muckleshoot Indian Reservation was to isolate the hostile Indians at a place where they could be watched. He picked the location near the juncture of the White and Green rivers because of its good agricultural land. Stevens's choice was in keeping with government policy. During the last half of the nineteenth century and the early part of the twentieth, a major focus of United States Indian policy was to turn Native Americans from hunting, fishing, and gathering—so-called savage pursuits—to the economically productive and civilized occupation of agriculture.

The policy often failed. The history of the Muckleshoot Indian Reservation reflects the policy's inherent contradictions, but the Muckleshoot Indians' experience differs from that of Indians on other reservations in that their story is one of successful adaptation despite the obstacles encountered.

In the spring of 1856, when the army had cut a road from Fort Steilacoom to Muckleshoot Prairie, Colonel Silas Casey noted that "there are several hundred acres of excellent land in that vicinity." The Indians who Stevens settled there in late 1856 came from a number of upriver bands loosely referred to as the Stuck or Stick Indians, with many related to the Puyallup, Nisqually, or other bands. Over the next several years, the Indians moved on and off the reservation. In time, those living there came to be called the Muckleshoots, taking their name from the reservation.[6]

The land adjacent to Puget Sound is composed of a variety of soil conditions. Much of the lowland consists of fine alluvial sediment washed down by the rivers; at the higher elevations, between the Sound and the Cascade Mountains, the soil is often loam. During the mid-nineteenth century, western Washington was heavily forested except for occasional openings that the pioneers called prairies. One of these openings was the Muckleshoot Prairie, which encompassed eight to nine hundred acres of land. The Muckleshoot differed from most of the other prairies only in the greater fertility of the soil, which was a mixture of Puget silt loam and Puget fine sandy loam.[7]

The reservations at the south end of the Sound were under the supervision of Indian Agent Michael Simmons, stationed at Tulalip, and various sub-agents and farmers assigned to the Puyallup, Nisqually, Duwamish, and other reservations. Under Simmons's supervision, the two sections of the Muckleshoot Reservation were surveyed to include the prairie lands. In October 1856, Simmons sent the plat to Stevens with his endorsement, and Stevens in turn forwarded it to the commissioner of Indian Affairs with the assurance that the land had been "carefully surveyed." President Franklin Pierce gave his approval to the new reservation on January 20, 1857.[8]

Simmons continued as Indian agent until the Civil War began. From time to time he reported to his superiors on activity at the Muckleshoot Reservation, where most effort was directed toward establishing farms. Simmons reported to Superintendent James W. Nesmith that the prairie lands of western Washington were generally poor, "except Muckleshoot." By the spring of 1859, Simmons wrote, the Indians at Muckleshoot were peaceable and eager to go to work, so he furnished the reservation with "a yoke of oxen, and plow, and some few tools, as well as with seed that he [the resident farmer] may assist, and instruct, them in planting and working their crops." That same summer, after a visit to the area, Simmons reported on his plan for the reservation:

> At Muckleshoot, the Station I have spoken of as having been recently turned over by the military to the Indian department, there is a prairie containing probably three hundred acres of good arable land. This has been surveyed and set aside for an Indian reservation. Early this spring I furnished the employee who is stationed there with a plow and one yoke of oxen for the use of the Indians. He has put in cultivation such land as the team was able to break, but, as I have ascertained from personal observation, it will require three good yoke of oxen to break the prairie to advantage. As this is the only reservation where there is any body of rich prairie land I think it should be made as profitable as possible, and I therefore propose to seed about one hundred acres of it in wheat this fall. At a moderate calculation this should reap two thousand bushels, which will feed all the needy Indians in that vicinity at least.[9]

The farming project moved forward, although it was difficult to find either competent employees or the necessary seeds and implements. Despite these problems, Simmons continued to believe the Muckleshoot could become a flourishing reservation. He recommended that the reservation be enlarged, so that

> all the country lying between Green and White rivers above the forks, as far east as the [?] meridian that is laid down on the map be given to these Indians. There are no other claimants upon this land, and it will give much fine bottom land suitable for raising vegetables which the prairie from its great elevation is not well adapted to, (while for grass and grain it can hardly be surpassed). Then these streams above the forks afford excellent fisheries and a fence across the peninsula on the line of the meridian would secure them from being trespassed upon by other persons stock, and would also confine their own for which there will be an ample supply of food growing both winter and summer.[10]

With the end of the Indian Wars and the beginning of the Civil War, the Muckleshoot Reservation was often ignored by government officials who succeeded Simmons. In 1862, the new Indian agent at Tulalip, S. D. Howe, visited the Muckleshoot Reservation and reported to the Washington superintendent for Indian Affairs that he was convinced "that the keeping up of that Reservation is a useless expenditure of money." Recommending that the Indians be moved to Port Madison Reservation, Howe concluded: "I am clearly of the opinion that Muckleshoot should be abandoned and that is also the opinion of nine tenths of the people at this place." No immediate action was taken, however, and by the next spring an assistant farmer assigned to the reservation, John Webster, described the Muckleshoots as "anxious to put in crops," particularly oats and wheat. Agent Howe was not persuaded and again wrote to his superior indicating the "Muckleshoot Reservation I intend to break up . . . and discharge Webster." [11] These conflicting views reflected the transitory nature of the reservation population, which left at the appropriate seasons of the year to hunt, fish, and gather berries.

During the post-Civil War period, George D. Hill, one of Howe's successors, reported:

> This reservation is occupied by the Muck-le-shook tribe, Lewis Nelson head chief; there is no white employee on the reservation. These Indians, or a majority of them, are what are known as "Stick" or Horse Indians, and differ materially in their habits from those that live on the Sound, as they subsist themselves more by hunting. . . . A few cultivate the soil; but as there is no white employee there to instruct them, they make but slow progress in civilization. These Indians possess about 50 horses; they have under cultivation several acres of land, having small patches of potatoes and other vegetables.

Hill recommended that a white employee be placed in charge.[12]

Neither Howe nor Hill nor Simmons was able to fully carry out his plans, and the Muckleshoot Reservation struggled on, although without a resident white employee for considerable periods. Policy changes during the Grant administration, however, gave renewed impetus to the agrarian policies elucidated by Simmons. Among other things, the Civil War had been a great moral crusade. After the war,

with slavery abolished and the Fourteenth and Fifteenth amendments
in place, the evangelical reformers turned to other problems. One that
could not be overlooked was the failure of the reservation system. The
Indian Office seemed incapable of managing the reservations, which
muddled on amidst corruption, crisis, and chaos.

The demand for reform of Indian and reservation policies led to
"Grant's peace policy"—basically a way of thinking, a determination to bring justice to the government's dealings with the Indians.
Although the policy is associated with the presidency of Ulysses S.
Grant (1869–1877), it predated his two terms in office. A key step was
the appointment by Congress in 1867 of the Indian Peace Commission,
which made recommendations for change. Treaties made with the
Sioux and other tribes at Fort Laramie in 1868 implemented some of
the commission's recommendations. The intent was to turn nomadic
tribes into farmers and to set aside additional arable land adjacent
to reservations that did not contain 160 acres for each Indian. The
treaties also provided rewards for Indians who were judged to be the
best farmers.[13]

In his inaugural address in 1869, Grant promised to consider new
ideas for dealing with the Indians. He was soon visited by Christian
philanthropists, who urged taking the reservations away from civilian
control and handing them over to the missionary arms of churches.
Grant was agreeable. Beginning in 1869, Quakers were assigned to
run a number of reservations, and the plan was soon expanded to include other denominations. By 1872, churches were running most of
the nation's reservations. The Catholic church complained bitterly that
it had the most experience in working with Indians but was assigned
to only a few reservations. One of the few was the Tulalip.[14]

Grant's new policy began with great promise, which soon turned to
disillusionment. Many of the churches were not very astute in select-
ing agents, and they often found that the best of intentions did not
automatically provide the means to deal with the realities of the reservation system. The sectarian schisms of that time led to recrimination,
with much of the venom directed toward the Catholics.

Grant's Indian policy was also maligned, particularly in the West,
because of the outbreak of hostilities during the 1870s. The Modoc War
on the Oregon-California line in 1872–1873 and the death of George

Custer and his men at the Little Big Horn in Montana three years later put the policy into serious question. On May 8, 1873, the *Puget Sound Express* complained bitterly of "the petted and favored wards of the government." The editor demanded: "let us have Peace Commissioners and let the governor apply to the government for them. Let them be one thousand strong and of the breech-loading variety." This despair at ever getting a handle on reservation administration together with the new interest in acculturation for the Indians led to an increased emphasis on allotment of lands in severalty.[15]

In Washington Territory, Superintendent Robert Milroy, a minister in the Methodist Episcopal church, was in step with the times when he presented his plan of action in January 1873. Milroy noted that "a large part of the Indians around Puget Sound work at the saw mills, coal mines, logging camps, or upon their reservations." He proposed to have them "exercise the right of American citizens" by allotting the

> head of each family a small tract of land to be managed and cultivated for their own use and benefit; and when they become sufficiently advanced in civilization and the science of government, they will sever their tribal relations, and become worthy members of society and useful citizens of the republic.

Milroy further predicted that "in ten years the Indian department of Washington Territory will be abolished." He expanded on these themes in a letter to the commissioner:

> I have for many years felt a deep interest in the civilization and elevation of the Indians, and from observation & reading, especially since my present appointment, I am fully convinced that the first vital and fundamental step towards the permanent civilization, christianization, and true elevation of Indian, and to properly prepare him for assuming the duties of an American citizen, is to give him a separate property in the soil and a fixed and permanent home, where he may confidently surround himself with the comforts of civilization by increasing and satisfying his wants; as the real difference between the savage and civilized man is, that the wants of the former, like those of the animal, are few and simple, requiring but little mental effort for their satisfaction, while those of the latter are many, demanding the most vigorous effort of mind and body for their supply.[16]

The Grant administration also proposed consolidating reservation lands prior to allotment. The government argued that consolidation would allow fewer administrators to keep an eye on the Indians, prevent problems with white intruders, and simplify the allotment process. Consolidation and allotment would lessen white pressure on Indian lands and give a surer title to those lands left in Indian hands; in addition, proceeds from land sales could be applied to the Indians' welfare. Finally, reformers believed that allotment would drive the Indians closer to an agrarian way of life. Thus, when the Muckleshoot Reservation was expanded from two to six sections in 1874, the action conformed to national policies and was intended to provide sufficient land for each Muckleshoot.[17]

The practical problems of allotment were numerous and were not limited to the Muckleshoot Reservation. An 1873 report from Superintendent Milroy to Commissioner of Indian Affairs Francis A. Walker regarding the Muckleshoot was one of a series, each dealing with one of the Washington reservations. The prevailing theme in the reports is similar: the early surveys of the reservation were not accurate; the surveyors' marks were no longer visible; and whites had taken claims on what appeared to be Indian lands. The government, Milroy judged, should immediately take steps to resurvey, clarify claims, and allot the lands in severalty.[18]

The immediate action Milroy sought did not occur, and the debate continued on the proper course for United States policy to take on the Indian question. The inability of church groups to effectively administer Indian affairs prompted questions about the viability of the reservation system. By the late 1870s reformers were convinced that the attempt to redeem the reservations had failed, and they had come to see that the problem was more fundamental than whether the army, civilians, or churches administered the reservations. The reformers believed that the key to any long-term reform was individual Indians, and the heart of their philosophy was an insistence on individual salvation. Reformers had become convinced that tribal customs, the old way of life, and the reservation system stood in the way of progress, civilization, and redemption. Merrill Gates succinctly summed up the beliefs of a generation of reformers when he wrote in 1900:

If civilization, education and Christianity are to do their work, we must get at the individual. They must lay hold of men and women and children, one by one. The deadening sway of tribal custom must be interfered with. The sad uniformity of savage tribal life must be broken up! Individuality must be cultivated. Personality must be developed. And personality is strengthened only by the direction of one's own life through voluntary obedience to recognized moral law. At last, as a nation, we are coming to recognize the great truth that if we would do justice to the Indians, we must get at them, one by one, with American ideals, American schools, American laws, the privileges and the pressures of American rights and duties.

The reformers had a ready-made vehicle to accomplish their goals—allotment. Lyman Abbott spoke for most Americans when he wrote:

I declare my conviction then that the reservation system is hopelessly wrong; that it cannot be amended or modified; that it can only be uprooted, root, trunk, branch, and leaf, and a new system put in its place. . . . I hold that the reservation barriers should be cast down and the land given to the Indians in severalty.[19]

Thus, the push for allocation came primarily from eastern reformers motivated by humanitarian impulses. Settlers in the Puget Sound area, however, agreed with the policy. As one editor put it, "let the Indians be incorporated as a part of the population of the country . . . ; throw them on their own resources, educate and civilize them. . . ." Members of the Indian commission who visited Puget Sound Indians reported they were laboring on farms and in sawmills and "receive the commendation of employers and agents." The commissioners observed that the Indians had adopted white customs and were rapidly acquiring white habits. Progress toward civilization was rapid, they agreed, although they warned that such progress also included acquiring the vices of whites as well as the virtues.[20]

Washington's governors, who had paid little attention to the territory's Indian population during most of the 1860s and 1870s, added their voices to the call for allocation and acculturation. In 1881, Governor William Newell argued:

The Indian question, which so vexes the public mind and strains the
public purse, is easy of solution in this Territory. Abolish Reservations,
conceding liberal homesteads, which shall be inalienable for a period of
years; dissolve tribal relations and subject Indians to the same authorities and laws by which other people are governed, then predatory and
hostile excursions will cease.[21]

These diverse voices combined reform motives with avarice for excess reservation lands, placing pressure on the politicians. Beginning
in 1879, Congress debated a general allotment act each session, but
final passage was delayed as the two houses disagreed on details and
became embroiled in partisan squabbles. The General Allotment Act,
or Dawes Act, finally passed late in 1886 and was signed by President
Cleveland in February 1887. The act was a key piece of legislation,
but it held no new policies; it extended and confirmed a trend that
had begun earlier in the century. The Dawes Act greatly accelerated
the process of allotting reservation lands, with about 5.5 million acres
being allotted by 1900.

At the same time, the Indian agent for the Muckleshoots inde-
pendently developed an allotment plan assigning reservation land to
heads of families. Coincidentally, he sent his plan to Washington,
D.C., only five days after passage of the Dawes Act. It was not a coincidence that the agent, W. H. Talbott, returned to the topic of allotment
a couple of months later when whites were surveying in the vicinity
and crossed onto the reservation. The legal right of the Muckleshoots
to the land had been in question since the reservation was first established. Before 1857, two white settlers had taken homestead claims
that included most of the reservation. Although the claims had been
appraised in 1859, Congress had neglected to appropriate funds to
pay for them, and as late as 1876 both settlers were threatening to re-
take their lands. Additional problems occurred on lands granted to the
Northern Pacific Railroad. Talbott believed that allotment would provide the key to resolve the disputes and would also provide incentives
to the Indians to clear and break the forested lands and to make other
improvements.[22]

While the debate on reservation policy raged, agricultural development moved ahead on the Muckleshoot Reservation during the 1870s

and 1880s. In 1874, Father Eugene Chirouse observed that the Muckle-shoots' crops were promising and "progress in agricultural pursuits [is] most remarkable." A few years later, agent John O'Keane found the crops on the Muckleshoot Reservation doing well. He reported: "the Lummi and Muckleshoot Indians especially are deserving of great praise for their farming; every year they cultivate new land, rear more stock, improve their dwellings and enlarge their barns and out-houses." O'Keane also noted, as had his predecessors, the fertility of the soil. He wrote: "of all the Reservations the Lummi and Muckle-shoot are the most prosperous which is owing in great measure to the superiority of the soil." Agent Patrick Buckley reported in 1884: "no real division of land has been allotted to these Indians in severalty, but it is fenced into small tracts and each family has control of all within their respective enclosures; about 2,000 acres are thus enclosed and much of it is well tilled and promises an abundant yield." Agent W. H. Talbott echoed these sentiments in 1887, noting that more ground had been planted than ever before and predicting: "I am convinced that in a very few years they will all have good farms and comfortable buildings." By 1893, a majority of the Muckleshoots were living on individual tracts, and the agent reported that "all the Indians are in favor of the allotment in severalty." As the century drew to a close, it was clear that much progress had occurred. The agent reported that on the Tulalip Agency reservations,

> some of the younger and more progressive Indians have well-cultivated farms and devote themselves almost entirely to agricultural purposes. This is especially the case upon the Swinomish, Lummi, and Muckle-shoot Reservations, where the land is rich and much better adapted to farming than on the Tulalip and Port Madison reservations. . . . Muckle-shoot Reservation, 25 miles south of Seattle, located between Green and White Rivers, has some of the finest land of any of the reservations. Its fertility makes it capable of producing anything adapted to the climate.[23]

The efforts of Indian Department employees and, most important, the hard work expended by the Muckleshoot Indians had produced results. By 1881, the Muckleshoots were growing wheat, oats, barley, and a wide variety of vegetables; had set ten miles of fencing; and were raising sixty cattle, fifty-five horses, and sheep, chickens, and hogs. In 1887, they produced 4,350 bushels of oats, 5,400 bushels of potatoes, 40 bushels of barley, 350 bushels of wheat, 300 bushels of vegetables, 400 pounds of butter, and 227 tons of hay. They owned 63 head of cattle, 80 horses, 36 sheep, 45 hogs, and 300 chickens. By 1892, the agent could respond to questions posed by the commissioner of Indian Affairs that all 161 Muckleshoots made their living by labor for themselves or others "in civilized pursuits." The commissioner also wanted to know the proportion of the Indians' subsistence obtained by "fishing, hunting, or root-gathering." The answer was none, and the same answer applied to the percentage provided by government rations. In 1890, the Tribal Census Roll listed all of the Muckleshoots as "farmers."[24]

In 1895, the Muckleshoots sold 180 bushels of berries. The women made wool socks spun from the fleece of reservation sheep, which sold in the cities for fifty cents a pair; in 1895, 840 pair were sold for $420. By contrast, the sale of fish during the same year brought in $75. In 1898, the farmer estimated that the 146 Muckleshoots gained nine-tenths of their support from farming and other "civilized pursuits," one-twentieth from fishing, and one-twentieth from government subsidies. In 1900, the percentages remained the same; in 1905, they altered slightly to 95 percent from "civilized pursuits," 5 percent from fishing, and no support from the government.[25]

Agriculture on the Muckleshoot Reservation mirrored developments that were taking place in other parts of the Green and White valleys and in the nearby Puyallup River Valley. White farmers settled along the rivers and produced potatoes and other vegetables, butter, eggs, hams, and wool. The most unusual crop, and for a time the dominant one, was hops. Ezra Meeker and his father experimented with growing hops during the late 1860s. They succeeded beyond their wildest dreams, and by the late 1880s, 3 million pounds of hops were produced each year in Pierce County and 1.7 million in King County. A small quantity of hops was grown on the Muckleshoot Reservation (three tons in 1892), but the Indians participated primarily as workers during the hop harvest, earning from $1.50 to $3.00 a day. Hops virtually disappeared from the area after the early 1890s, when hop lice severely damaged the crop.[26]

Despite these advances in agriculture on the Muckleshoot Reservation, the bureaucracy of the Indian Service focused its attention on the larger reservations when it implemented the Dawes Act. From the 1880s through 1903, the major issue for agency officials and for the Muckleshoots was the allocation of reservation lands. In addition to Agent Talbott's proposal for allocation in 1887, others apparently developed similar plans. Agent Charles Buchanan argued in 1902 that at least as far back as 1887, Muckleshoots had expressed their desire to hold the land in severalty and "that this desire of the Indians has never been carried out is no fault of the Muckleshoot Indians and should not, therefore, be allowed to militate [sic] against any advantages or interests which the fact might bestow." The commissioner of Indian Affairs finally acted in April 1902 to authorize allotment of the Muckleshoot Reservation lands, which was to be carried out based on the terms included in the treaty with the Omahas of March 16, 1854. On receiving the news, Reservation Farmer Charles Reynolds responded: "I am sure the Muckleshoots will be pleased with the prospect of allotment." In 1903, 3,357.16 acres were divided into thirty-nine allotments averaging 81.97 acres (one quarter-section was not allotted until a later date).[27]

Division of the Muckleshoot lands coincided with the appointment of Charles Reynolds as the farmer assigned to the reservation. Reynolds remained in this position for more than twenty-five years. Further administrative stability was provided by the long tenure of Charles Buchanan as superintendent of the Tulalip Agency. Both men worked long and diligently with and for the Muckleshoots. After the 1903 allotments, work went ahead on the reservation to clear additional lands, build fences, and construct roads. Reynolds's annual reports and correspondence during the first decade of the century reflect these activities. In 1905, for example, he reported that the reservation contained 800 acres of "rich black soil," although some of the land was still heavily covered with timber. Of the economic activities, "farming is the principal industry." Reynolds also noted that "when the Indians are not employed at home they find work near the Reservation at fair wages. They work on farms in sawmills in lumber camps in hopyards etc." Of the thirty-nine families who received allotments, twenty-five were living on and cultivating their lands. In 1905, Reynolds reported "a good crop of hay, a fair crop of potatoes but not much grain." New fences were put up, old ones repaired, new barns and houses built, drainage ditches constructed, and road work carried out.[28]

Two years later, the same report was submitted with some variation. Reynolds noted:

> the industries are farming and stockraising; a majority of the Indian families reside upon and are improving their allotments. There are a few however who cannot be induced to make any improvements; hay is the principal crop and is about an average crop.

One factor that Reynolds pointed to in 1907 remained a constant for the next several decades and even to the present. "Owing to the high wages which the Indians receive outside of the reservation," he reported, "less plowing and planting was done this year than formerly. They can get more ready money working for wages than farming their land." Although the Muckleshoots worked off the reservation at farms and in canneries, most of the labor was in the woods or in mills where they acquired a reputation as knowledgeable and able workers.[29]

In the years immediately after allotment, government officials were reluctant to allow leasing of allotted land or the sale of timber rights. This reluctance derived from a concern that unscrupulous individuals would take advantage of the Indian rights holders. Under pressure from potential white lessees, the policy was soon modified to allow leasing when it could be advantageous to the Indians involved. There were two aspects to the new approach. First, for those who were judged not competent to handle complex legal and financial matters, such as minors, elderly, or widows who held or inherited land allotments and were not able to work them, the white farmer and agent aided in making the arrangements. The second group included those members of the tribe, usually adult males but also females, who were deemed competent to handle their own affairs. Among those who leased all or part of their land to whites or other Indians at the end of the first decade of the century was William Nason, who leased most of his allotment for pasture and agriculture. Nason received a fair rental and also acquired resulting improvements, such as fencing, ditching, and clearing. Gilbert Courville leased his allotment for two years for $500 a year. Others did the same, and Reynolds reported that those who leased a part or all of their lands received more income than they would have otherwise: "Alex Morris, William Nason, Philip Starr, Joe Wilson, and Frank Ross are each doing very well." [30]

During the second decade of the century, the Muckleshoot Reservation was shifted to the jurisdiction of the Cushman School superintendent. The change may have retarded efforts at economic development, as the superintendent's major concern was the school; in 1920, responsibility for the reservation was moved back to the Tulalip Agency. In any event, the trends established during the first decade of the century continued to the depression of the 1930s. Visitors to the reservation in 1927, observed that "the land in the main is good" and "the Indians are mostly farmers." In 1913, a State College of Washington (now Washington State University) agricultural experiment station at Puyallup provided information on the best varieties of crops and livestock and the proper methods of cultivation and care. The scientists recommended alfalfa because of soil conditions, and Muckleshoot farmers made several seedings of that crop with the "very finest results."

For the reservations under the Tulalip and Puyallup agencies, it was generally recognized that the effort made during the nineteenth and early twentieth centuries to turn the Indians to farming was most successful with the Muckleshoots and with the neighboring Puyallups. In both instances, the existence of sufficient good agricultural land was a critical factor. For the Muckleshoots, the diligence of the resident farmer was also important. Another factor was the Muckleshoots' heritage. Many were descended from upriver bands that traditionally were more diversified in their economic activities than those who lived on the coast or the Sound.[31]

The Muckleshoots continued to produce hay, fruit, wool, potatoes, and a variety of other garden products. When the Tulalip agent organized exhibits for the Western Washington State Fair in 1924, he singled out the Muckleshoots for their agricultural exhibits, noting in particular their "very fine gardens." One new development was dairying, which had begun in the White-Puyallup River areas in the 1890s and was given a boost by the establishment of a Carnation Milk plant in Kent in 1899. The big expansion in dairy farming took place during the 1920s, and in 1926 three Muckleshoot families were in the business on a commercial scale using purebred bulls and new feeding practices. Two families sold the milk, and one sold cream and used the skim for feed. The agency school at Tulalip kept a dairy herd and provided training in dairying.[32]

The depression of the 1930s brought hard times to the Muckleshoot Reservation, as it did to all of rural America. Most of the good agricultural lands were leased to whites during the 1920s and 1930s. Many of the original allotment holders were elderly, and the younger men tended to work off the reservation in the mills and forests or in other occupations. By the mid-1930s, various New Deal programs began to have an impact on the reservation. In a reversal of earlier attempts to destroy tribal affiliation and native customs, in 1936 the government granted tribal status to the Muckleshoots. That same year, the tribal council made successful application for a loan through a Department of Agriculture program that provided funds for improving agricultural land.[33]

A second project, run by the Agriculture Extension Service, promoted family gardens. Families were paid to improve and extend their gardens with the yield accruing to themselves. The tribal council discussed and apparently endorsed this project. In 1937, the Muckleshoots' gardens yielded 18,480 pounds of potatoes, 240 pounds of onions, 2,400 pounds of cabbages, 1,840 pounds of red beets, 2,960 pounds of beans, 4,800 pounds of squash and pumpkins, 8,600 pounds of carrots, 400 pounds of turnips, 1,600 pounds of peas, and 14,000 pounds of cucumbers for a total of 55,320 pounds.

By the end of the 1930s, most families on the reservation were engaged in a variety of agricultural activities. They produced hay, apples, cherries, pears, raspberries, and loganberries for sale. The women continued to make woolen socks, and families sold poultry, milk, and livestock. The Starr family, for example, owned cattle and raised hay, grain, potatoes, and other vegetables. Louis Starr said they had good land and produced enough to feed the family. He later remembered: "in them days, you had to raise it. There was no such thing as welfare or anything like that. We had to get out and hustle in the spring and get ready for the winter."[34]

The Muckleshoot Reservation remains an agricultural area that is known as a center of the dairy industry. Examination of the reservation readily reveals that the reports made by agents, farmers, and others over the years in regard to the agricultural value of this land were correct. The evidence indicates that since the creation of the reservation, a major economic activity has been agriculture. Agent after agent and report after report document that the land was well suited for farming and stock raising and that the Muckleshoots, aided by government agents, took advantage of this opportunity. Agriculture on the Muckleshoot Reservation had its ups and downs as it followed the pattern of economic cycles, but it remains a persistent feature of the reservation.

The argument has often been made that it was futile to attempt to turn Native Americans into white Americans by making them farmers. This was true; but given the long agrarian heritage of some native peoples, promoting agriculture as the best economic alternative to the decline of traditional food sources was not necessarily a futile gesture. It was clearly not the best answer for everyone, but even in a region dominated by fishing, the Muckleshoots' experience indicates that it was a viable alternative for some.[35]

Notes

1. Isaac I. Stevens to Commissioner George Manypenny, December 26, 1853, Manypenny to Section of Interior, February 6, 1854, S. Ex. Doc. 34, 33rd Cong., 1st sess. (Serial 698).

2. Stevens to Michael Simmons, March 22, 1854, *Records of the Washington Superintendency of Indian Affairs, 1853–1874* [WSIA], RG 75, Letters Sent, National Archives, Washington, D.C.: Colonel B. F. Shaw, "Medicine Creek Treaty," *Proceedings of the Oregon Historical Society* (1901), 27–29.

3. Stevens to the Officer Commanding the Troops, December 13, 1855, in *Pioneer and Democrat* (Olympia, Washington), January 11, 1856; Message of Governor to Third Annual Session of the Legislative Assembly of the Territory of Washington, January 21, 1856, in Charles M. Gates, ed., *Messages of the Governors of the Territory of Washington to the Legislative Assembly, 1854–1889*, vol. 12 (Seattle: University of Washington, 1940), 25.

4. Ezra Meeker, *Pioneer Reminiscences of Puget Sound* (Seattle, 1905), 270.

5. Murray Morgan, *Puget's Sound* (Seattle: University of Washington Press, 1979), 102–7; Maurice Maloney to Charles Mason, November 6, 1855, John Nugen to James Tilton, November 4, 1855, E. D. Keyes to Charles Mason, December 7, 1855, Indian War Documents, University of Washington Libraries, Seattle; E. D. Keyes, *Fifty Years' Observation of Men and Events* (New York, 1884), 251–3; H. H. Bancroft, *History of Washington, Idaho and Montana*

(New York, 1890), 122–3; S. S. Ford, Journal, July 23, July 30, 1856, WSIA, Letters from Employees Assigned to the Puget Sound District; Stevens to Manypenny, May 5, August 28, August 31, 1856, Stevens, Circular to Indian Agents, April 13, 1856, WSIA, Letters Sent.

6. *Pioneer and Democrat*, March 21, 1856.

7. *Atlas of Washington Agriculture* (Olympia: Washington State Department of Agriculture, 1963), 3–4; Michael L. Olsen, "The Beginning of Agriculture in Western Oregon and Western Washington" (Ph.D. diss., University of Washington, Seattle, 1970), 190–1; James R. Gibson, *Farming the Frontier: The Agricultural Opening of the Oregon Country, 1786–1846* (Seattle: University of Washington Press, 1985), 96–97; A. Lars Nelson, *Recent Rural Settlement . . . and Agricultural Development in the State of Washington* (U.S. Resettlement Administration, Region XI, 1937), 22–24.

8. Simmons to Stevens, October 1, 1856, Stevens to Commissioner of Indian Affairs, December 5, 1856 (draft), Robert McClelland to the President, January 20, 1857, WSIA, Puget Sound District Agency.

9. Simmons to James Nesmith, October 15, 1858, March 31, 1859, Simmons to Edward Geary, July 1, 1859, WSIA, Puget Sound District Agency.

10. Simmons to Edward Geary, October 26, December 13, 1859, WSIA, Puget Sound District Letters.

11. S. D. Howe to C. H. Hale, October 13, 1862, June 27, 1863, John Webster to C. H. Hale, June 18, 1863, WSIA, Tulalip Agency Correspondence.

12. George D. Hill to Samuel Ross, September 1, 1870, Report of Secretary of the Interior, 41st Cong., 3d sess. (Serial 1449).

13. Francis Paul Prucha, *The Great Father* (Lincoln: University of Nebraska Press, 1984), 493.

14. Ibid., 522–3.

15. *Puget Sound Express* (Steilacoom), May 8, 1873.

16. *Puget Sound Express*, January 2, 1873; Robert Milroy to F. A. Walker, Commissioner of Indian Affairs, September 3, 1872, Letters Received by Commissioner of Indian Affairs.

17. Zachariah Chandler, quoted in Prucha, *The Great Father*, 565.

18. Milroy to Commissioner of Indian Affairs, January 20, January 27, February 4, February 17, March 10, March 20, 1873, Letters Received by Commissioner.

19. Quoted in Prucha, *The Great Father*, 621, 657.

20. *Puget Sound Express*, July 3, 1873; *Weekly Pacific Tribune* (Olympia), January 27, 1872.

21. Message of Governor William A. Newell, October 5, 1881, October 3, 1883, in Gates, *Messages of the Governors*, 227, 243.

22. *Annual Report of the Commissioner of Indian Affairs, 1876*, 140; W. H. Talbott to Commissioner of Indian Affairs, April 2, July 11, 1887, Tulalip Agency, Letters Sent to the Commissioner of Indian Affairs.

23. *Report of the Secretary of the Interior, 1896,* 315; Eugene Chirouse to Milroy, July 30, 1874, Chirouse to Commissioner of Indian Affairs, August 1, 1874, Puget Sound District Agency; John O'Keane to Commissioner of Indian Affairs, August 2, 1881, June 2, 1879, Talbott to Commissioner of Indian Affairs, June 1, July 1, 1887, Tulalip Agency, Letters Sent to Commissioner of Indian Affairs; *Annual Report of the Commissioner of Indian Affairs, 1884,* 169; *Tulalip Agency Annual Report,* October 2, 1893.

24. *Tulalip Agency Annual Report,* Circular of December 15, 1881; *Tulalip Agency Annual Report,* June 23, 1892; Talbott to Commissioner of Indian Affairs, August 15, 1887, Tulalip Agency, Letters Sent to Commissioner of Indian Affairs; Tulalip Agency, Tribal Census Rolls, Muckleshoot Census, 1890.

25. *Tulalip Agency Annual Report,* 1898, 1900, 1905; Burton Axe to D. G. Gowan, August 19, 1895, Tulalip Agency, *Annual Reports.*

26. Olsen, "Beginning of Agriculture," 190–4; *King County 1909: Its History, Resources, Development, Present Conditions and Opportunities* (1909); Ezra Meeker, *Seventy Years of Progress in Washington* (Seattle, 1921), 183–4.

27. Talbott to Commissioner of Indian Affairs, July 11, December 10, 1887, Charles Buchanan to Commissioner of Indian Affairs, February 17, June 17, 1908, December 1, 1909, Acting Commissioner of Indian Affairs to Buchanan, April 29, 1902, Tulalip Agency, Letters Sent to Commissioner of Indian Affairs; Reynolds to Buchanan, May 14, 1902, June 30, 1905, October 30, 1903, Affidavits of Gilbert Courville, Snohomish Joe, and Alexander Morris, October 15, 1903, Tulalip Agency, Letters Received from Tulalip Agency Reservations; *Annual Reports of the Department of the Interior, 1902,* 364.

28. Reynolds to Buchanan, June 30, 1905, Tulalip Agency, Letters Received from Tulalip Agency Reservations; Reynolds, *Annual Report,* July 6, 1905, Tulalip Agency, *Annual Reports.*

29. Reynolds, *Annual Report,* June 30, 1907, Tulalip Agency, *Annual Reports.*

30. Reynolds to Buchanan, June 21, 1909, Tulalip Agency, Letters Received from Tulalip Agency Reservations; Reynolds, *Annual Report,* July 10, 1908, June 30, 1909, Tulalip Agency, *Annual Reports;* Buchanan to Reynolds, February 13, 1902, Tulalip Agency, Letters Sent from Superintendent of Tulalip Agency Reservations.

31. *Forty-ninth Annual Report of the Board of Indian Commissioners, 1918,* 74–75; *Tulalip Agency Annual Report, 1927;* Benton Stookey, "Alfalfa in Western Washington," *Monthly Bulletin* (Puyallup: State College of Washington, Agriculture Experiment Station, November 1913), 15.

32. Olsen, "Beginning of Agriculture," 266–7; *Tulalip Agency Annual Report, 1927;* Reynolds, *Annual Report,* 1923, 1926, 1929, Tulalip Agency, *Annual Reports;* W. F. Dickens to Joseph Schlageter, September 18, 1924, Tulalip Agency, Decimal File, Correspondence with Tulalip Resident Farmer; H. L. Blanchard, "What Dairy Farming Means," *Monthly Bulletin* (March 1914).

33. George LaVatta to Commissioner of Indian Affairs, December 13, 1939,

H. D. McCullough to Commissioner of Indian Affairs, December 2, 1936,
O. C. Upchurch to Commissioner of Indian Affairs, November 18, 1936, Tulalip Agency, Decimal File, Muckleshoot Reservation.

34. *Annual Report of Extension Workers*, Tulalip Agency, Muckleshoot Reservation, 1937, 1939; *Dry Farm Statistics*, Tulalip Agency, Muckleshoot Reservation; Louis Starr, interview, August 5, 1986. A 1937 letter from several citizens
confirmed Starr's statement that the Muckleshoot Indians were not receiving
welfare at this time. Bertha Bowman et al. to Commissioner of Indian Affairs,
March 17, 1937, Tulalip Agency, Decimal File, Muckleshoot Reservation.

35. Most recently, this view is represented in R. Douglas Hurt, *Indian Agriculture in America* (Lawrence: University Press of Kansas, 1987), chaps. 9
and 10.

3

The Reservation as Place
A South Dakota Essay

FRANK POMMERSHEIM

For Stanley Red Bird (1917–1987)

From the Indians we learned a toughness and a strength; and we
    gained
A freedom: by taking theirs: but a real freedom: born
From the wild and open land our grandfathers heroically stole.
But we took a wound at Indian hands: a part of our soul scabbed over.
                       —Thomas McGrath[1]

INDIAN RESERVATIONS ARE OFTEN DESCRIBED AS ISLANDS OF POV-
erty and despair cast adrift from the mainstream of national progress.
Less often, they are extolled as places luckily isolated from the cor-
rosive predations of the twentieth century. Each description invokes
the complex field of Indian law as a touchstone of both the past and
the future, as either a driving wedge for Indian natural resources and
cultural breakup or a countervailing force of restraint and an element
of cultural renewal. Hidden in these descriptions and claims is the
important notion of the reservation as place—as a physical, human,
legal, and spiritual reality that embodies the history, the dreams, and
the aspirations of Indian people, their communities, and their tribes.
The reservation is a place that not only marks the enduring survival
of Indian communities from a marauding western society, but it also
holds the promise of fulfillment. As Lakota people say, "hecel lena
Oyate nipikte [that these people may live]."[2] The reservation constitutes an abiding place full of quotidian vitality and pressing dilemmas
that define modern Indian life.

South Dakota has often resisted the notion that reservations either
endure or possess any positive significance for the state. The history
of litigious animosity is long and bitter, with continuous disputes over

reservation boundaries, water rights, the Black Hills, and state authority on the reservation. Yet, at this centennial juncture it might be worthwhile to suggest another angle of vision that might, in turn, suggest an "angle of repose"—a vision infused by mutual understanding and common interest.[3]

The perspective of this essay centers on the continuing process of cultural self-scrutiny and intercultural contact between Indians and non-Indians and between Indian tribes and state and federal governments. This notion of "contact," which began with the arrival of the first Europeans, is continuous.[4] As a process, it is not related to the ethnocentric concepts of manifest destiny, progress, and cultural superiority but to an examination of the forces at play in the "contact" and the rubric of *choices* that emerges. Choice, whether conscious or not, has real implications for individuals, communities, and tribes. Choice is not always apparent, and the failure to be aware of it often results in loss and forfeited opportunity. It is important, therefore, to highlight and clarify these choices as they emerge from the consideration of the reservation as place and eternal center—choices that are not merely grounded in considerations of efficiency but are also located in the larger space of culture and meaning.

Figures on Mother Earth

Indian people often cannot conceive of life without land. They are a part of it and it is a part of them; it is their Mother. This is not just a romantic commonplace. For most Indian groups, including the Lakotas of South Dakota, land is a cultural centerpiece with wide-ranging implications for any attempt to understand modern reservation life. Beyond its obvious historical provision of subsistence, land is the source of spiritual origins and sustaining myth, which in turn provide a landscape of cultural and emotional meaning.

The land often determines the values of the human landscape.[5] The harsh lands of the prairie helped to make Lakota tribal communities austere and generous, places where giving and sharing were first principles.[6] The people needed the land and each other too much to permit wanton accumulation and ecological impairment to the living source of nourishment. Much of this, of course, is antithetical to western history and culture. As one commentator suggested, the western ethos reflects a commitment

> to *take* possession without being possessed: to take secure hold on the lands beyond and yet hold them at a rigidly maintained spiritual distance. It was never to merge, to mingle, to marry. To do so was to become an apostate from Christian history and so be kept in an eternal wilderness.[7]

Such differing conceptions between Indians and non-Indians about the nature of land only added to the likelihood of adversity and misunderstanding. And sure enough, one of the results of more than three centuries of Indian and non-Indian contact has been the severance of much of this cultural taproot that connects Lakota people to the land. Impaired but not eradicated, this root is now being rediscovered and tended with renewed vigor and stewardship. The importance of land has been a recurrent theme in recent Indian literature, which involves the loss of the old guardian spirits of place and how they might be made to speak again—how the land can become numinous once more.[8]

This, then, is one pull of the land, the source of vital myth and cultural well-being. But there is also the complementary idea of a homeland where generations have lived out their lives and destiny. Many reservations are rural and isolated and, like the Rosebud Indian Reservation, are quite beautiful, captivating in the way that the subtle paintbrush of the prairie often is. The Rosebud and other reservations like it hold no appeal for tourists, but a long stay makes lasting impressions on the psyche. The notion of homeland, of course, is not unique to Indians; and despite the obvious irony, it is valued by many non-Indians, including non-Indian residents of reservations.

These attractions and connections do not prevent people from leaving their reservations, but they do make it difficult. People do leave, most often for greater economic opportunity and sometimes to escape violence and what they consider to be inferior schools. But most who leave also return. Robert Logterman, a longtime, non-Indian rancher on the Rosebud Indian Reservation, may have said it best: "they ought to send someone from the reservation into outer space because then they would be sure that they would return safely."[9] Even the federal government learned this lesson and abandoned its program of "relocation," which attempted to take people from the reservation and resettle them in major urban areas where there were greater economic opportunities.[10] Few Indians would participate, however, and many of those who did refused to stay on the fringes of urban ghettos.

The reservation is home for Indians. It is a place where the land lives and stalks people, where the land looks after people and makes them live right, where the earth's ways provide solace and nurturance.[11] Yet, it is also a place where the land has been wounded and the sacred hoop has been broken, a place where there is the stain of violence and suffering. It is this painful dilemma that also stalks people and their Mother.

The Formation of Reservations

Any attempt to understand modern reservation life requires an understanding of what reservations are and how they came to be. Without an understanding of the legal and cultural roots involved in the formation of reservations, it is impossible to comprehend much of the current social reality and political atmosphere that dominates individual and institutional life in Indian country. The particular history of any reservation can then augment this general understanding. Particulars include whether the reservation is located within a tribe's aboriginal homeland, whether more than one tribe is "confederated" there, and the numbers of permanent non-Indians. All of these elements ionize expectations and struggles in the modern refraction of old promises and commitments—the covenant with the past.

The concept of an Indian reservation is best defined as the guarantee of a "measured separatism" to Indian people as the result of negotiated treaties and settlements reached between tribes and the federal government.[12] Most of the treaties between mutual sovereigns were signed during the nineteenth century through negotiations that represented political and legal adjustments between the western march of an expansionary, American society and the staunch resistance of established, tribal societies.

The treaties that established reservations did much more. They helped create an enduring and special legal and moral relationship between the federal government and Indian tribes. Treaties also reflect a set of sovereign promises and expectations that continues to be at the heart of defining the modern contours of this relationship. It is instructive, then, to explore the roots of these interactions and legal exchanges because they affect so much of what continues in this dynamic, though often misunderstood and wrongly construed relationship.

The meetings of tribes and representatives of the federal government brought together people with different languages, cultures, and worldviews. Those often extreme divergences must have gravely affected emotions and understandings. Perhaps under no other set of circumstances—except those of raw, historical necessity involving one sovereign in the face of another—could these disparate human configurations come together. The treaties represent the documents of that unprecedented exchange where, in part, each side cast its future on the integrity and goodwill of the other.

Treaties represent a bargained-for exchange, and it is important to understand what the exchange was. The Indians usually agreed to make peace and cede land—often vast amounts of it—to the federal government in exchange for a cessation of hostilities, the provision of some services, and, most important, the establishment and recognition of a reservation homeland free from the incursion of both the state and non-Indian settlers.

The quality of the exchanges varied significantly. In some cases, the federal government had the strong military upper hand, and many tribes were forced to agree to small reservations in regions removed from their aboriginal territories. In other cases—particularly involving the Lakota of the Great Sioux Nation in South Dakota—there was a military standoff and the reservations were established in the heart of the Indians' traditional homeland.

Much of the negotiations surrounding the treaties focused on the government's promises and guarantees to protect tribes from white settlement. For example, the Chippewas, Ottawas, and Potawatomies were told that

the Great Spirit has ordained that your Great Father and Congress should be to the Red Man, as Guardians and Fathers. . . . soon . . . you shall be at a permanent home from which there will be no danger of your moving again, you will receive their full benefit.[13]

The need for reservations and for homelands of a "measured separatism" was the one point upon which both the tribes and federal government could readily agree. Such entities met important policy objectives for each side. The United States wanted to regulate and reduce the contact of Indians with future settlers in order to minimize the likelihood of violence. This federal policy was consistent from the beginning of the Republic. Non-Indians could not live harmoniously with Indians, and the federal government early on regulated contact between Indians and non-Indians. Non-Indians (and the states) could not purchase lands from individual Indians or tribes without the approval of the federal government. The federal government also regulated trade, the interdiction of liquor, and criminal activity in Indian country.[14]

This non-intercourse policy was complemented by the policy of removal. When non-Indians continually pressed on Indian lands and settlements, Indians were often "removed" and relocated west of the Mississippi River. The most dramatic example of this policy is the Trail of Broken Tears in 1831, when President Andrew Jackson, under conditions imposed in the Treaty of Dancing Rabbit Creek, removed the Cherokees, Creeks, Choctaws, Chickasaws, and Seminoles to their new "homes" in Indian Territory. In the West, removal was untenable because the continent ended at the not-so-distant West Coast, and many tribes, including the Lakota of the Great Sioux Nation, were not sufficiently "subdued" to have such conditions imposed on them.

The tribes, for their part, wanted to be left alone. The Fort Laramie Treaty of 1868 was typical, providing that the reservation was

> set apart for the absolute and undisturbed use and occupation of the Indians herein named . . . and the United States now solemnly agrees that no person except those herein designated and authorized so to do, . . . shall ever be permitted to pass over, settle upon, or reside in the territory described in the article.[15]

Much of what federal negotiators said and did was a mixture of grandiloquence and ash, the expedience of the day grounded in the clash between binding promises and mere holding actions. For the Indians, more was at stake. Theirs was not simply the need for a place to live, but the need to preserve the land that was critical for cultural survival and spiritual succor. Despite these contrasting needs and expectations, the notion was born that reservations were to exist as islands of Indianness within an ever-expanding, encroaching society.[16] Whatever their shortcomings—and there are many—reservations continue to provide the opportunity to strengthen and fulfill the national commitment to a vital, pluralistic society and to preserve the promise of a "measured separatism."

Despite this history of bargained-for exchange, treaties and reservations are often misconstrued as unilateral, revocable acts of majority and federal largesse. Tribes gave up much for what they received— homelands, often reduced in size, with the right to govern their own affairs. If this mutuality had been preserved and legally vouchsafed, then the original purpose of reservations might have been achieved and maintained. But the treaty-based promises were often eroded and the "strong fences" of federal protection torn down.

"Measured Separatism" Under Assault

Western expansion did not abate with the signing of treaties, and the federal policy of "measured separatism" soon gave way to a policy of vigorous assimilation. The homelands were cut open, and the line separating Indians and non-Indians was obliterated. Much Indian land was lost as non-Indian settlers came into Indian country. Cultural ways were strained, and traditional tribal institutions were undermined and weakened. For many tribes, this was the most devastating historical blow to traditional Indian life.[17]

The linchpin for this policy was the Dawes Severalty Act, also known as the General Allotment Act of 1887. President Theodore Roosevelt forcefully described the act as "a mighty pulverizing engine to break up the tribal mass. It acts directly upon the family and the individual."[18] The General Allotment Act authorized the Bureau of Indian Affairs to allot 160 acres of tribal land to each head of household and 40 acres to each minor. Allotments were originally to remain in trust for twenty-five years, where they would be immune from

local property taxes during the transition from a tribally owned communal resource to an individually owned piece of land managed like
surrounding non-Indian farms and ranches.

The twenty-five-year trust period was undermined by the Burke
Act of 1906, which allowed the transfer of a fee patent to "competent" Indians prior to the expiration of the trust period. Competency
commissions were quickly established to determine whether or not
individual Indians were "competent" to receive fee patents that would
remove restrictions against alienation and tax obligations. The commissions often made competency determinations based on the most
perfunctory of findings, including whether the individual was one-
half degree Indian blood or less. In addition to authorizing allotments,
the act permitted the opening of "surplus" reservation lands for homesteading by non-Indians.

The allotment policy may be best understood as a land reform policy
imposed from above without tribal input and consent; grossly under-
capitalized, providing ten dollars and less per allottee for implements,
seeds, and instruction; insensitive to the hunting and food gathering traditions of nonagricultural tribes; and devoid of any cultural
understanding of the roles of the *tiyospaye* (the extended family of
the Lakota) in which the allotments that were assigned to individuals
were often located outside their home communities. Seen from this
perspective, it is not difficult to understand why the allotment policy
failed.

The results of the policy were devastating. The national Indian land
estate was reduced from 138 million acres in 1887 to 52 million acres in
1934. More than 26 million acres of allotted land were transferred from
tribes to individual Indians and then passed to non-Indians through
sale, fraud, mortgage foreclosures, and tax sales.[19]

Sixty million of the 86 million acres lost by Indians during the allotment era were lost because of the "surplus" land provisions of the
Burke Act. Thirty-eight million acres of unallotted tribal lands were
declared "surplus" to Indian needs and were ceded to the federal
government for sale to non-Indians. The federal government opened
another 22 million acres of "surplus" tribal land to homesteading.[20]
The ravages of the allotment policy were halted only by the Indian Reorganization Act of 1934, which permanently extended the trust status

of all existing allotments and halted the issuance of new allotments.

These ravages had equally scarring collateral effects. For the first time, the reservations became checkerboards of lands owned by tribes, individual Indians, individual non-Indians, and corporations. Individual Indian allotments quickly fractionated within two to three generations, often resulting in dozens or even hundreds of heirs. Even land that remained in trust was more often leased to non-Indians than used by the allottees.

More difficult to assess is the direct effect of the allotment process on tribal government and institutions. When the reservations were opened, some commentators have argued, true traditional governments were essentially doomed in most tribes, and the authority of any form of tribal government was undermined.[21] The great influx of non-Indian settlers coupled with the loss of communal lands and the attendant yoke of federal support of these policies eradicated much of the tribes' ability to govern. In the resulting void, the Bureau of Indian Affairs, in league with Christian missionaries, became the true power brokers and the *de facto* governing forces.

The missionaries wreaked a debilitating havoc on the tribes with their religious and educational programs, particularly the boarding school program that took Indian children from their families for long periods of time and forbade the speaking of tribal languages in school.[22] Under these circumstances, it is not difficult to perceive the strain and pressure placed on traditional Indian culture. The strain was even more apparent when these policies were joined with Bureau of Indian Affairs directives outlawing traditional religious practices, such as the Sun Dance. The heart of the culture was driven underground.

Many people on the reservation vividly recall those times. Albert White Hat, an instructor of Lakota thought and philosophy at Sinte Gleska College on the Rosebud Sioux Reservation, remembered many times when he and his classmates at St. Francis Indian School had their mouths washed out with soap for speaking Lakota. As White Hat eloquently summarized: "You gave us the Bible, but stole our land. You taught us English only so we could take orders, not so that we might dream."[23]

The point here is not to assign blame, but to comprehend more deeply the forces at work on reservations. The governmental and religious policies of assimilation were clearly mistakes, but they were at least partly driven by worthy motives. The more sinister motives of greed, ethnocentrism, and religious exclusivity are clear, and even glaring, but there were also many well-meaning individuals and groups who believed that the policies of allotment and assimilation were the only ways to stave off the obliteration of Indian culture by the forces of manifest destiny. The leading historian of the allotment era, D. S. Otis, concluded:

> That the leading proponents of allotment were inspired by the highest motives seems conclusively true. A member of Congress, speaking on the Dawes bill in 1886 said, "It has . . . the endorsement of the Indian rights associations throughout the country, and of the best sentiment of the land."[24]

A minority of congressional opponents on the House Indian Affairs Committee saw it differently in 1880:

> The real aim of this bill is to get at the Indian lands and open them up to settlement. The provisions for the apparent benefit of the Indian are but the pretext to get at the lands and occupy them. . . . If this were done in the name of greed it would be bad enough; but to do it in the name of humanity, and under the cloak of an ardent desire to promote the Indian's welfare by making him like ourselves whether he will or not is infinitely worse.[25]

The cultural and institutional loss was inevitable.

The federal government's endorsement of these policies was reversed with the Indian Reorganization Act of 1934, which ended the allotment era and supported the development of tribal self-government. The IRA reforms, including explicit authorization and assistance in the adoption of tribal constitutions, sought to engender recovery from stultification. Yet, the "new" opportunity held out in the IRA often was—and still is—perceived on reservations as further evisceration of traditional tribal government with its emphasis on the "white man's way" of holding elections, speaking English, and communicating by writing. For some, the apparatus of IRA tribal governments further disturbed the cultural balance necessary to support traditional forms of self-rule that are often associated with tribal governance when treaties were made. As a result, IRA-elected tribal governments often remain controversial and occasionally have a hint of illegitimacy about them.

The dismal effects of allotment and assimilation have been halted and the thrust of self-rule reworked and reinvigorated. But the scars of the severe loss of land and the reminders of social weakening serve to verify the inextricable bond that connects the people, the culture, and the land.

The South Dakota Experience

All reservations in South Dakota have felt the battering of the allotment and assimilation process.[26] Some, such as the Sisseton-Wahpeton and the Yankton Sioux reservations, were completely allotted, with the remainder ceded to the federal government and subsequently made available to non-Indian homesteaders.[27] On both of these reservations, only 15 to 20 per cent of the original reservation's territory was allotted to tribal members. No longer is any land held in common by these tribes. In other instances, such as on the Pine Ridge and Rosebud reservations, the tribes were able to retain approximately one-third of the reservation land, with approximately one-third held by Indians and one-third by non-Indians.[28]

Along with the allotment and assimilation processes was the related process of diminishment, which often reduced the boundaries of a reservation. The diminishment issue focuses not on the question of who *owns* the land, but more precisely on whether the process through which the federal government obtained "surplus" unallotted tribal lands for non-Indian homesteading resulted in a corresponding reduction of the reservation's boundaries. The concept of diminishment addresses the size of the reservation, not the composition of landownership patterns within the reservation. Therefore, the question of diminishment focuses most directly on the potential territorial scope of tribal governmental authority.

The principal legal issue in diminishment cases has been whether Congress, in "opening" unallotted portions of reservations for non-

Indian settlement, intended to reduce the size and boundaries of the reservation or whether it simply intended to allow non-Indians to settle on the reservation.[29] The authority to do either is clearly within the scope of Congress' plenary authority in Indian affairs; but because Congress never directly addressed the issue in any of the acts that encouraged non-Indian settlement in Indian country, the question has tended to center on congressional intent.[30] It seems remarkable that Congress never directly addressed the issue, given the potentially serious consequences attendant on its actions.

The Supreme Court noted the incongruity. Justice Marshall pointed out in his dissent in *Rosebud Sioux Tribe* v. *Kneip:*

> Congress manifested an "almost complete lack of . . . concern with the boundary issue." This issue was of no great importance in the early 1900s as it was commonly assumed that all reservations would be abolished when the trust period on allotted lands expired. There was no pressure on Congress to accelerate this timetable, so long as settlers could acquire unused land. Accordingly, Congress did not focus on the boundary question. . . . For the Court to find in this confusion and indifference a "clear" congressional intent to disestablish its reservation is incomprehensible.[31]

The test for determining congressional intent in diminishment cases finds its most recent elucidation in *Solem* v. *Bartlett*.[32] Justice Marshall, writing for a unanimous Court, held that a 1908 act of Congress opening part of the Cheyenne River Sioux Reservation to non-Indian settlement did *not* evince any congressional intent to diminish the boundaries of the reservation.[33] The Court stated that diminishment will not be lightly inferred and that the examination of surplus land acts requires that Congress clearly evince an "intent" to change "boundaries" before diminishment will be found.[34] Pertinent indicia of congressional intent include the statutory language used to open the Indian lands, regarded by the Court as "most probative," as well as surrounding circumstances, particularly the manner in which the transaction was negotiated and the tenor of congressional reports.[35] "To a lesser extent," the Court has "looked to events that occurred after the passage of a surplus land act to decipher Congress's intentions." And finally, "on a more pragmatic level, [the Court] recognized that who actually moved into open reservation lands is also relevant to deciding whether a surplus land act diminished a reservation."[36]

Five reservations in South Dakota have been diminished under this analysis: Sisseton-Wahpeton, Yankton, Rosebud, and Pine Ridge.[37] The result in each instance was to reduce the boundaries of the reservation and, in effect, to contract the size of the "homeland." Diminishment can also have the anomalous effect of placing substantial numbers of Indian people and their communities *outside* the reservation. For example, one of the results of the Supreme Court's decision in *Rosebud Sioux Tribe* v. *Kneip,* which upheld the diminishment of the Rosebud Sioux Reservation, was to place two thousand tribal members and seven recognized tribal communities outside the official reservation boundaries.[38] The social, cultural, psychological, and legal effects of such decisions clearly exacerbate the stress and burden of attempting to maintain individual and tribal well-being and integrity.

This wrenching epoch of allotment and diminishment was not the last of its kind in South Dakota. Another round of federal "takings" of Indian lands occurred during the 1940s as part of the Missouri River Basin Development Program, better known as the Pick-Sloan project. Pick-Sloan was a joint water development plan developed by the Army Corps of Engineers and the Bureau of Reclamation in 1944 for the Missouri River Basin.[39] As adopted by Congress, the Pick-Sloan plan included 107 dams, 13 of which had previously been authorized. The key structures were the five Corps of Engineer dams on the Missouri: the Garrison Dam in North Dakota and the Oahe, Big Bend, Fort Randall, and Gavins Point dams in South Dakota.[40] The primary goals of the project were to provide flood control, irrigation, and hydroelectric power.

The five main stem dams destroyed more than five hundred and fifty square miles of tribal land in North Dakota and South Dakota and dislocated more than nine hundred Indian families. Most of this damage was sustained by four Sioux reservations in South Dakota: Standing Rock and Cheyenne River, reduced by the Oahe project; Yankton, affected by Fort Randall Dam; and Crow Creek and Lower Brule, damaged by both the Fort Randall and Big Bend projects.[41] Army Corps of Engineer dams on the Missouri inundated another 200,000 acres of Sioux land and uprooted an additional 580 families.[42]

The results of this destruction were summarized by a leading chronicler of the Pick-Sloan project:

> [Sioux families were] uprooted and forced to move from rich sheltered bottomlands to empty prairies. Their best homesites, their finest pastures, croplands and hay meadows, and most of their valuable timber, wildlife, and vegetation were flooded. Relocation of the agency headquarters on the Cheyenne River, Lower Brule, and Crow Creek reservations seriously disrupted governmental, medical, and educational services and facilities and dismantled the largest Indian communities on these reservations. Removal of churches and community centers, cemeteries, and shrines impaired social and religious life on all five reservations. Loss not only of primary fuel, food, and water resources but also of prime grazing land effectively destroyed the Indians' economic base. The thought of having to give up their ancestral land, to which they were so closely wedded, caused severe psychological stress. The result was extreme confusion and hardship for tribal members.[43]

The Sioux knew little about the Pick-Sloan project until long after Congress had approved the plan. Despite treaty rights mandating that land could not be taken without their consent, none of the tribes were consulted prior to the program's enactment. The Bureau of Indian Affairs was fully informed, but it made no objections to Congress and did not inform tribes of their impending loss until 1947, three years after the project was approved. Financial settlements, generally regarded as grossly inadequate, were not achieved until 1957.[44]

Vine Deloria Jr. observed that this flooding of ancestral lands ruthlessly took away old memories and led to the tribe's material and spiritual impoverishment. He characterized the Pick-Sloan plan as "the single most destructive act ever perpetrated on any tribe by the United States."[45] Yet, this legacy of loss has not reduced but has extended and deepened the emotional and cultural commitment of Lakota people to the land as the enduring repository of their ultimate well-being. Without the land, there is no center to resist the historical pressures created by the dominant society.

"The American West as Living Space"

Despite the pervasive conflict between tribes and state and federal governments and between Indians and non-Indians, there are some unitive factors that are often not perceived and occasionally even ignored. One such factor is the geographical conditions of living in the West—a unique environmental and ecological system that exacts a premium for successful living. The key attributes of this habitat are space and aridity.[46] Writer and critic Wallace Stegner has aptly described this western "living space":

> In the West it is impossible to be unconscious of or indifferent to space. At every city's edge it confronts us as federal lands kept open by aridity and the custodial bureaus; out in the boondocks it engulfs us. And it does contribute to individualism, if only because in that much emptiness people have the dignity of rareness and must do much of what they do without help, and because self-reliance becomes a social imperative, part of a code. . . . It encourages a fatal carelessness and destructiveness because it seems so limitless and because what is everybody's is nobody's responsibility. It also encourages, in some, an impassioned protectiveness. . . . it promotes certain needs, tastes, attitudes, skills. It is those tastes, attitudes, and skills, as well as the prevailing destructiveness and its corrective, love of the land, that relate real Westerners to the myth.[47]

The West is also arid, which is not only a physical and often brutal fact, but is also a determinant of the social fabric:

> Aridity and aridity alone makes the various Wests one. The distinctive western plants and animals, the hard clarity . . . of the western air, the look and location of western towns, the empty spaces that separate them, the way farms and ranches are either densely concentrated where water is plentiful or widely scattered where it is scarce, the pervasive presence as dam builder and water broker, the snarling state's-rights and antifederal feeling whose burden Bernard DeVoto once characterized in a sentence—"Get out and give us more money"—those are all consequences . . . of aridity.[48]

Aridity and space have combined to establish a unique environment in which there is often a sharp sense of independence poised against an encroaching federal authority. Despite the vastness of the land and the claims of individualism and tribal sovereignty, there is significant and seemingly intractable dependence on and resentment of the federal presence in Indian country and the West. Stegner keenly summarized this bleak history: "Take for granted federal assistance, but damn federal control. Your presence as absentee landlord offends us, Uncle. Get out, and give us more money."[49]

This description contains the necessary seeds to cultivate a renewed examination of the role that federal money and the federal government play in Indian country and the West. Although Indian tribes are often casually described as too dependent on the federal government, it is less often noted that many of their non-Indian "rugged individualist" neighbors are equally dependent, whether through federal farm subsidies or the below-cost access and use of water and grazing rights on federal lands. This knot of common dependency must be examined to determine whether or not there is sufficient common ground on which Indians and non-Indians, tribes and states, might define a clearer, more productive, and more satisfying relationship with the federal government.

This is not an easy matter. Tribal dependency on the federal government is based on a "trust relationship" that is grounded in the mutual covenants of the treaties. The object is not, or should not be, to end this important relationship but to redefine its contours so that the relationship is less asymmetrical and has a renewed infusion of mutuality. At the same time, western farmers and ranchers need to depend less on federal subsidies and the profligate use of the public domain. There is the potential for state and tribal conflict here, but the risk must be taken if there is to be a realignment of interests by people and entities that call the West home.

This federal dependence also has its nongovernmental analogue in the western suspicion and distrust of outsiders and do-gooders and the resultant insularity of vision. The history of the West

> is a history of colonialism, both material and cultural. Is it any wonder we are so deeply xenophobic, and regard anything east of us as suspect? The money and power always came from the East, took what it wanted, and left us, white or Indian, with our traditions dismantled and our territory filled with holes in the ground.[50]

This insularity, at least in South Dakota, remains more prominent in the non-Indian than in the Indian community, as tribes increasingly look to and find more congenial support for their efforts outside the state.[51] Yet, it remains true for both communities that difficulty and exploitation have often come from outsiders. The aggravated insularity of South Dakotans needs to be set aside to allow each group to consider the potential coalition *against* outside exploiters and support *for* outsiders who have genuine empathy and commitment to both the Indian and non-Indian communities.

Implicit in the process of clarifying relationships with both governmental and non-governmental "external" forces is the opportunity to embrace a new concern for improving "internal" relations between Indians and non-Indians, between tribes and the state. This process is necessary if there is to be any unity on the issues central to the existence and reinvigoration of Indian and non-Indian rural communities, which often share the attributes of being underdeveloped, isolated, and easily ignored by the powers that be.

Indians and non-Indians, the tribes and the state, have more in common than they might think. Despite a history of conflict, their future is inextricably linked. Many of the dominant forces—such as the scarcity of capital, the shortage of human resources, the increased reliance on technology, and a disappearance of markets—act with equal devastation on Indian and non-Indian communities. But each side must accede to a condition before any common agenda can be addressed. Each group must recognize the permanency and legitimacy of the other.

What both sides already have is space and aridity. What they need most is a sense of place to meet the deep human need of belonging. Yet, this is unlikely without some painful introspection, particularly in the non-Indian community. The mythology of the non-Indian West is grounded in conquest and possession, and it no longer works. As writer William Kittredge suggested:

> Our mythology doesn't work anymore. . . . We find ourselves weathering a rough winter of discontent, snared in the uncertainties of a transitional time and urgently yearning to inhabit a story that might bring sensible order to our lives—even as we know such a story can only evolve through an almost literally infinite series of recognitions of what,

individually, we hold sacred. . . . There is no more running away to
territory. This is it, for most of us. We have no choice but to live in community. If we're lucky we may discover a story that teaches us to abhor
our old romance with conquest and possession.[52]

The outworn mythology has also been fueled by the excesses of
individualism that have hindered the development of communities
and traditions. American individualism, much celebrated and cher-
ished, has developed without its essential corrective, which is *belonging*.[53] In South Dakota, particularly in the rural areas on or near Indian
country, this sense of belonging in the non-Indian community may
not be so sharply attenuated, which again suggests the potential for a
coming together on these issues. There are many complex issues, such
as the use of Missouri River and Oglala Aquifer water and the Black
Hills issue, that have the potential to bring Indians and non-Indians
together, but the development of a greater ethic or story is needed to
hold them together. Of course, no one knows exactly how to do this,
yet important work has begun:

> We need to develop an ethic of place. It respects equally the people of
> a region and the land, animals, vegetation, water, and air. An ethic of
> place recognizes that Western people revere the physical surroundings
> and that they need and deserve a stable, productive economy that is
> accessible to those of modest incomes. An ethic of place ought to be a
> shared community value and ought to manifest itself in a dogged deter-
> mination of the society at large to treat the environment and its people
> as equals, to recognize both as sacred, and to insure that all members of
> the community not just search for, but insist upon, solutions that fulfill
> the ethic.[54]

Within this ethic of place, there must be a recognition that Indians

> possess individuality as people and self-rule as governments, but they
> are also an inseparable part of the larger community, a proud and valu-
> able constituent group that must be extended the full measure of respect
> mandated by an ethic of place.[55]

Along with these encouraging beginnings, there are other signs
of the Indian and non-Indian communities coming together. These

signs are found most often in the area of education, specifically in the Indian-controlled colleges in South Dakota. Sinte Gleska College at Rosebud and Oglala Lakota College at Pine Ridge, both funded during the early 1970s, represent successful acts of self-determination by local tribal leaders to meet the educational needs of tribal people.[56] At the same time, 10 per cent to 15 per cent of students and staff at these institutions are non-Indians who are preparing to be teachers, nurses, and counselors. The more extraordinary aspect of this arrangement is that the colleges have provided rare forums in which Indians and non-Indians have opportunities for face-to-face communication, which fosters personal, cultural, and political respect and understanding.

Conclusion

Gerald Clifford, an Oglala and chairman of the Black Hills Steering Committee, said, "Our relationships to one another as Lakota are defined by our relationship to the earth. Until we get back on track in our relationship to the earth, we cannot straighten out any of our relationships to ourselves, to other people."[57] The difficult question is *how* to get back on track. For many Indians on reservations, the relationship to the land has become more passive than active. The land does not provide economic livelihood for very many, and the detritus of the dominant society often invades and mars the landscape. The observations of one visitor to a reservation in the Southwest are salutary:

> I was . . . impressed by the amount of junk on the reservation—the usual modern American assortment of cars and bottles, plastic jugs, old cars, blowing paper, etc. The junk surprised me, most people who write or talk about Indians, I think, try to see or imagine them apart from the worst—or at least the most unsightly—influence of white society. But of course one should not be surprised. When junk is everywhere— better hidden in some places than others—why should one not expect to find it here?[58]

The rupture in the relationship of Indians to the land has also had adverse social effects. Ronnie Lupe, former chairman of the White

Mountain Apache Tribe in New Mexico, vividly articulated this view: "Our children are losing the land. It doesn't work on them anymore. They don't know the story about what happened to these places. That's why some get into trouble."[59] At Rosebud and other reservations in South Dakota, problems of teenage alcoholism and juvenile crime provide dispiriting confirmation of Lupe's observation. Yet, as Stanley Red Bird, founder and former chairman of the board of directors at Sinte Gleska College, observed: "You white people got a lot of our land and a lot of our heart, but we know you were wrong and now with the help of the Great Spirit, and the new warriors of education, we will live again."[60]

The land must be retained, restored, and redefined. Its economic role must be resuscitated, its spiritual role must be revivified, and its healing role must be revitalized. The land must hold the people and give direction to their aspirations and yearnings. In this way, the land may be seen to be part of the "sacred text" of Lakota religion and culture. As part of the "sacred text," the land is a principal symbol of— perhaps *the* principal symbol of—the fundamental aspirations of the tradition. In this sense, the "sacred text" constantly *disturbs*, serving a prophetic function in the life of the community.[61] The land constantly evokes the fundamental Lakota aspirations to live in harmony with Mother Earth and to embody the traditional virtues of wisdom, courage, generosity, and fortitude. The "sacred text" guarantees nothing, but it does hold the necessary potential to successfully mediate the past of the tradition with its present predicament.

This concept of a "sacred text" also challenges non-Indians to examine their own traditions. For many in South Dakota, this would include a review of the Christian tradition and whether its aspirations include solidarity with the struggles of others for justice and self-realization. Non-Indians need to consider the deeper quandary of their Lakota neighbors' commitment to a "sacred text" so often assaulted by western history. Within the legal profession, this might include an examination of the aspirations of our constitutional "faith."[62]

The breath of despair once so prevalent in Indian country seems to be yielding to the air of hope. The answers to the troubling questions about the land and its economic, cultural, and spiritual roles do not readily insinuate themselves, but they are increasingly recognized and energetically posed. These questions also unerringly pierce the larger society's continuing assumptions about cultural diversity and the use and exploitation of the earth to sustain economic prodigality and waste.

Notes

1. Thomas McGrath, *Letter to an Imaginary Friend: Parts I & II* (Chicago: Swallow Press, 1970), 190.

2. "Lakota" is the traditional linguistic reference used by the Teton Sioux to describe themselves in their own language. "Sioux," a French corruption of a Chippewa word meaning snake or adder, was used by the Chippewas in a derogatory fashion to describe their traditional enemy, the Lakotas. For this reason, "Lakota" is the preferred term, although popular and legal usage has made "Sioux" a much more conventional and better known term. The terms are used here interchangeably.

The Teton, the Santee, and the Yanktonai Sioux are the three main divisions of the Sioux people. The Santees were basically woodland people who lived in Wisconsin and Minnesota; the Yanktonais were primarily riverine people who lived in Minnesota and eastern South Dakota; and the Tetons lived in the plains of the Dakotas. The Teton people spoke their language with an L(akota) emphasis, the Yanktonai with a D(akota) emphasis, and the Santee with an N(akota) emphasis. See, for example, James Satterlee and Vernon Malan, *History and Acculturation of the Dakota Indians*, Bulletin 613 (Brookings: Rural Sociology Department, South Dakota State University, 1973).

In South Dakota, the Santee division of Sioux people are found primarily on the Lake Traverse (Sisseton-Wahpeton) and Flandreau Santee reservations; the Yanktonais are on the Yankton, Standing Rock, and Crow Creek reservations; and the Tetons are on the Rosebud, Pine Ridge, Lower Brule, Cheyenne River, and Standing Rock Sioux reservations. It is reasonably accurate to state that today the strongest identification of Indians in South Dakota is with their reservation, rather than with their major Sioux branch. See, for example, M. Lawson, *Dammed Indians* (1982), 31–32.

3. Wallace Stegner, *Angle of Repose* (Garden City, N.Y.: Doubleday, 1971). This extraordinary novel has nothing to do with Native-Americans or South Dakota, yet the title and introspection of the work seem especially resonant in the context of this essay. "Angle of repose" is an engineering term that refers to the angle between the horizontal and the plane of contact between two bodies when the upper body is just about to slide over the lower. Repose, then, in the sense of rest, not from the demands of mutual problem solving but from antagonism.

4. See, for example, Francis Jennings, *The Invasion of America: Indians, Colo-*

nialism, and the Cant of Conquest (Chapel Hill: University of North Carolina Press, 1975), 32–42.

5. See, for example, Leslie Silko, "Landscape, History, and the Pueblo Imagination," in *On Nature*, ed. D. Halpern (1987), 83–94; Barry Lopez, *Crossing Open Ground* (New York: Scribner's, 1988), 61–71.

6. See, for example, Wendell Berry, *The Gift of Good Land: Further Essays, Cultural and Agricultural* (San Francisco: North Point Press, 1981), 50–52. Berry discusses the Papago Indians of the Southwest, but his descriptions are equally pertinent in the Lakota context.

7. Frederick W. Turner, *Beyond Geography: The Western Spirit Against the Wilderness* (New York: Viking Press, 1980), 238.

8. Frederick W. Turner, "Literature Lost in the Thickets," *New York Times Book Review*, February 15, 1987, 35. See also N. Scott Momaday, *House Made of Dawn* (New York: Harper & Row, 1968); Leslie Silko, *Ceremony* (New York: Viking, 1977); James Welch, *Winter in the Blood* (New York: Harper & Row, 1974); Welch, *Fools Crow* (New York: Viking, 1986); Louise Erdrich, *Love Medicine* (New York: Holt, Rinehart and Winston, 1985); Erdrich, *Tracks* (New York: Henry Holt, 1988).

9. Robert Logterman, interview with author, May 1986.

10. This policy of the Bureau of Indian Affairs was prominent from 1955 through 1961, the latter part of the termination period (1945–1961), when it was believed that reservations were inhospitable anachronisms that people should be encouraged to leave. See Donald Lee Fixico, *Termination and Relocation: Federal Indian Policy, 1945–1960* (Albuquerque: University of New Mexico Press, 1986).

11. See, for example, Keith Basso, " 'Stalking with Stories': Names, Places, and Moral Narratives Among the Western Apache," in *On Nature*, 95–116. See also Momaday, *House Made of Dawn*, 115.

12. Charles F. Wilkinson, *American Indians, Time and the Law: Native Societies in Modern Constitutional Democracy* (New Haven, Conn.: Yale University Press, 1987), 4. It is important to note that the Lakota did not see the treaty as mere expedience and the power politics of the day, subject to future accommodation to other emerging national interests. See comments by Father Peter John Powell in Roxanne Dunbar Ortiz, *The Great Sioux Nation: Sitting in Judgment on America* (Berkeley, Calif.: Moon Books, 1977), 141–2.

13. Treaty with Chippewas, Ottawas, and Potawatomies, 9 Stat. 853 (1846); Speech of Commissioner in *Journal of Proceedings* (November 12, 1845).

14. See, for example, Francis Paul Prucha, *American Indian Policy in the Formative Years: The Indian Trade and Intercourse Acts, 1780–1834* (Cambridge, Mass.: Harvard University Press, 1962).

15. Art. II, 15 Stat. 635 (1868).

16. See, for example, Wilkinson, *American Indians*, 14–19.

17. Ibid., 19–23.

18. Quoted in S. Lyman Tyler, *A History of Indian Policy* (Washington, D.C.: Bureau of Indian Affairs, 1973), 104.

19. Wilkinson, *American Indians*, 20.

20. Francis Paul Prucha, *The Great Father: The United States Government and the American Indians* (Lincoln: University of Nebraska Press, 1984), 896.

21. See, for example, Wilkinson, *American Indians*, 21; Walcomb E. Washburn, *Red Man's Land/White Man's Law: A Study of the Past and Present Status of the American Indian* (New York: Scribner's, 1971), 75–76.

22. See, for example, D. W. Adams, "Fundamental Considerations: The Deep Meaning of Native-American Schooling, 1880–1900," *Harvard Educational Review* 58 (1988): 1.

23. Albert White Hat, interview with the author, May 1983.

24. Delos Sacket Otis, *History of the Allotment Policy*, Hearings on H.R. 7902 Before the House Committee on Indian Affairs, 73d Cong., 2d sess., pt. 9, 428–89.

25. Ibid.

26. This discussion does not include the 7.7 million acres taken as part of the Black Hills Act of 1877, Act of February 28, 1877, 19 Stat. 254, or the 9 million acres lost as part of the Great Sioux Agreement of 1889, Act of March 2, 1889, 25 Stat. 889. The 1889 agreement carved out the six West River reservations (Pine Ridge, Rosebud, Cheyenne River, Standing Rock, Lower Brule, and Crow Creek) from the Great Sioux Reservation established as part of the Fort Laramie Treaty of 1868.

27. See the discussion in *DeCoteau v. District County Court*, 420 U.S. 425 (1975); *Wood v. Jameson*, 130 N.W.2d 95 (S.D. 1964).

28. See the discussion in *U.S. ex rel Cook v. Parkinson*, 525 F.2d 120 (8th Cir. 1975); *Rosebud Sioux Tribe v. Kneip*, 420 U.S. 584 (1977).

29. *Rosebud Sioux Tribe v. Kneip*, 586.

30. Ibid., 585–6. See also *Lone Wolf v. Hitchcock*, 187 U.S. 553 (1903), for a discussion of Congress's plenary authority in Indian affairs.

31. *Rosebud Sioux Tribe v. Kneip; Rosebud Sioux Tribe* at 430 U.S. 629–30 (Marshall, J., dissenting).

32. *Solem v. Bartlett*, 465 U.S. 463 (1984).

33. Act of May 29, 1908, ch. 218, 35 Stat. 460; *Solem v. Bartlett*, 466.

34. *Solem v. Bartlett*, 470.

35. Ibid., 471.

36. Ibid.

37. *DeCoteau v. District County Court; Wood v. Jameson; Cook v. Parkinson; Rosebud Sioux Tribe v. Kneip*.

38. *Rosebud Sioux Tribe*, 616.

39. Lawson, *Dammed Indians*, xxi.

40. Ibid., 20.

41. Ibid., 27.

42. Ibid., 29.

43. Ibid.

44. Ibid., 45, 95–107.

45. Vine Deloria Jr., Foreword to *Dammed Indians*, xiv.

46. Wallace Stegner, *The American West as Living Space* (Ann Arbor: University of Michigan Press, 1987), esp. 5. For this essay, I have included all of South Dakota in the West. It is interesting that most of the Indian population and Indian land in South Dakota are in the western part of the state, and there is a clear east/west distinction marked by the Missouri River in that state. East of the river the traditional crop agriculture of the Middle West dominates, and west of the river cattle ranching is prevalent.

47. Ibid., 80–81.

48. Ibid., 8–9.

49. Ibid., 15.

50. William Kittredge, *Owning It All* (St. Paul: Graywolf Press, 1987), 88. See also Patricia Nelson Limerick, *The Legacy of Conquest: The Unbroken Past of the American West* (New York: Norton, 1987).

51. The congressional bill for return of the Black Hills (S. 705) could not find a sponsor in the South Dakota delegation. The original sponsor was Senator Bill Bradley (D.-N.J.), who first heard about the Black Hills issue when conducting summer basketball clinics for the children of Pine Ridge.

52. Kittredge, *Owning It All*, 67–68.

53. Stegner, *American West as Living Space*, 22–23.

54. Charles Wilkinson, "Law and the American West: The Search for an Ethic of Place," *Colorado Law Review* 59 (1988): 401, 405.

55. Ibid., 407.

56. Each of these colleges has an enrollment of more than five hundred students with growth rates of 5 per cent or more annually. See, for example, *Lakota Times*, January 31, 1989. There are also smaller reservation-based colleges on the Cheyenne River, Standing Rock, Yankton, and Sisseton-Wahpeton reservations in South Dakota. More than twenty such colleges are located throughout Indian country. The national organization is known as the American Higher Education Consortium.

57. Quoted in William Grieder, "The Heart of Everything That Is," *Rolling Stone*, May 7, 1987, 62.

58. Berry, *Gift of Good Land*, 71–72.

59. Quoted in Basso, " 'Stalking with Stories,' " 95.

60. Stanley Red Bird, interview with the author, May 1986.

61. Michael J. Perry, *Morality, Politics, and Law* (New York: Oxford University Press, 1988), 137.

62. See, for example, William Brennan, "The Constitution of the United States: Contemporary Ratification," *Southern Texas Law Review* 27 (1986): 433,

434. Brennan concluded: "the Constitution embodies the aspiration to social justice, brotherhood, and human dignity that brought this nation into being. . . . we are an aspiring people, a people with faith in progress. Our amended Constitution is the lodestar of our aspirations."

4

"March of Civilization"

Standing Rock and the Sioux Act of 1889

CAROLE BARRETT

ON JULY 4, 1889, ONLY THIRTEEN YEARS AFTER NEWS OF CUSTER'S debacle at the Little Big Horn reached a shocked nation, five hundred Standing Rock Sioux, many of whom had been on the battlefield in 1876, converged on Bismarck to take part in the festivities that marked the opening of the Constitutional Convention and the impending statehood of North Dakota. In 1889, Bismarck was the territorial capital, but still a frontier town with dirt streets and wooden plank sidewalks. Panic still occasionally seized the citizenry when rumors of an Indian attack spread through the city.[1] But on this day the Indians, special guests of the territory of North Dakota and the city of Bismarck, were hailed by Bismarck's mayor as "Representatives of the Original Owners of these Great Prairies."[2]

Major James McLaughlin, Indian Agent at Standing Rock, arranged five hundred Sioux men, women, and children in an elaborate parade formation he called the "March of Civilization." McLaughlin grouped the Indians in five platoons, which were to symbolize and proclaim their progression into modern times.[3] Three men comprised the first contingent. Hairy Chin, chief of the Yanktonai Sioux and a prominent orator, led the Indians and was decked out as Uncle Sam. Walking behind Hairy Chin was Black Bull, a former warrior, who carried the American flag. Filling out the contingent was Red Horse, a partisan of Sitting Bull's who had fought in the Battle of the Little Big Horn; Red Horse shouldered the lead banner proclaiming "March of Civilization."

The next section of the parade was a troop of Indian men, women, and children arrayed in traditional buckskin clothing and carrying a banner announcing "Dakota as a Territory." This section represented the older, nomadic way of life, with ponies and dogs hitched to travois as if marching across the plains.[4] Sitting Bull marched in this column, wearing what was known as citizen's dress. The Bismarck paper reported him as "resplendent in a black Prince Albert coat," a stylish double-breasted frock coat. Sitting Bull's reputation was legendary. The general public held him responsible for the Custer disaster at the Little Big Horn, and he was judged a "nonprogressive" because of his unwillingness to adopt white ways and his opposition to the reservation system and government interference in Indian affairs. McLaughlin barely tolerated Sitting Bull, labeling him "the most noted disaffected Indian of modern times."[5]

Thirty United States Indian police, sporting navy blue uniforms and shouldering an American flag and a banner proclaiming them the representatives of "Law and Order," comprised the next group in the parade. Favored by Major McLaughlin, the police were appointed and supervised by him and thereby undermined the authority of the traditional chiefs. Within the next year, a number of the Standing Rock policemen, along with Sitting Bull, would be dead as a result of carrying out McLaughlin's orders to arrest Sitting Bull in his camp on the Grand River.[6]

The three judges of the Indian Court made up the next division in the parade. They carried a banner inscribed with a scale and weights and the word "Justice." The 1889 appointees to the court were Gall, John Grass, and Mad Bear, all former warriors who were renowned for their oratorical abilities and who McLaughlin had chosen because they were respected by their people as leaders and were moderate in their political outlook. These men were known as "progressives," those Indians who generally sought to follow the path set by the Indian agents because they believed that through compromises with the whites they could preserve some of their culture. Government agents dubbed them "progressives" because of their willingness to persuade fellow tribesmen of the benefits of cooperation.

The final section of the parade consisted of about two hundred Indian people, chiefly young and middle-aged. All of the men were outfitted with new hats and linen dusters, and the women were arrayed in snowy white dresses that conformed to the dictates of 1889 fashion. This last group carried the United States flag and a banner bearing the inscription "State of North Dakota, 1889."[7]

The "March of Civilization" was more than a festive procession. The parade of Sioux was meant as a representation of the people's progression from the traditional days of dog and horse drags to modern times. It was also a visual symbol of federal Indian policy that sought to assimilate or "christianize and civilize" the Indians. An 1889 Commissioner of Indian Affairs report clearly set forth the government's goal in Indian affairs:

> The Indians must conform to "the white man's ways," peaceably if they will, forcibly if they must. They must adjust themselves to their environment, and conform their mode of living substantially to our civilization. This civilization may not be the best possible, but it is the best the Indians can get. They cannot escape it, and must either conform to it or be crushed by it.[8]

As agent at Standing Rock, McLaughlin was charged with carrying out the official government policy of assimilation. He echoed the official policy in a letter he wrote in April 1889: "From the very nature of things Indians must either fall in with the march of civilization and progress or be crushed by the passage of the multitude. . . ."[9] Three months later McLaughlin took the five hundred Standing Rock Sioux to Bismarck to parade in the "March of Civilization."

The "March of Civilization," a parade formation representing the Standing Rock Sioux as the original inhabitants of this land as well as the inheritors of the American way of life, was a particularly appropriate and possibly ominous metaphor for Indian life in 1889. Some of the Standing Rock Sioux tried to follow the path set by McLaughlin while others, loosely clustered around Sitting Bull, opposed the agent and his policies. Sitting Bull exhorted this conservative or "non-progressive" element to cling to the old order of things and warned that government programs signaled the destruction of their race. For seven years, Sitting Bull steadfastly thwarted government interference in Indian life and the break-up of the Great Sioux Reservation. But in 1889 the Sioux lost nine million acres of their lands. While North

Dakota passed into a new era of statehood, North Dakota's Indians marched uneasily forward into a profoundly different world.

With the passage of the Omnibus Bill of 1889, which provided for the statehood of Washington, Montana, North Dakota, and South Dakota, residents of Dakota Territory agitated to reduce the size of the Great Sioux Reservation, an area that encompassed a major portion of South Dakota west of the Missouri River and extended into North Dakota. There was a desire to open this land for homesteading and to establish an eastern entry into the Black Hills area, which had been annexed from the Great Sioux Reservation in 1876. The reservation established by the 1876 agreement kept more than 43,000 square miles off limits to white settlement and economic development and cut the Black Hills off from the rest of Dakota Territory.[10]

Dakota promoters who sought to reduce the Great Sioux Reservation allied themselves with zealous humanitarian Christian reformers in the eastern United States who believed that eliminating reservations and giving the Indians individual plots of land would be the "entering-wedge by which tribal organization is to be rent asunder."[11] In response to this clamor, Congress passed the Sioux Act of 1889, which proposed the break-up of the Great Sioux Reservation. Although Indians had not been dealt with by treaty since 1871, the government still negotiated with them and Congress passed acts or agreements that had the force of law.

With the passage of the Sioux Act of 1889, President Benjamin Harrison appointed three negotiators—known as the Sioux Commission—who were charged with representing U.S. government interests in talks with the Indians. Only one of the presidential appointees to the commission, General George Crook, had any significant association with Indians. Although Crook had met the Sioux on the battlefield and was a reminder of the Plains wars, he was seemingly well-respected by the Indians for his courage and bravery. At Standing Rock, the Indians jokingly dubbed Crook "the pony and grub man," referring to his seizure of Indian ponies at their agency soon after the Battle of the Little Big Horn and to the feasting he arranged for the Standing Rock Sioux during the 1889 council meetings.[12] Neither of the other Sioux commissioners—Charles Foster, ex-governor of Ohio, or Major William Warner of Missouri—had any previous experience in Indian matters. Nonetheless, commission members were firmly in support of federal Indian policy that sought to put the Indians squarely "in the paths of civilization." [13]

The Sioux Commission had responsibility for presenting and explaining the Sioux Act to the Indians in large public councils and then obtaining the signatures of three-quarters of the adult Sioux males, as required by the 1868 Treaty.

On July 25, 1889, three weeks after the Standing Rock Indians returned from the Fourth of July celebration in Bismarck, the commission arrived at their agency. Standing Rock was the last agency to be visited, and the *Bismarck Daily Tribune* reported: "This is the important agency and all depends upon the success or failure here." [14] The Sioux Commission needed six hundred adult male signatures to enact the bill that would open nine million acres of the Great Sioux Reservation to homesteading and effectively catapult the Sioux into a dark period in their history.

Once word got out that the commissioners had arrived, the Standing Rock Sioux began gathering at the agency in large numbers, setting up tipis and camping near the agency buildings. Congress had made a substantial $25,000 appropriation when it passed the Sioux Act, "which sum shall be expended . . . for procuring the assent of the Sioux Indians to this act. . . ." [15] With this money, General Crook bought cattle from individual Sioux and throughout the duration of the council Crook sponsored lavish feeds, and he even permitted the dances that had been banned by the Indian Bureau.

Formal council proceedings opened on July 26, and with the aid of interpreters, the commissioners explained the major points of the act which proposed that the Sioux give up nine million acres of land with the remainder to be divided into six smaller reservations. Unceded lands would be sold on the open market over a ten-year period, during which prices would gradually descend from $1.25 to 50 cents per acre. Any lands not sold after ten years would be bought by the United States government for 50 cents an acre and would become public domain. Proceeds from the land sale would go into a government account known as a "civilizing fund" to pay for the education of Indian children and to purchase farm implements. The Sioux Act also proposed that each Indian family would receive 320 acres of land that eventually would become their private property. Supporters of the act believed that land allotment was the only way to force individual ownership of land and break up the tribal system in which land was used in common. The Sioux Act of 1889 was built around education and farming, the keystones of the civilizing policies of the federal government.[16]

Two similar bills, with basically the same land provisions but with less monetary compensation, had been put before the Sioux in 1882 and 1888; both had been overwhelmingly rejected. But greed and humanitarian zeal had combined, and during the winter of 1888 proponents of the Sioux Act had drafted a modified version that expanded and increased key terms. The 1889 bill provided for larger allotments; more money for the ceded lands; more liberal fringe benefits in the form of cash, livestock, and farm implements; and payments for pony seizures.[17]

National attention focused on events at Standing Rock as the council got underway. The *Bismarck Daily Tribune* circulated an alarming report over the wires: "It is evident that the Sioux here are under the perfect control of the chiefs, and it will require some pretty fine work on the part of the commissioners to make a break in favor of the treaty." Correspondents anticipated opposition from "the wily old warrior" Sitting Bull, who was later reported "to have been quietly scheming to block the work of the commissioners." Public hope and attention focused on John Grass, Gall, and other moderates who were usually more willing to compromise. But then news accounts stated that none of the Indians was working more assiduously than John Grass to defeat the Sioux Act. Both progressives and nonprogressives among Standing Rock Sioux stood united in their opposition to the act. Government officials and the general public seemed to agree with newspaper views that "matters were in bad shape if a lot of breech clouted blanket Indians" were allowed to prevent the opening of nine million acres of land to settlement.[18]

At every agency, the commission members had insisted their biggest obstacle had been the control the old chiefs had over the people. It was no different at Standing Rock. In keeping with tribal custom, the Sioux appointed spokesmen who did all the speaking for their people during council sessions, even though the commissioners earnestly sought "to break up the control of chiefs and to deal only with individuals." At Standing Rock, John Grass represented the Blackfeet Sioux, Gall the Hunkpapa, Big Head the Upper Yanktonai, and Mad Bear the Lower Yanktonai. Although McLaughlin later indicated that Sitting Bull and Gall often clashed over politics, both opposed the Sioux Act and Gall represented Sitting Bull and his people in this matter.[19]

The Sioux Act had united the factions at Standing Rock. Government programs aimed at "civilizing the wild Indians" had relentlessly chewed away at the old culture and the old ways until the Sioux were determined not to give up any more of their land. When the Sioux Commission came to Standing Rock, progressives and nonprogressives stood together to deliver a litany of grievances and wrongs they had been made to endure since they had been moved onto the agency some thirteen years before.

The Indians did not wish to own individual parcels of land, and Mad Bear told the commissioners: "The Great Spirit gave this large piece of land to the Indians for them to live upon in their way."[20] Furthermore, the Indians argued farming was impossible on this land. In the summer of 1889, crops burned up and blew away in severe drought conditions. Even as the clamor by whites for Indian lands was reaching a high pitch, many farmers in the Dakotas were abandoning their homesteads and heading for a better climate.[21] The Dakota winters were harsh, and coupled with the drought conditions of the previous few years, stock-raising was nearly impossible. McLaughlin himself wrote to the Commissioner of Indian Affairs in 1889: "I have always advocated an agricultural life . . . for the Indians . . . but until some climatic changes take place . . . I am now prepared to advocate the abandonment of agriculture."[22] But the government's allotment of land to individual Indians was not negotiable. It was the basis of federal Indian policy, and whether or not the land was productive was entirely irrelevant.

Other government programs also came under attack during the council. The architects of Indian policy conceived the ration system as a way of forcing Indian dependency on the U.S. government after the wholesale slaughter of the buffalo on the northern Great Plains had left the Sioux destitute. But the quality and quantity of the food rations were inadequate and substandard—wormy flour, bony cattle, and rancid bacon—and the superintendent of schools had supported the Sioux' claims that the Indians' poor health at Standing Rock was due, in part, to lack of adequate foodstuffs. The Indian speakers at Standing Rock pleaded with the commissioners not to reduce their rations, especially since their crops were once again withering in the fields. The commissioners assured the Indians that the Sioux Act would not affect their rations.[23]

Also in the interests of promoting civilization, the government had instituted an annuity system, whereby clothing was issued to the Indians on a yearly basis. If Indians dressed like whites, so the argument went, they would begin to act like whites and conform to their way of life. Gall requested that the government give the Sioux money rather than the ill-fitting annuity goods, and the commissioners noted in their report that the quality of clothing was so poor that many Indians declined to wear "civilized garb."[24]

The Sioux also complained to the commissioners about the schools their children were being forced to attend. The children were taken from their families, put into boarding schools—often far from home— harshly disciplined, and intentionally taught that the old ways were bad. The Indians pointed out that many of the children who went to these schools died while away from home or soon after their return. Parents who objected to the government's terms of educating their children were jailed or had their rations cut off. The Sioux sought more local day schools and less severe discipline for their children, but their pleas fell on deaf ears. The Sioux also argued that previous treaties had included educational provisions and as yet many of those promises were unfulfilled, so it was unnecessary to secure more assurances of schooling.[25] The government viewed education as the one sure path to civilization; in an 1889 government circular the Commissioner of Indian Affairs directed teachers to remember that the work of education involves "the destruction of barbarous habits by the substitution of civilized manners." McLaughlin would later write that "there can be no questions as to [schools'] beneficial effects in breaking up the old Indian customs, and gradually supplanting white men's ways, and it is only through such system . . . that we may hope for the ultimate civilization of the Indians." Education was not a negotiable item either.[26]

Government interference in all facets of Indian life had made the Standing Rock Sioux virtual prisoners on their own reservation, subject to the whims and foibles of government policy. In 1889, for example, the Commissioner of Indian Affairs issued directives regulating how the rationed beef were to be killed. "During the killing children are specially prohibited from being present . . . butchering must be done by men," and "the consumption of the blood and intestines is strictly prohibited." These regulations were enacted as "an object lesson to [the Indians] of the difference . . . between civilized man and savage."[27] Licensed traders at the agencies were prohibited from selling playing cards to Indians and the Indian Office forbade gambling by Indians.[28] Indian men could not wear blankets in camp, an old courting practice in which the Indian man and his betrothed would walk around camp wrapped in the man's blanket. "Robeing in a sheet," as it was termed, would land a Standing Rock Sioux in the guardhouse in 1889. Indians were to conform to the courting practices of the white society and marry in church.[29] The government intruded even further into Indian life in 1889 when the Commissioner of Indian Affairs promulgated orders that Indians would not be permitted to travel with Wild West shows. It had been hoped that Indians who appeared in the shows would "become familiar with the manners and customs of civilized life," but by 1889 the Commissioner judged the shows to be demoralizing in an extreme degree because the Indians become

> . . . strongly imbued with the idea that the deeds . . . which they portray in their most realistic aspects, are especially pleasing to the white people, whom they have been taught to regard as examples of civilization.

The Wild West shows presented facets of the older way of life and glorified Indian traditions of warfare and the hunt, images particularly abhorrent to the government in 1889.[30] The government also forbid all expressions of traditional religion and banned the sun dance, the most solemn religious ceremony of the Sioux people. With the loss of the sun dance, the Sioux religious framework gave way. This was a shattering blow to the people, and it created a void in their lives.

By 1889, the government had transgressed into every aspect of Sioux life, and the Standing Rock Sioux—both progressives and non-progressives—stood united in their opposition to the Sioux Act. To the Sioux, the land was all they had left. John Grass, Gall, Big Head, and Mad Bear usually backed McLaughlin, but in this instance they clearly and openly stated their refusal to give up any land. Sitting Bull vehemently insisted that for the Sioux the land was not negotiable. His feelings, which were well-known to his people, were poetically expressed in a speech delivered at Fort Rice in 1868:

> I wish all to know that I do not propose to sell any part of my country, nor will I have the whites cutting our timber along the rivers, more especially, the oaks. I am particularly fond of the little groves of oak trees. I love to look at them, because they endure the wintry storm and the summer's heat, and—not unlike ourselves—seem to flourish by them.[31]

When the government proposed to break up the Great Sioux Reservation in 1882, Sitting Bull had stridently pleaded with his people to stand together in opposition to the plan:

> I do not wish to consider any proposition to cede any portion of our tribal holdings to the Great Father. If I agree to dispose of any part of our land to the white people I would feel guilty of taking food away from our children's mouths, and I do not wish to be that mean. . . . My friends and relatives, let us stand as one family as we did before the white people led us astray.[32]

Confident that the 1889 version of the Sioux Act would not be approved by his people, Sitting Bull retired to his camp on the Grand River, some forty miles south of Fort Yates, sometime after the first council session. Gall was the official delegate for Sitting Bull's band at the meetings.

John Grass, Mad Bear, and the other Indian spokesmen at the council raised astute questions about the provisions of the Sioux Act. In particular, they objected to the inadequate compensation offered for the land and the government's disregard of major provisions in other treaties and agreements, especially the Treaty of 1868. On the second day of the council, John Grass concluded that there was no need to sign this new act because all the provisions were already guaranteed through prior treaties and agreements. To great applause from the Indian audience, John Grass announced:

> We have considered this matter as well as we could, and we have come to the conclusion that there is nothing in there for us, no more than there has been in the past, and we would not gain anything by that. And that is the conclusion of all you see around here, and they have concluded they will not sign.[33]

As soon as the cheering subsided, Commissioner Foster praised the Indians, beginning, "My friends, it is a very great pleasure to us to listen to intelligent discussion." But then he confided that whites "are camping on the other side of the Missouri" and indicated that the commissioners were being pressured. The unspoken possibility seemed to be that the reservation land might be opened even without Sioux assent. Although Foster minimized these outside forces, he continued:

> It does not make a bit of difference to us whether you sign or don't sign, except that we believe it is right and would be glad to succeed. We are glad to meet you in such good spirit, and above all, we are glad to know that we are able to have an intelligent discussion of the question.

The commissioners continued to flatter the Indians until the council ended for the day and arrangements were made to sponsor a feast.[34]

At the next council session, John Grass and the other Indian delegates demonstrated they were unmoved by the artifice of speech or the abundance of beef, by continuing to enumerate their objections to the Sioux Act. With obvious exasperation, John Grass announced:

> I . . . told you yesterday that my people you see here, they can't bring their names there and put them on that paper. I don't know how many times you expect me to refuse, but this is the second time I have refused. If I respect a man and think he is a man, and I ask him to do anything, and if he refuses me, well I think he has refused and that is sufficient.

Although the Indians applauded John Grass's remarks, General Crook replied straightforwardly: "One of the many features that you have to consider in case you do not accept this bill, is that Congress may open [your land] without asking your consent again." Crook's rejoinder was not so much a threat as an attempt to be forthright about the situation and its probable outcome.[35] But Mad Bear immediately re-stated the Sioux position:

> The Great Spirit gave this piece of land to the Indians for them to live upon in their way. . . . When we had plenty of land in the past we sold it cheap and thought nothing of it, but now we have come down to the last piece of land we have to spare . . . the probability is that if we don't take [the price you have offered] the land will be taken anyhow. All people that are created on the face of the earth here are all of one blood. I speak for myself individually, that if I was to see something that belongs to another person and I offered him so much for it and he refused it, I would not go and take it away from him. The reason I get up here and speak these words is the people you see around here they use us as their speakers, and they say so, far as we can understand, that they don't wish to sign the paper, and of course for us to tell it for them.[36]

The Sioux enthusiastically applauded Mad Bear's words, but a sense of futility was beginning to take hold. The threat that the land would simply be taken by the government was clear. It was repeated the next day by General Crook who warned the Sioux:

> Now I said to you yesterday that the probabilities were that this land would be opened by the Government, if you did not accept this proposition. I will give you my reasons for the statement I máde yesterday. This territory of Dakota, Montana, and Washington Territory have three representatives in Washington, and those three men can take part in the discussions, but they can't vote on questions. Now, in three months this Territory of Dakota will be divided into two States, Montana will come in as a State, and Washington Territory will come in as a State. Now, those States will send eight Senators to Congress, and five representatives, that will be 13 in all, and each of those people will have a vote. And it is from these people that the pressure is going to come to open your land.[37]

Crook then reminded the Sioux, especially the headmen, that their old way of life was rapidly passing. "Since you have started in the

white man's way," Crook said, "you must keep going on, going on
and improving every year. . . . It is the march of progress and you
must keep up with it."[38]

As the council meetings continued, it became clear to the Sioux
that their careful questioning as well as their opposition to surrender-
ing more land to the government had no effect on the proceedings.
Crook stated the impending threat clearly: "Now this rush of people
is coming, and none of us can prevent it not even the President of the
United States." The Indians assailed the commissioners with many
grievances and problems, but the commissioners responded that they
had no authority to remedy their complaints. Commissioner Warner
reminded the Sioux: "In the discussion of this bill we have no authority
to add or take one word from it"; and the commission described itself
as a "mouth-piece of General Government."[39] Behind the scenes, the
Sioux commissioners stressed to McLaughlin that if the Indians did
not sign the agreement, Congress assuredly would seize the land and
offer no renumeration; to prevent legal complications down the road,
however, the signatures were needed. The Sioux Act was hanging in
the balance at Standing Rock.

The cooperation of the Standing Rock Sioux was a point of honor
for McLaughlin, who often referred to the Indians as his children.
McLaughlin did not want to appear powerless to the commissioners,
the president, or the people of the Dakotas, so he set up a clandes-
tine evening meeting with John Grass at a house five miles from the
agency. Grass was so afraid of being seen with McLaughlin that he
insisted on meeting in an outbuilding behind the house. At this par-
ley, McLaughlin stressed that the Sioux Act was the most liberal bill
the government would offer and Grass should take the lead and ratify
it. McLaughlin told him that if the Sioux did not accept the agreement, they would lose both their lands and the monetary compensation. After many hours of McLaughlin's cajoling and pleading, a defeated John Grass reluctantly accepted the inevitability of the Indians'
losses. Years later, McLaughlin recalled: "Grass was an honest man
and always stood for the best interest of his people, but in order to
meet my views now, he would have to recede from the position he
had maintained in council and in private for a long time." Before the

night was over, McLaughlin also spoke with Gall, Big Head, and Mad Bear "and got them to agree to support the proposition."[40]

Late on the afternoon of August 3, John Grass addressed the council, stressing the weaknesses in the act and blaming the Sioux at other agencies for signing. He indicated that he believed it was necessary for the Sioux at Standing Rock to sign "so that the people of Standing Rock Agency can have a separate reservation of their own." He ended: "I am not fully satisfied with what is in the bill, yet I am willing. Of course the bill is not what we wish it would have been, but it is the weakness of my friends that has pulled me down, until now I say I am willing. That is all."[41]

A routine procedure was to be followed in ratifying the bill. Headmen were to sign the agreement first, followed by tribal members. The Indians would sign their names or make their marks, which would then be witnessed, and each would receive a certificate with his name on it as a keepsake. The government councilors praised John Grass for his change of heart, and he was given the privilege of being the first to sign to the document that would break up the Great Sioux Reservation. Other leaders lined up to sign, but just as the headmen began to sign, Sitting Bull and twenty of his followers rode up. Sitting Bull chided the men for signing the agreement and threatened to stampede through the council area to prevent further confirmation. McLaughlin had anticipated opposition from Sitting Bull, however, and the Indian police were tightly cordoned around the council area, reinforced by Two Bears's band of Lower Yanktonai. As Sitting Bull and his followers were forced to leave the area, he bitterly told a reporter: "There are no Indians left but me."[42]

The Indians continued the signing as their headmen had asked them to do, and the break-up of the Great Sioux Reservation was accomplished. The commissioners left with 685 signatures, a little more than half of the Standing Rock Sioux males over eighteen years of age.[43]

The ratification of the Sioux Act shook the Teton Sioux with greater force than anything in their history, and it threw into sharp focus the resentments and frustrations built up during a decade of reservation life. Two weeks after the commissioners left Standing Rock, a census of the people was taken and rations were significantly trimmed back;

the cutback was not connected with the Sioux Act, but this was not clear to the Indians. The Sioux commissioners protested the cutbacks to the president, but the foodstuffs were not restored, and physician reports indicated that the Sioux were suffering from the effects of starvation. Epidemics of measles, whooping cough, and the grippe seized all Sioux camps on Standing Rock and deaths far exceeded births in 1889. Blighting hot winds and drought continued throughout the summer; even the prairie grass withered and dried up. The grayness of poverty and misery surrounded the Sioux.[44]

The Sioux were offered a glimmer of hope in the summer of 1889; word came of an Indian messiah in the West called Wovoka, whose promise was for all Indians. He told of a world inhabited only by Indians, a world where the buffalo were once again plentiful, and a world where all dead relatives would return. He foretold a return to the old ways.[45] All summer long talk of the Ghost Dance continued, with much of the news ironically being spread by Indian students who had learned to read and write English in government schools. By the fall of 1889, the Sioux had sent delegates to see and speak with the messiah. News arrived that a millennium was coming, a time of great prosperity and peace. In the meantime, Indians were to be kind toward all people, sing, and Ghost Dance. Those who practiced the Ghost Dance often went into a visionary trance where they spoke of seeing dead relatives and had a glimpse of the world to come.[46]

The Sioux at Standing Rock and at all the newly defined Sioux reservations were starving, in poor health, and were witnessing the rapid disintegration of their tribal way of life. The signing of the Sioux Act of 1889 accentuated the grievances of the people and caused sharp division between progressives and nonprogressives. Sitting Bull openly spoke against those who signed the agreement and on ration days and at other public gatherings signers and non-signers taunted each other. McLaughlin reported similar conflicts in the day schools among the children. At Standing Rock, as on the other Sioux reservations, the Ghost Dance was practiced mainly by those who had refused to sign the 1889 agreement. Sitting Bull continued to be the leading opponent of the government's "civilizing policies," and his camp became the rallying place for the dissatisfied conservative element that clung to the old order of things.[47] Although Sitting Bull did not accept the tenets of the Ghost Dance religion, he did permit its ceremonies to go on in his camp and he used the Ghost Dance as a way of making known his dissatisfaction with government policies.[48]

The Sioux world in 1889 was one of shattered dreams, broken promises, and deep suffering. In the winter of 1889, the progressives, among them John Grass and Gall, went to Washington, D.C., to protest conditions on the reservation and to list grievances in the way the government was fulfilling its obligations through the Sioux Act. The only response by the Commissioner of Indian Affairs was that if the civilizing policies had been successful "we would be speaking in English now."[49] There was no remedy forthcoming from the government, only an increased tempo in the "march toward civilization." Neither allotments nor surveys of the diminished reservation were made; bowing to pressure from the Dakotas, President Harrison pronounced the Sioux Act law on February 10, 1890, as recommended by Secretary of the Interior John Noble.

Nine million acres of Sioux land opened for settlement in the newly proclaimed states of North Dakota and South Dakota. And the words spoken by the Sioux commissioners on the opening day of the Standing Rock council, July 26, 1889, echoed across the prairies:

> The object of the bill is something far higher than the mere selling of some land. Every intelligent Indian must recognize that his hope in the future is in the adoption of the white man's ways. The buffalo is gone, and his old means of getting a subsistence is gone. What your white brethren wants is to see you advance in civilization and the white man's ways, and the white man of this country is going to furnish you the means, if you will accept it to push you forward as fast as you will go in the direction of the white man's ways. . . . The object of the white man and this act is to build you up.[50]

The "march of civilization" was a torturous trek for the Sioux people, and there would be no turning back; those who broke rank could not be tolerated. It is with some pride that McLaughlin ended his 1889 annual report to the Commissioner of Indian Affairs with these words: "I desire to state that the Indians of this agency, with few exceptions, show steady progress and wholesome advancement in civilization."[51]

Sitting Bull died some months later at the hands of the Indian police

because McLaughlin viewed him as an ardent opponent to the civilizing policies that he, as agent, was entrusted to carry out.[52] In April
1889, McLaughlin had written: "Indians must either fall in with the
march of civilization and progress or be crushed by the passage of
the multitude."[53] Sitting Bull's death, followed soon by the deaths of
almost three hundred men, women, and children in the barren gullies
and draws of Wounded Knee, was a profound sign that a new way of
life was upon the people.

Federal policy sought to erase all traces of the Indian way of life
within the time of one generation; but the harshness of early reservation life on Standing Rock, and on all the newly formed Sioux
reservations, caused the people to grip tenaciously onto their culture
rather than surrender it. And the government policies that took so
much from the Sioux, and that by 1889 left them numbed with their
powerlessness, also contributed to their sense of oneness as a people.
Ultimately, the smaller land areas left them after the break-up of the
Great Sioux Reservation contributed to the Sioux developing a sense
of nationhood; they were a defined people with a homeland. With the
passage of the Sioux Act of 1889, the Sioux people did take their place
in the forced march into a profoundly different world, but they carried
with them a vision of the older times. And this past gives strength
and direction on the winding road into the future.

Notes

1. George F. Bird and Edwin J. Taylor, *History of the City of Bismarck, North
Dakota: First One-Hundred Years, 1872–1972* (Bismarck: Bismarck Centennial
Association, 1972), 89.

2. *Bismarck Daily Tribune*, July 5, 1889.

3. McLaughlin to Clement Lounsberry, July 10, 1917, in Louis Pfaller, ed.,
Microfilm Edition of the James McLaughlin Papers (Richardton, N.D.: Assumption Abbey Archives, 1968), Roll 8, Frames 23–24 [McLaughlin Papers]. Also
in Clement Lounsberry, *North Dakota History and People: Outlines of American
History* (Chicago: The S. J. Clarke Publishing Company, 1917), 417–20.

4. *Bismarck Daily Tribune*, July 5, 1889; *McLaughlin Papers*, Roll 8, Frame 23;
Lounsberry, *North Dakota History*, 417–20.

5. *Bismarck Daily Tribune*, July 4, 1889; McLaughlin to Brother at St. Mary's
Training School, DesPlaines, Illinois, February 14, 1884, McLaughlin Papers,
Roll 20, Frames 179–180.

6. McLaughlin to Commissioner of Indian Affairs, December 16, 1890, McLaughlin Papers, Roll 20, 1890–39602. Casualties among the Standing Rock Police force who participated in the attempted arrest of Sitting Bull were Lieutenant Henry Bullhead, Lieutenant Charles Shavehead, Sergeant James Little Eagle, Private Paul Akicitah, Special Police John Armstrong, and Special Police David Hawkman.

7. McLaughlin to Clement Lounsberry, July 10, 1917, McLaughlin Papers, Roll 8, Frames 23–24; Lounsberry, *North Dakota History*, 417–20.

8. Commissioner of Indian Affairs [CIA], *Annual Report* (1889), 3.

9. McLaughlin to General Armstrong, Hampton Institute, April 12, 1889, McLaughlin Papers, Roll 20, Frames 817–818.

10. Robert M. Utley, *The Last Days of the Sioux Nation* (New Haven, Conn.: Yale University Press, 1963), 41–42.

11. "Indian Rights Association's Statement of Objectives," 1885, in Francis Paul Prucha, *Americanizing the American Indian: Writings by the "Friends of the Indian" 1880–1900* (Lincoln: University of Nebraska Press, 1973), 43.

12. S. Ex. Doc., 51st Cong., 1st sess., Document 48, 215. Correspondence and transcript of councils of the Sioux Commission of 1889.

13. CIA, *Annual Report*, 1890, xxxix.

14. *Bismarck Daily Tribune*, July 28, 1889. Nine million acres of land were to be opened with passage of the Sioux Act; popular accounts often mistakenly cited the figure eleven million acres.

15. "An Act to Divide the Great Sioux Reservation, March 2, 1889," is reprinted in *Treaties and Agreements and the Proceedings of the Treaties and Agreements of the Tribes and Bands of the Sioux Nation* (The Institute for the Development of Indian Law, n.d.).

16. Ibid., secs. 29, 17, 27.

17. For an interesting popular account of the earlier proceedings, see George F. Hyde, *A Sioux Chronicle* (Norman: University of Oklahoma Press, 1956), 107–44. Correspondence and transcript of the councils of the Sioux Commission of 1888 are in S. Ex. Doc., 50th Cong., 2d sess., Document 17, 1888, 131.

18. *Bismarck Daily Tribune*, July 28, 1889; *Yankton Press and Dakotan*, July 2, 1889; *Bismarck Daily Tribune*, July 28, July 19, 1889.

19. James McLaughlin, *My Friend the Indian* (Seattle: Superior Publishing Company, 1970), 75.

20. S. Ex. Doc., 51st Congress, 1st sess., Document 48, 1889, 201.

21. *Bismarck Daily Tribune*, July 1889. The drought and poor farming conditions in the Dakotas were news throughout the summer of 1889.

22. CIA, *Annual Report*, 1889, 166.

23. CIA, *Annual Report*, 1890, 276–7.

24. S. Ex. Doc., 51st Cong., 1st sess., Document 48, 1889, 25–26.

25. S. Ex. Doc., 51st Cong., 1st sess., Document 48, 1889, 194–9.

26. CIA, *Annual Report*, 1890, ix–x; McLaughlin to General Armstrong, Hampton Institute, March 24, 1891, McLaughlin Papers.

27. CIA, *Annual Report*, 1890, viii, clxvi.

28. McLaughlin to M. H. Angevin, Indian Trader, September 18, 1890, McLaughlin Papers, Roll 20, Frame 269.

29. McLaughlin Papers, Roll 21, Frames 315–324.

30. CIA, *Annual Report*, 1890, viii, lvii–lviii. Despite the orders, however, Indians, especially the Sioux, continued to appear in the Wild West shows touring the eastern United States, Canada, and Europe until well past World War I.

31. Stanley Vestal, *Sitting Bull: Champion of the Sioux* (Norman: University of Oklahoma Press, 1969), 102.

32. W. C. Vanderworth, comp., *Indian Oratory* (New York: Ballantine Books, 1971), 184–88. Sitting Bull's quotation is from proceedings of Dawes Commission in 1883.

33. S. Ex. Doc., 51st Cong., 1st sess., Document 48, 1889, 196.

34. S. Ex. Doc., 51st Cong., 1st sess., Document 48, 1889, 196, 197.

35. S. Ex. Doc., 51st Cong., 1st sess., Document 48, 1889, 200.

36. S. Ex. Doc., 51st Cong., 1st sess., Document 48, 1889, 201.

37. S. Ex. Doc., 51st Cong., 1st sess., Document 48, 1889, 207.

38. S. Ex. Doc., 51st Cong., 1st sess., Document 48, 1889, 208.

39. S. Ex. Doc., 51st Cong., 1st sess., Document 48, 1889, 31–32.

40. McLaughlin, *My Friend the Indian*, 76.

41. S. Ex. Doc., 51st Cong., 1st sess., Document 48, 1889, 209, 210.

42. McLaughlin, *My Friend the Indian*, 76; Vestal, *Sitting Bull*, 262.

43. McLaughlin, *My Friend the Indian*, 76.

44. CIA, *Annual Report*, 1890; letter from Amble Caskie, Agency Physician at Standing Rock to McLaughlin, August 12, 1889, McLaughlin Papers, 1889–22959. Caskie requested the Department of the Interior to release medicine for 1889–1890 due to "the unprecedented prevalence of sickness, epidemic, and otherwise amongst our Indians during the past and present fiscal years."

45. Elaine Goodale Eastman, "The Ghost Dance War and Wounded Knee Massacre of 1890–91," *Nebraska History* 26 (1945): 28. Eastman noted that early word of the Ghost Dance religion spread into the Sioux camps during council meetings connected with the implementation of the Sioux Act.

46. James Mooney, *The Ghost Dance Religion and the Sioux Outbreak of 1890* (Chicago: University of Chicago Press, 1965), 64*ff.*

47. CIA, *Annual Report*, 1891, 126, 328–30.

48. There is considerable controversy over the depth of Sitting Bull's participation in the Ghost Dance. The dance definitely went on in Sitting Bull's camp, and McLaughlin called Sitting Bull the "high priest and leading apostle of this latest Indian absurdity" in a letter to T. J. Morgan, Commissioner of Indian Affairs, October 17, 1890, McLaughlin Papers, Roll 21, Frames 369–

381. But at no time did McLaughlin actually witness Sitting Bull taking part in the Ghost Dance. Most of Sitting Bull's family say he did not reject his traditional religion in favor of this imported religion. In particular, Isaac Dog Eagle, a descendant of Sitting Bull in South Dakota, stated this at a seminar opening an exhibition "The Last Years of Sitting Bull" at the North Dakota Heritage Center, Bismarck, on June 1, 1984. Mooney in *The Ghost Dance Religion* and Vestal in *Sitting Bull: Champion of the Sioux* also reported that Sitting Bull was not an adherent or practitioner of the Ghost Dance religion.

49. Sioux Delegation Proceedings, McLaughlin Papers, Roll 34, 1890–614.

50. S. Ex. Doc., 51st Cong., 1st sess., Document 48, 1889, 189.

51. CIA, *Annual Report*, 1890, p. 4.

52. McLaughlin to Herbert Welsh, November 25, 1890, McLaughlin Papers, Roll 20, Frames 931–934.

53. McLaughlin to General Armstrong, Hampton Institute, April 12, 1889, McLaughlin Papers, Roll 20, Frames 817–818.

5

Persistence and Adaptation
The Emergence of a Legal Culture in the Northern Tier Territories, 1853–1890

JOHN R. WUNDER

THE PERILS OF PRACTICING LAW ON THE FRONTIER WERE PROBABLY never as bad as experienced by George F. Cowan during the summer of 1877. Cowan, born in Columbus, Ohio, in 1842, arrived in Helena, Montana Territory, when he was twenty-three years old. He had studied the law and was ready to begin his practice. He chose to locate in Radersburg, the county seat of Jefferson County, and in 1875 he married a Montanan, Emma Carpenter. During the hot, dry August of 1877, Cowan decided to take a break from his law practice. He joined his wife, his wife's brother and youngest sister, and five other men for a holiday trek to Yellowstone National Park, about one hundred miles to the south.[1]

The holiday party left Radersburg on August 6 and made its way up the fork of the Madison River and on to the Lower Geyser Basin. After two weeks of pleasant camping, the Cowan tourists began the trip homeward. On this return trip, they encountered the Nez Perces, who had left their homeland in Idaho and Oregon and who were being chased by the U.S. Army. Shots rang out, two men of the party escaped into the brush, and Cowan was wounded above the knee. After the Indians arrived, much to Emma Cowan's horror, a Nez Perce shot George Cowan in the head.[2]

Emma Cowan was taken to the main Nez Perce band, thinking her husband was dead. But George had survived the attack. He crawled for four days and nights without food or water only to be nearly burned to death in a brush fire. After General Oliver O. Howard's troops found him, Cowan was placed in a carriage that rolled away from its moorings and dumped the injured man down a cliff. Cowan was retrieved and brought to a hotel where a doctor treated him in a bed that collapsed, hurling Cowan to the floor. This nearly did the poor man in, but again he recovered. Cowan was eventually reunited with his family, and his persistence and adaptability, not to say his durability, allowed him to live to the age of eighty-four. In 1901, he moved to Spokane, Washington, where he continued a successful legal career.[3]

Most Montanans and most settlers in the new territories of the Northern Tier of the United States did not have to go through the ordeal that George Cowan did in order to continue a relationship with the law. Nevertheless, this incident did occur in frontier Montana and Wyoming, and it is doubtful that other areas of the United States could claim this particular kind of hardship. Any functioning legal system in these new territories required sacrifice and creativity in order to establish a foothold. It was men like George Cowan who helped anchor law in the new territories.

The legal history of Washington, Idaho, Montana, Wyoming, North Dakota, and South Dakota during their territorial years is rich in substance, and it has been examined, albeit in limited detail, by legal historians.[4] But any number of questions remain to be explored. Was there a common legal experience among the six states? Did a "northwestern jurisprudence" emanate in American law from the early years of the Northern Tier territories? Were legal doctrines borrowed wholesale, adapted, or created to meet perceived needs? What was the status of crime and punishment, and how did criminal law evolve? Did civil law foster or inhibit economic development? Was law used to protect and expand civil liberties or to deny civil rights? How did the bar develop, and did judges at all levels dispense a high quality of justice? What was the attitude of frontier residents toward American law, and did attitudes encourage or discourage extra-legal activities?

This essay will offer an overview by which these and other questions might be placed within a legal historical framework for the Northern Tier. More specifically, its overarching theme will be to determine to what extent, if any, the frontier territories of the Northern Tier developed a regional legal culture. Other regions of the United States have claimed a unique legal history. Puritan New England, the antebellum South, and to some degree Gilded Age California have each been identified as having created separate, distinctive legal cultures that had an impact on national life.[5] Might the same be true for another region, the Northern Tier, an emerging settled area united in time by territorial status and statehood, a complex geography and environment that transcends geopolitical boundaries, and a retained cultural diversity?

To begin the consideration of this important question, three legal areas will be investigated. First will be basic issues of the Northern Tier territorial appellate courts, specifically substantive adjudication rates. Second, the legal doctrine surrounding the laws of divorce will be discussed with reference to grounds and residency requirements. The last section will consider the laws of evidence of the Northern Tier territories that concern the competency of Native Americans to testify in local courts. Each of these discussions will provide clues as to the nature of any legal culture that is distinctive to the Northern Tier territories.

Appellate Court Adjudication Rates

Washington Territory was the first of the Northern Tier territories to be created. Separated from Oregon Territory in 1853, Washington Territory covered an immense area, including the present states of Washington, Idaho, and portions of Wyoming and Montana.[6] In the 1860s, Congress legislatively organized the rest of the Northern Tier territories. Dakota Territory was shaped out of the unorganized areas of the upper Louisiana Purchase lands in 1861.[7] In 1863, Washington Territory was reduced to its present dimensions with the creation of Idaho Territory. One year later, Montana Territory came into being, and Wyoming Territory was formed in 1868.[8] Each of these territories went through the various stages associated with the American territorial system. An organic act was passed setting up governmental and legal frameworks, and territorial officers—such as governors, secretaries, and supreme court justices—were appointed. When these officials assumed power, a legislature was chosen, a territorial delegate to Washington, D.C., was elected, and the first codes of law were adopted.

Numerous officials governed the Northern Tier territories. From

1853 to 1890, sixty-six territorial governors were appointed. Not all actually served in the territories, but most did. Idaho Territory proved to be the appointment least likely to result in longevity, with twenty-one governors appointed, serving an average term of fifteen months each. The Northern Tier experienced 54 secretaries and 126 territorial supreme court justices, with three to seven per territory at any given time. Secretaries and judges were much more frequently reappointed, which allowed them to use their acquired expertise to better advantage.[9]

The territorial supreme courts first began to hear appeals from their own lower courts in the 1850s, and all were functioning within two years of the creation of each territory. The initial decision of any appellate court in the Northern Tier territories occurred in 1854 from Washington Territory's Supreme Court. The case, *Nesqually Mill Company* v. *Taylor*, concerned an action brought by James S. Taylor for compensation for labor and merchandise he furnished a Thurston County mill company. The lower court had ruled in Taylor's favor, but the mill company appealed, alleging numerous petty errors in the record. Justice Obadiah B. McFadden and the rest of the Washington Territory Supreme Court admitted that there were errors, but they refused to overrule the decision because the merits of the case had been adjudicated.[10]

The first case decided by the Wyoming Territory Supreme Court involved a civil suit by a telegraph company to recover the costs of telegraph poles. In *Western Union Telegraph* v. *Monseau*, the Wyoming justices determined when a jury verdict could be set aside. The defendant had won at the lower court, and the telegraph company appealed, asking to set aside the jury verdict because it did not have sufficient evidence upon which to base its findings. Wyoming Territory's Supreme Court did not find this argument convincing. Instead, they decided that the only time a jury verdict could be overruled was if the jury clearly misunderstood evidence and if the jury was carried away by passion or prejudice. Because that had not been the case, the court upheld the decision of the lower court, and in the process the justices struck a blow for placing confidence in frontier settlers' abilities to make fair decisions.[11]

Idaho Territory's first appellate case concerned water damage to cigars. J. B. Bloomingdale of Idaho City had ordered 6,500 cigars delivered by B. M. Du Rell & Company, which ran a carrier business from Umatilla, Oregon, to Idaho City. During the trip, the cigars had become waterlogged. Bloomingdale did not discover this damage immediately, but once he did he notified the owner, a man named Webb. The residents of Idaho City could not procure cigars at Bloomingdales, a bad situation that its owner wished to rectify. Du Rell & Company did nothing, so Bloomingdale sued, naming Webb and the company in the petition. Once the parties got into court, Webb announced that he no longer owned the company. The defendants claimed that the petition was faulty and asked for dismissal, which was granted by the lower court judge. The plaintiff appealed. The Idaho Territory Supreme Court would have nothing to do with this subterfuge and held that because Webb was not the owner, he could not be sued. But this did not stop the action. Du Rell & Company were clearly responsible for his losses.[12]

These three cases are indicative of the kinds of legal disputes that came before the Northern Tier territorial appellate courts. Most resolved commercial disputes or fine-tuned the law so that territorial residents could be comfortable with established procedures. Most cases were civil rather than criminal, and the imbalance suggests a litigious commercial society.

Consider the following table:

Northern Tier Appellate Court Decisions, 1853–1890 [13]

Territory	Civil Law Opinions		Criminal Law Opinions	
Dakota	241	81%	57	19%
Idaho	193	71%	78	29%
Montana	447	77%	135	23%
Washington	225	74%	77	26%
Wyoming	172	80%	42	20%

Several observations can be made here. First, the territories' appellate courts seemed to be fairly busy. This is the result of an active economy, aggressive bars in each territory, and quality appellate judging. Second, the range of division between civil and criminal law business is roughly four to one. This is a reasonable distribution based on a non-statistical comparison to other state courts, notably in the West. And third, internal distributions suggest that some territories, notably Montana and Dakota, had more appellate activity than others. It should be noted that both Montana and Dakota territories were larger geographically than the other three Northern Tier territories during most of their territorial existence. Geography, therefore, may not have inhibited the use of the legal system.

What can be concluded about the Northern Tier appellate courts? Certainly, these courts dispensed a significant quantity of justice, which reflected the growing, frontier economies of the region. In addition, the supreme courts wrote quality, dynamic opinions that provided frontier residents with a stable jurisprudential base. Furthermore, criminal law/civil law ratios were not particularly disparate.[14] Such a conclusion mirrors what other researchers have concluded for other American courts and other western regions.

Northern Tier Territorial Divorce Law

The judiciary, the bar, and the legislatures set out to establish the law in these territories and in the process they created a unique legal environment. One aspect of this new legal culture can be seen in divorce law.

Two kinds of divorce could be granted under the American system: legislative and judicial. Legislative divorce was accomplished by persuading a legislature to pass as a private law a specific act abolishing a particular marriage. Legislatures were prone to avoid divorce bills, and those few that were passed involved prominent state or territorial citizens. A legislature had the authority to pass private divorce laws unless it was expressly prohibited by its state constitution or territorial organic act. None of the Northern Tier territories were prohibited from passing legislative divorces, although most states were.[15]

Judicial divorces were granted where a court was given divorce jurisdiction. In the law of judicial divorce, two aspects separate the legal development of states and territories. These can be found in an examination of the grounds for divorce and in residency requirements. In a 1989 paper, historian Glenda Riley discussed what she calls "three key divorce mills of the 1890s."[16] Two of these mills were located in the new Dakota states, at Sioux Falls and Fargo. These settlements in Dakota Territory became divorce mills or at least had the reputation of being divorce mills because the territory had liberal residency requirements and allowed ample grounds for divorce.

From its origins, Dakota Territory was confronted with the issues of divorce. In 1862, the legislature granted its first legislative divorce through a private law. In the process they jokingly placed all divorce petitions under the jurisdiction of the "Committee on Internal Improvements."[17] In 1865–1866, the first judicial divorce law was enacted, placing jurisdiction in the territorial courts and making life imprisonment and adultery the only grounds available. The grounds were later increased fivefold and included cruelty and neglect, which lent themselves to broad interpretation by local courts. More importantly, a residency requirement of only 90 days was established.[18] Dakota Territory had probably the most accessible divorce mechanism in the country.

All of the Northern Tier territories may have been affected by divorce provisions in Utah Territory. Utah courts could entertain divorce proceedings for any party who was or who *wished to become* a Utah resident. Moreover, Utah Territory allowed irreconcilable differences as one of the grounds for divorce. This liberal provision was also adopted by Washington Territory and South Dakota after statehood.[19] These pathbreaking provisions for divorce law in Utah were designed to protect and support polygamy, but many Americans nevertheless went to Utah Territory to obtain a divorce. Once they left Utah, however, their divorce decrees were subject to attack.[20] Thus, the surrounding territories may have adopted short residency requirements and greater numbers of grounds for divorce in order to control divorce laws within their own jurisdictions and prevent their citizens from journeying to Salt Lake City, never to return.

Divorce in the United States was increasing during this time. In 1860, there were 7,380 divorces granted, or 1.2 per 1,000 marriages; by 1920, there were 167,105 divorces, or 7.7 per 1,000 marriages.[21] In response to religious and reform pressures and the public perception of the increase in divorces, both South Dakota and North Dakota toughened their residency requirements shortly after statehood.

Dakota Territory was not alone in developing a unique divorce doctrine. Montana territorial legislators grappled with legislative divorces from the beginning. By 1866, divorces made up the second largest number of special bills before the legislature.[22] That same year, Acting-Governor Thomas Meagher returned two legislative divorce bills to the Montana solons because no grounds for the divorces were a part of the legislation. Meagher stated that legislative divorces "are multiplying in such a measure to bring our social condition into grave disrepute, and give to strangers the impression that Montana is a paradise for all belligerent wives and husbands."[23] Even so, the Montana territorial legislature continued to handle legislative divorces until 1874; shortly after Meagher's rebuke, they passed laws allowing for judicial divorce.

Montana Territory's divorce laws gave local courts great discretion in determining proper grounds for divorce, and the Montana territorial Supreme Court encouraged this exceptional trend. Divorce could be obtained if one proved impotency, adultery, bigamy, abandonment for one year, willful desertion, conviction of a felony, habitual drunkenness, and extreme cruelty.[24] This was in contrast to national trends where only a few grounds were available, such as in New York where a judicial divorce could be obtained only if one proved adultery.

Extreme cruelty as a concept proved to be the subject of judicial interpretation in Montana Territory. It was also one of the most popular grounds for divorce. The courts had to work out the nuances of "extreme cruelty," the conditions of physical and mental abuse. In his 1887 treatise, legalist David Stewart defined legal cruelty as "the willful and persistent causing of unnecessary suffering, whether in realization or in apprehension, whether of body or of mind, in such a way as to render cohabitation dangerous or unendurable."[25] From this extremely broad definition, states and territories narrowed its meaning.

Ahead of its time, the Montana Territory Supreme Court declared in *Albert* v. *Albert* (1885) that physical cruelty could be proven with only "one beating or whipping" rather than the "three incidents test" that courts had been following. Even with *Albert* v. *Albert* available as precedent, some Montana courts refused to implement it. Local courts that readily complied with the precedent also expanded the meaning of mental cruelty to encompass sexual abuse, verbal abuse, and public embarrassment. After statehood, Montana adopted a new code of laws that incorporated much of the divorce law previously created in Montana's territorial courts, which had broadly construed the definition of legal cruelty in promoting the fundamental concepts of nineteenth century compassionate marriage. By the turn of the century, thanks to the legal experiments of Montana Territory, cruelty had become the most common ground for divorce in the United States.[26]

In these ways, the Northern Tier territories contributed to the growing liberalization of divorce law in the United States. By being more flexible in terms of residency requirements and the grounds for divorce, many more people who needed this legal sanction could attain it. In many ways Northern Tier territorial domestic relations law anticipated twentieth century developments in other legal cultural areas within the United States.[27]

Native American Competency Evidence Law

Native Americans were frequently denied access to the American legal system during the nineteenth century.[28] This denial took a variety of forms, but the most basic legal discrimination prevented Indians from testifying in courts of law. For example, Georgia in 1828 and 1829, as a part of its successful attempts to remove Cherokees from the state, passed laws nullifying all Indian laws and customs and denying all Indians the right to testify in court cases involving whites.[29] In California, the legislature in 1850 passed a statute providing that "No Black or Mulatto person, or Indian, shall be allowed to give evidence in favor of, or against a white man" in civil or criminal law proceedings. This was later expanded to include Chinese witnesses in *People* v. *Hall* (1854).[30] Two years later, Indiana's Supreme Court voided the will of Catharine Lasselle, daughter of Miami chief Richardville. Lasselle bequeathed that a huge chunk of land never be divided and that it never leave Indian hands, but the court ruled that the document had no legal standing because an Indian was not competent to devise a will.[31]

Nebraska also considered the competency of Native American testimony. In *Priest and Walker* v. *State of Nebraska*, the Nebraska Supreme Court found that Holly Scott, a Winnebago, could not testify against two men who had admitted to him that they had murdered a white man on the Winnebago Indian Reservation. The court reasoned that Native Americans could not testify because they were "incapable of receiving just impressions of the facts respecting which they are examined, or of relating them intelligently and truly."[32] This case was later discussed in another Nebraska dispute in 1909 when a defendant's counsel wished to disqualify the testimony of a Japanese witness. Nebraska's highest court reinforced *Priest and Walker*, reasoning that Indian incompetency to testify was justified, but that the "Japanese . . . are a civilized people, and have at least three recognized religions—Buddhism, Shintoism, and Christianity."[33]

During the nineteenth and early twentieth centuries, legal scholars wrote a variety of treatises concerning evidence. Few commented on the competency of Native American testimony.[34] But one who did was John Henry Wigmore. In his 1904 four-volume treatise on evidence law, Wigmore found that most discriminatory rules against Indians in evidence law had disappeared, a development he termed "enlightened progress." By the twentieth century there remained several state statutes that included forms of evidentiary discrimination against Indians, such as those in Minnesota, Nebraska, and Washington, but Wigmore thought they were probably voided by federal courts and the federal code.[35]

Wigmore was probably referring to an 1897 Federal Circuit Court of Appeals case from Alaska Territory. In this case a man named Shelp was charged with illegally selling liquor to Indians. At the trial court, the defendant's attorney argued that all Native American testimony had to be disregarded because

the evidence of ignorant, half-civilized barbarians, whose moral and religious sense was not developed, and who did not understand and appreciate the binding force of an oath as understood by Christian people, and who had little or no appreciation of our religious ideas, from which the oath gets its binding force and efficacy, and who had no appreciation of the enormity of perjury,—that the evidence of such witnesses was not entitled to as much credit as the evidence of a witness whose moral ideas were more fully developed. . . .[36]

The trial judge then charged the jury that

(1) it is a fact that Indians lie, and it is also a fact that white men lie, and some of the more civilized and cultured men are among the greatest liars. The evidence of Indian witnesses is entitled to as much credit and weight as the evidence of white men. . . . [but] (3) you have the right to use your own knowledge of this country, the habits and disposition of the Indians, and your knowledge and observation of the fact that whisky peddlers cruise about this coast, going from one Indian village to another, selling vile whisky to the natives.[37]

The federal circuit court ruled that the judge had given an incorrect, discriminatory charge to the jury and reversed the lower court's jury finding of innocence. Wigmore viewed this circuit court opinion, which was not appealed, as the new "law of the land."

Wigmore attributed these past creations of legal incompetency rules to whites' regard of Native Americans as "an object of selfish exploitation and unscrupulous plunder; for this brutal spirit is likely enough to combine with greed for the Indian's land a distrust of his testimony."[38] If this holds to be the primary motivation, then one would expect similar restrictions as found in California, Indiana, Nebraska, and other states to be a part of the legal culture of the Northern Tier territories.

The Northern Tier territories had several characteristics in common. All had significant populations of Native Americans; all had adopted similar legal systems for implementation; and all approved new state constitutions that included a disclaimer such as that found in Idaho's constitution recognizing exclusive federal control over lands "owned or held by any Indians or Indian tribes."[39]

Almost immediately upon their creation, Northern Tier territorial supreme courts had to deal with evidentiary issues concerning Native Americans. The second case before the Dakota Territory Supreme Court squarely faced the question of Indian competency. A man named Bruguier was charged with selling whiskey to Pa-la-ne-a-pa-pe, a Sioux chief. One of the issues the defendant raised was whether any Indians could be competent witnesses. The court ruled that "there should not be any distinction made so far as color or race is concerned."[40] Previously, the Dakota Territory Legislature had made it quite clear who might testify in court. In an 1862 statute, Dakota territorial law declared that "every human being of sufficient capacity to understand the obligations of an oath, is a competent witness in all cases, both civil and criminal."[41] At least in Dakota Territory, Native Americans were declared "human beings" who had "legal capacities."

Montana Territory also allowed for Indian testimony. In two cases involving whites who were charged with selling liquor to Indians on Indian reservations, Montana's courts allowed Native American testimony. In *U.S. v. Carr*, an affidavit from an Indian named Strangle Wolf was allowed into evidence.[42] Montana Territory went so far as to scrutinize the quality of Native American testimony so as to prevent any language misunderstandings. In *Territory v. Big Knot on Head et. al.*, the lower court had admitted testimony against the Piegan defendants from an interpreter who could not have made known his views to Big Knot on Head and others. Such fraudulent testimony was not tolerated by Montana Territory's Supreme Court, and the conviction for horse stealing was reversed.[43]

Indians did not fare as well in Washington Territory. Of the first six cases heard before the Washington Territory Supreme Court, four involved Native American testimony. All testimony was allowed to stand; but where the defendants were non-Indians who had been convicted of selling liquor to Indians, the convictions were overturned. In two other cases, one of them involving a prominent Indian leader, Leschi, the Supreme Court was able to find the means to affirm murder convictions of Indian defendants.[44]

Of the Northern Tier territories, only Washington and Idaho placed restrictions on Native American testimony, and they were placed in law shortly after statehood.[45] Idaho's constitution prevented Indians from serving on juries and from testifying in court, and Washington's statutes were quite unclear.[46] An 1897 law provided that "witnesses competent to testify in civil cases shall be competent in criminal prosecutions; . . . Indians shall be competent as hereinbefore provided [which does not exist], or in any prosecutions in which an Indian may be a defendant." The statute also specifically singled out Indians as competent to testify in any prosecutions for selling liquor to Native Americans.[47]

Native Americans were allowed to testify in the civil and criminal courts of the Northern Tier territories; and in at least two, Dakota and Montana, such testimony was carefully monitored to prevent discriminatory actions by lower courts, lawyers, and juries. This is a unique development in legal doctrine in terms of time and place in the United States.

Conclusion

The significance of the frontier legal experience has been explored by many scholars. Some have assessed it in terms of violence, extra-legal violence, and non-violence. Others have attempted to place the legal frontier within a Turnerian landscape. Some historians have found it worthwhile to analyze key participants in the legal system. Only recently have full-scale examinations of legal doctrine been composed for the West, and it will be here, in the study of the jurisprudence of the West, that the question of western legal exceptionalism will be answered.

The regional evolution of legal doctrine, and with it a legal culture, has been determined for the South, where the key ingredients are race and secession. In this way, eleven states have been grouped for research purposes along with the inevitable sub-regional variations. But the West is a much larger area. One can certainly argue that the West is more complex in evolution and that in terms of the development of legal doctrine and a legal culture it is more multi-faceted than the South. Sub-regions of the geographical West may be more likely, therefore, to take on the characteristics of distinctive full regions of the legal West.

Might a unique legal culture exist in the Northern Tier territories? Did this area, united by the common bonds of similar settlement patterns, territorial status, and 1889–1890 statehood, develop special legal doctrinal forms that distinguish it from other areas of the West and the nation?

Preliminary evidence suggests that in at least two areas of legal doctrine specific jurisprudential aspects single out this northwestern region. First, divorce law as it developed in the Northern Tier territories was both pathbreaking and reactive. The result was a pioneering effort breaking the restrictive nature of domestic relations law. The creative usages of extreme cruelty as a ground for divorce and the focus less on residency and more on the problems of a failed marriage were strangely found in Northern Tier territories during the late nineteenth century.

Second, allowance of Native Americans to testify in courts represents a fundamental divergence from precedent. Especially important was the failure of California law on Native American competency to spread to Idaho, Montana, Washington, Wyoming, and the Dakotas. For a region that many scholars have seen as dependent on the California experience, if not incapable of developing its own peculiar jurisprudence, the Northern Tier territories added a significantly new dimension to the laws of evidence.

Northern Tier appellate courts were clearly within the mainstream of American judicial development. Their ability to provide a dynamic forum for diverse dispute resolutions belies some previous scholarship that does not place credence on the territorial supreme court as a court of importance. These Northern Tier courts were frequently at the forefront of new developments in legal doctrine. It remains for further detailed investigation of the law in the Northern Tier territories and states to verify this preliminary suggestion of regional legal distinctiveness.

Notes

1. Emma Carpenter Cowan, "Holiday in Yellowstone Part," in *Montana Margins: A State Anthology*, ed. Joseph Kinsey Howard (New Haven, Conn.: Yale University Press, 1946), 125–41.

2. Ibid., 126–30.

3. Ibid., 125, 136–41.

4. Some of the history of the legal systems in some, but not all, of the Northern Tier territories have been the subject of recent scholarly inquiry. On civil law doctrine, see Gordon Bakken, *The Development of Law on the Rocky Mountain Frontier: Civil Law and Society, 1850–1912* (Westport, Conn.: Greenwood Press, 1983); on the judiciary, see John D. W. Guice, *The Rocky Mountain Bench: The Territorial Supreme Courts of Colorado, Montana, and Wyoming, 1864–1912* (New Haven, Conn.: Yale University Press, 1972); on property law, see John Phillip Reid, *Law for the Elephant: Property and Social Behavior on the Overland Trail* (San Marino, Calif.: Huntington Library Press, 1980); on the lower courts, see John R. Wunder, *Inferior Courts, Superior Justice: Justices of the Peace on the Northwest Frontier, 1853–1889* (Westport, Conn.: Greenwood Press, 1979); Bernard J. Hyatt, "A Legal Legacy for Statehood: The Development of the Territorial Judicial System in Dakota Territory, 1861–1889," 2 vols. (Ph.D. diss., Texas

Tech University, 1987); Paula Petrik, "If She Be Content: The Development of Montana Divorce Law, 1865–1907," *Western Historical Quarterly* 18 (July 1987): 261–82.

5. See David T. Konig, *Law and Society in Puritan Massachusetts, Essex County, 1629–1692* (Cambridge, Mass.: Harvard University Press, 1979); William E. Nelson, *Dispute and Conflict Resolution in Plymouth County, Massachusetts, 1725–1825* (Chapel Hill: University of North Carolina Press, 1981); David J. Bodenhamer and James W. Ely Jr., eds., *Ambivalent Legacy: A Legal History of the South* (Oxford: University of Mississippi Press, 1984); Lawrence M. Friedman and Robert V. Percival, *The Roots of Justice: Crime and Punishment in Alameda County, California, 1870–1910* (Chapel Hill: University of North Carolina Press, 1981).

6. Washington Territory Organic Act, U.S., *Statutes at Large* (1853), 172–9.

7. Dakota Territory Organic Act, U.S., *Statutes at Large* (1861), 241–3.

8. For the unique circumstances behind the creation of Idaho Territory, see John R. Wunder, "Tampering with the Northwest Frontier: The Accidental Design of the Washington/Idaho Boundary," *Pacific Northwest Quarterly* 68 (January 1977): 1–12.

9. Earl S. Pomeroy, *The Territories and the United States, 1861–1890: Studies in Colonial Administration* (1947; reprint, Seattle: University of Washington Press, 1969), 119–23, 127–31, 134–44. See also Charles H. Sheldon, *A Century of Judging* (Seattle: University of Washington Press, 1988), esp. 14–26; Ronald H. Limbaugh, *Rocky Mountain Carpetbaggers: Idaho's Territorial Governors, 1863–1890* (Moscow: University of Idaho Press, 1982); Guice, *The Rocky Mountain Bench*.

10. *Nesqually Mill Company v. Taylor*, 1 Wash. Terr. 1–3 (1854).

11. *Western Union Telegram v. Monseau*, 1 Wyo. Terr. 17–19 (1870).

12. *Bloomingdale v. Du Rell & Co.*, 1 Ida. Terr. 33–41 (1866).

13. *Dakota Territory Supreme Court Reports*, vols. 1–6 (1867–1889); *Idaho Territory Supreme Court Reports*, vols. 1–2 (1866–1890); *Montana Territory Supreme Court Reports*, vols. 1–9 (1868–1889); *Washington Territory Supreme Court Reports*, vols. 1–3 (1854–1888); *Wyoming Territory Supreme Court Reports*, vols. 1–3 (1870–1890).

14. An examination of the criminal and civil cases of the lower courts of Washington Territory found an even greater disparity. Civil cases constituted 92 per cent of all J.P. court activity. See Wunder, *Inferior Courts, Superior Justice*, 147.

15. David Stewart, *The Law of Marriage and Divorce As Established in England and the United States* (San Francisco: Bancroft-Whitney Company, 1887), 172–3. By 1980, legislative divorce was prohibited in thirty states: Alabama, Arkansas, California, Florida, Georgia, Illinois, Indiana, Iowa, Kansas, Kentucky, Louisiana, Maryland, Massachusetts, Michigan, Minnesota, Missouri, Mississippi, Nebraska, New Hampshire, New Jersey, New York, Nevada, North Carolina, Ohio, Pennsylvania, Tennessee, Texas, Virginia, West Virginia, and

Wisconsin. Shortly thereafter, South Carolina prohibited both legislative and judicial divorce.

16. Glenda Riley, "Untying the Knot: Divorce Mills on the Great Plains during the 1890s" (paper delivered at the Missouri Valley History Conference, Omaha, Nebraska, March 1989), 1.

17. Howard Roberts Lamar, *Dakota Territory, 1861–1889: A Study of Frontier Politics* (New Haven, Conn.: Yale University Press, 1956), 93.

18. George H. Hand, ed., "Chapter I: The Contract of Marriage, Article II, 'Dissolution'," *The Revised Codes of the Territory of Dakota, 1877* (Yankton, Dakota Territory: Bowen and Kingsbury, 1880), 215–19; A. B. Levisee and L. Levisee, eds., "Chapter I: The Contract of Marriage, Article II, 'Dissolution'," *The Annotated Revised Codes of the Territory of Dakota, 1883* (St. Paul, Minn.: West Publishing Company, 1885), 747–51; "Chapter I: The Contract of Marriage, Article II, 'Dissolution'," *The Compiled Law of the Territory of Dakota, 1887* (Bismarck: Dakota Territory, 1887), 545–51, in Riley, "Divorce Mills on the Great Plains," 2–8, 18.

The usual residency requirement was one year, and courts were especially sensitive to making sure that the litigants were permanent residents. A fraudulent residency meant a voiding of the divorce decree. See Stewart, *Marriage and Divorce*, 196–8. Some courts did allow for a wife to have a residency separate from her husband and for husbands to have more than one residency. See Joel Prentiss Bishop, *New Commentaries on Marriage, Divorce, and Separation As to the Law, Evidence, Pleading, Practice, Forms and the Evidence of Marriage in All Issues on a New System of Legal Exposition* (Chicago: T. H. Flood and Company, 1891), 2: 56–60.

19. *Laws of Utah Territory*, "An Act in Relation to Bills of Divorce, Sections 2, 3," 1851–1852. See also George Elliott Howard, *A History of Matrimonial Institutions*, 3 vols. (Chicago: University of Chicago Press, 1904).

20. Bishop, *New Commentaries on Marriage*, 2:22.

21. Kermit L. Hall, *The Magic Mirror: Law in American History* (New York: Oxford University Press, 1989), 166.

22. Clark C. Spence, *Territorial Politics and Government in Montana, 1864–1889* (Urbana: University of Illinois Press, 1975), 184.

23. Acting-Governor Thomas Francis Meagher to the Montana Territory Legislature, April 4, 1866, *Council Journal*, 2 Session (1866), 217–18, cited in Spence, *Territorial Politics*, 184.

24. See Petrik, "If She Be Content," 261–89, esp. 263; Carroll D. Wright, *A Report on Marriage and Divorce in the United States, 1867 to 1886*, rev. ed. (Washington, D.C.: United States Government, 1891), 144–5.

25. Petrik, "If She Be Content," 271; Stewart, *Marriage and Divorce*, 237.

26. *Albert v. Albert*, 5 Mont. Terr. 578 (1885); Petrik, "If She Be Content," 274–8, 285–7; Hall, *The Magic Mirror*, 165.

27. It took South Carolina until the 1960s and 1970s to adopt fully modern divorce law and domestic relations statutes.

28. See Felix S. Cohen, *Handbook of Federal Indian Law* (Washington, D.C.: Government Printing Office, 1941), and its reprinting, *Felix S. Cohen's Handbook of Federal Indian Law* (Albuquerque: University of New Mexico Press, n.d.), esp. chap. 8, sec. 6, "Right to Sue." See also Stewart Rapalje, *A Treatise on the Law of Witnesses* (New York: Banks & Brothers, 1887), 26.

29. *A Compilation of the Laws of the State of Georgia* (W. Danson, Comp., 1831), Act No. 545 of December 20, 1828, and Act No. 546 of December 19, 1829, 198, cited in Joseph C. Burke, "The Cherokee Cases: A Study of Law, Politics, and Morality," *Stanford Law Review* 21 (February 1969): 503.

30. *Cal. Statutes*, "An Act Concerning Criminal Proceedings," Section 14, and "An Act Concerning Civil Cases," Section 394; *People v. Hall* 4 Cal. 399 (1854). In a curious expansion of logic, the California Supreme Court reasoned that Chinese because they came from Asia and Indians whose origins were also Asian were sufficiently related so that the legislative act could be interpreted to include the Chinese as well. See also John R. Wunder, "Chinese in Trouble: Criminal Law and Race on the Trans-Mississippi West Frontier," *Western Historical Quarterly* 17 (January 1986): 25–41.

31. *Doe d. LaFontaine v. Avaline*, 8 Ind. 6–17 (1856).

32. *Priest and Walker v. State of Nebraska*, 10 Neb. 393 at 397 (1880).

33. *Pumphrey v. State of Nebraska*, 84 Neb. 636 at 640 (1909). Taking the opposite view was Mississippi, where an Indian was recognized as a competent witness. Rapalje, *Treatise on the Law of Witnesses*, 26, citing *Coleman v. Doe*, 4 Sm & M 40 and *Doe v. Newman*, 3 Sm & M 585.

34. For example, Simon Greenleaf, in his *A Treatise on the Law of Evidence*, 13th ed. (Boston: Little, Brown, and Company, 1876), does not mention Native Americans once in his volumes, let alone in Chapter 2, "Of the Competency of Witnesses," sections 326–430. One author who did comment was Stewart Rapalje in his *Treatise on the Law of Witnesses*, 26.

35. Ibid. See note 15 especially and *Washington Annot. Code and Statutes*, sections 6940 and 7316.

36. *Shelp v. United States*, 81 Fed. 694 (1897). See also John Henry Wigmore, *The Principles of Judicial Proof* (Boston: Little, Brown, and Company, 1913), 314–22.

37. *Shelp v. United States*, 81 Fed. 694 (1897).

38. John Henry Wigmore, *A Treatise on the Anglo-American System of Evidence in Trials at Common Law* (Boston: Little, Brown, and Company, 1904), 1:645.

39. *Ida. Constitution*, Article 21, Section 19. See also Philip J. Rassier, "Legal Jurisdiction on Indian Lands: Authority in Transition," *Idaho Yesterdays* 25 (Spring 1981): 60–67.

40. *Bruguier v. United States*, 1 Dak. Terr. 8 (1867). See a fuller discussion of

this case in Hyatt, "A Legal Legacy for Statehood: The Development of the Territorial Judicial System in Dakota Territory, 1861–1889," 1:138–44.

41. *Dakota Territorial Statutes*, Article 308, 99 (1862). Quoted in *Bruguier* v. *United States*, 1 Dak. Terr. 9 (1867).

42. *U.S.* v. *Sacramento*, 2 Mont. Terr. 239–242 (1875); *U.S.* v. *Carr*, 2 Mont. Terr. 234–236 (1875).

43. *Territory* v. *Big Knot on Head et al.*, 6 Mont. Terr. 242–243 (1886).

44. *Palmer* v. *United States*, 1 Wash. Terr. 5–6 (1854); *Fowler* v. *United States*, 1 Wash. Terr. 3–5 (1854); *Wassissimi* v. *Washington Territory*, 1 Wash. Terr. 6–7 (1854); *Leschi* v. *Washington Territory*, 1 Wash. Terr. 13–30 (1857).

45. See Wigmore, *Treatise on Evidence* (1904), 1:600–1 (Idaho); 611 (Montana); 616–17 (North Dakota); 622 (South Dakota); 626–7 (Washington); 628–9 (Wyoming).

46. *Ida. Constitution*, Art. 6, Sec. 3.

47. *Washington Annot. Code and Statutes*, Sections 6940, 7316 (1897).

6

The Long Arm of the Law
Crime and Federal Law Enforcement in the Northern Tier Territories

ROLAND L. DE LORME

HISTORIANS OF THE AMERICAN WEST HAVE RECENTLY BEEN SUM-moned to observe the birth of the nation's fundamental law by examining the West's legal culture. Such study, Kermit L. Hall has written, "will contribute not only to the debate about the West's exceptionalism but provide a worthwhile comparative dimension to American legal history as a whole."[1] The undertaking is particularly appropriate in the case of the Northern Tier territories, for their one hundred-year anniversaries fall within the dates marking the bicentennials of both the federal constitution and the United States Supreme Court. Unquestionably, the history of the contributions of constitutional law and Supreme Court decisions to the region's civil and criminal law courts are vital facets of that task. Of equal importance is the careful examination of the nature and extent of crime and the response of federal law enforcement agencies in the region.

No aspect of frontier life has assumed more mythic proportions than its alleged propensity for violence. The frontier as a haven for criminals is a central theme of popular fiction, from the nineteenth century's dime novels to the books, motion pictures, and television programs of the twentieth century. Until recently, most scholarly accounts accepted the myth as established fact. According to this view, representatives of formal justice agencies arrived late in the territories and were too few in number and often too incompetent or corrupt to provide a level of law enforcement comparable to that enjoyed in the more settled parts of the United States. In the interim, an embattled minority of law-abiding frontier residents sought to keep disorder at bay, succeeding only occasionally and in only a handful of communities.

For the most part, the Northern Tier territories escaped the depredations of the West's most notorious badmen (and the exploits of its most famous lawmen), but many of the treatments of the region's history rest on the assumption that lawlessness was as true of the northwestern territories as of the Middle Border or the Southwest.[2] Moreover, there is an abundance of eyewitness accounts that appear to support the conclusion that these territories suffered dangerous levels of criminal activity.

As early as the 1840s, Elijah White, who first ventured into the Oregon Country with Jason Lee, reported that crimes throughout the vast region were "multiplying with numbers among the whites, and with scarcity of game with the Indians." White documented his perception with a letter from another observer with mission connections, H. A. G. Lee, who described "lawlessness bands [of Indians], along the river from Fort Walla Walla to the Dalles" that threatened the property and lives of emigrants. White also reported to officials in Washington, D.C., that he had found it necessary to arrest eight persons, mostly on charges of stealing horses and grain.[3]

The private correspondence of residents in the region agree, for the most part, with the published observations of Robert Bailey and Nathaniel Langford in their portrayal of deteriorating conditions during the gold stampedes of the late 1850s and 1860s. The two men described wide-open towns in eastern Washington, Idaho, and Montana, where saloons and streets were dominated by gamblers and gunfighters like Ferd Patterson, a red-haired, six-foot-tall Texan who carried an ivory-handled .45 and a razor-sharp bowie knife. Patterson allegedly murdered, among others, Sumner Pinkham, a former sheriff, at Warm Springs, Idaho, before dying himself in a gun battle in Walla Walla. Other lawbreakers included "Cherokee Bon" Talbert, who was accused of having killed two or three soldiers in a Walla Walla theater; Bill Mayfield, a fugitive from the Nevada Territorial Prison; Bill Bunton, an alleged murderer and horse thief; and, of course, the celebrated Henry Plummer, who, one historian has claimed, led "the most efficient organization of highway robbers in the history of the frontier."[4]

Careful detective work by genealogist R. E. Mather and historian
F. E. Boswell has cast considerable doubt on the view that Plummer
organized a gang or, for that matter, was guilty of robbery and murder.
The vigilantes who hanged Plummer and his suspected accomplices
produced no compelling evidence of guilt. Similarly, the vigilante attacks on alleged cattle rustlers and horse thieves on the Montana
range during the early 1880s and vigilance committee actions directed
against Chinese laborers in Seattle and Tacoma later in that decade
sprang from suspicions that apparently neither needed nor rested on
hard evidence of criminal conspiracies. The methodical gathering and
sifting of evidence are requirements of due process, but vigilantism
is the antithesis of due process.[5] Yet, even the vigilantes' most severe
critics (though they doubt the pervasiveness of outlaw gangs, exclud-
ing the vigilantes themselves) agree that violent crime was a problem
in the Northern Tier territories.[6]

James Stout, a Land Office employee, described Idaho in 1869 as a
"corrupt, demoralized, congregated slough. . . . Life and property is
so insecure—bad men so plenty [sic] and good men so scarce." Stout
wanted his complaints to remain anonymous, "for this is a section
where men pay off their grudges in the dark."[7] One of Idaho's U.S.
attorneys, Joel Huston, estimated that there had been at least twenty
homicides in the territory during 1869. It was essential, he reported,
that there be "some change in the manner of enforcing or rather as it
has been carried out here, not enforcing the laws."[8] As late as 1883,
Katherine Johnson, the wife of a Boise attorney, complained that Idaho
Territory's capital was "full of roughs, and there [sic] is breaking in
again every night."[9]

Montana and Dakota pioneers described similar conditions. Authorities appeared helpless in the face of large-scale, illegal sales of
liquor to the Indian population. Some officials, it was charged, prof-
ited from the trade, and juries often refused to convict the traders.[10]
In one suit, a liquor trader brought charges against the commanding
officer of a U.S. Army unit who had arrested the trader for dealing
with the Indians. The U.S. attorney in that district had been directed
to defend the officer, but he did not appear at the trial and $4,000 in
damages were assessed in default.[11] Granville Stuart described shoot-
outs between criminals and the residents of Montana's small towns

and claimed that even in the 1880s ranchers had to sleep with their rifles because of the boldness of rustlers.[12] In Dakota, long-nurtured rumors of immense gold deposits in the Black Hills proved too much for federal agencies, including the army, which cordoned off the area. Among the thousands of prospectors who founded Custer City and Deadwood were enough outlaws to make stagecoach robbery a common occurrence.[13]

The most judicious review of such evidence still results in the conclusion that the Northern Tier territories contained serious amounts of violent crime. This conclusion appears to uphold the legend of the frontier as a violent place. Still, it is a view drawn *in vacuo*, with little thought given to comparisons with the extent of crime in other, more settled portions of the nation. This is true, in part, because the governing assumption of a violent frontier has obscured the necessity of drawing comparisons. It is also true because most historians, as well as the observers they cite, have neglected statistical evidence, producing essentially anecdotal accounts.

Although revisionists like Frank Prassel and W. Eugene Hollon have questioned the traditional view, neither they nor their adversaries have made much use of crime statistics or comparative data.[14] One reason for this oversight surely is the fact that few historians feel comfortable working with statistics. Also, the study of crime in a regional context, as well as the search for casual links between physical environment and criminal activity, have proved difficult and inconclusive.[15]

To be sure, statistics concerning crime and its detection in the West are difficult to gather and to interpret. It will probably prove impossible to measure with exactitude the incidence of crime and the effectiveness of law enforcement in the Northern Tier territories or, for that matter, any portion of the frontier in the years before statehood. The traders, merchants, miners, ranchers, and farmers who settled on the frontier may have carried with them Anglo-American concepts of justice and occasionally even the written statutes that issued from them, but they seldom kept complete or consistent records of the attempts at enforcement. Much of the available statistical evidence follows no standard set of definitions, contains significant inconsistencies, or is of questionable objectivity.[16] Yet, assessed with care, the evidence can provide significant clues to the extent of the region's crime. Even incomplete records can help correct the biases inherent in other contemporary accounts and are "sensitive enough to reflect the otherwise unknowable movements in the 'actual' incidence of criminal activity."[17] That evidence is essential if the debate on frontier violence is to be based in substance.

The comparison of crime rates in the Northern Tier territories with those in states and territories that were the principal sources of population for the region offer interesting results.[18] In 1860, Washington Territory, which embraced most of the Northern Tier region outside the Dakotas, suffered a crime rate of 129.38 per 100,000 population. The crime rates in the territories and states providing most of the region's white population (arranged in order of their approximate population contributions) were Utah, 59.59; Minnesota, 19.18; Missouri, 43.65; Illinois, 47.43; and Maine, 193.39. In 1870, these crime rates were reported: Dakota, 14.10; Washington, 83.49; Idaho, 173.34; Montana, 114.53; Utah, 31.11; Minnesota, 48.67; Missouri, 87.30; Illinois, 61.11; New York, 124.88; and Maine, 68.75.[19]

The system of criminal justice and law enforcement with which twentieth century citizens are familiar was only just emerging during the mid-nineteenth century. By the 1840s, Boston and New York had borrowed the idea of a uniformed, municipally controlled police force from London's Scotland Yard and was gradually adapting the concept to American political and social conditions. By the onset of the Civil War, city police forces could be found in a number of the nation's larger urban centers, but smaller towns and rural jurisdictions often relied on town marshals, constables, and county sheriffs.[20]

The very concept of justice as a public responsibility and the institutionalization of that concept in the form of empowered officials whose functions included the instigation of criminal proceedings remained novel. The idea was still subject to testing by nervous elites who sometimes preferred the swift certainty of vigilante action to the preoccupation with due process that marked the newer public system of law enforcement.[21] Moreover, the level of violence in larger communities, while perhaps somewhat below that in eighteenth century cities, was considerably higher through most of the 1800s than would be the case after 1890. The perception of violence as the work of a criminal "dangerous class" and the consequent concern with a rising crime wave were not entirely nineteenth century phenomena; the anxious postulating of crime waves has been traced back at least to the medieval period. But the increased socio-economic frictions and divisions that accompanied industrialization, population mobility, urbanization, and the consolidation of capitalism during the 1800s sharply increased such anxieties. Improved statistical and demographic techniques supplied those vague fears with seemingly factual support. In addition, the spread of evangelical Christianity, with its intolerance of drinking and gambling, spurred a broadening definition of crime and provided the basis for an apparent rise in criminal activities.[22]

Widespread fears of a rising tide of crime flourished without reference to the accumulating evidence of a downturn in actual crime levels. One scholar has pointed out that even though official figures reflected a decreasing crime rate in England, Ireland, and France beginning in the 1840s, both press reports and serious studies attempted to explain a rise in crime.[23] The most exacting analyses to date of available data for the United States in the second half of the nineteenth century indicate that crime, at least in large urban areas, dropped an average .5 per cent annually between 1860 and 1920—33 per cent in sixty years. The decline took place, as Lynn McDonald pointed out, "even in the face of increases in all those factors that are supposed to produce crime—waves of immigrants from southern and eastern Europe, migration from the south, rapid population growth and poor living conditions."[24]

Yet, helping to sustain the fears of many observers, there were several crime waves during this period: in 1861–1862, 1865–1866, 1870, and 1876.[25] It may be, then, that those who arrived in the cattle and mill towns, mining camps, and ports of the Northern Tier territories during this period were predisposed to look for violence; that those from the larger cities looked in vain for uniformed police; and that those with substantial economic interests at stake feared the worst from the boisterous, polyglot population in the region. Moreover, neither tourists nor settlers liked being reminded that the Northern Tier territories were part of the frontier. As Ray Allen Billington observed, since the eighteenth century novelists and travelers had depicted the frontier as not only a land of promise but also as "a Babylon of barbarism, an updated Sodom and Gomorrah."[26]

The crime rates estimated for the Northern Tier during the formative years through 1870, in comparison with those for the territories and states that served as principal sources of population, cast some doubt on the premise that frontier areas invariably confronted higher crime levels than the more settled parts of the country. By 1870, the estimated crime rate for Washington Territory was below that of Missouri and well below that of New York. Dakota's estimated crime rate was the lowest cited. But Washington's crime rate a decade earlier and the rates estimated for Idaho and Montana in 1870 (after they had been carved largely from Washington Territory) are significantly higher than all others estimated, except for New York.

An examination of county crime statistics reveals that crime rates were comparatively higher in counties that contained the region's most economically active communities. In Ada County, Idaho, where Boise was a bustling mining center and territorial capital, in 1870 suffered from a crime rate of 224.30 per 100,000 population, significantly above Idaho's high territory-wide rate. Idaho's other counties reported much lower levels; in at least one county, the deputy court clerk informed a U.S. attorney that there had been no criminal cases in a year.[27] The same pattern existed throughout Washington's territorial years, particularly obvious in cases of violent crime. Leading in the number of assault and murder cases were King County, where Seattle was rapidly becoming an urban center; Jefferson County, where Port Townsend, as port of entry for the Puget Sound Customs District, hosted a highly mobile, volatile population; Walla Walla County, where Walla Walla was a busy agricultural trading center and an important stop for overland emigrants and miners on their way to the Idaho diggings; Pierce County, where Tacoma was the terminus for the Northern Pacific Railroad; and Thurston County, which embraced the territorial capital Olympia, a busy port and business center.[28]

The findings lend further support to the thesis advanced by Elliott West, who subjected census data for the Idaho mining communities of Centreville, Idaho City, Pioneer, Placerville, and Silver City to computer analysis. West suggested that the unruly nature of the people in such towns might be traced to a lack of social cohesion. All that accounted for such aggregations of people was the search for quick riches, and such a focus, West maintained, may well promote discord rather than harmony.[29] It is a good working paradigm, although it should be tested by examining other, potentially significant variables that have been suggested by criminological research, including possible linkages between age and gender, the nature and level of crimes, the tendency of high rates of crime to run in families, and the correlation of crime with educational levels of the population.[30]

Whatever the results of such inquiries may be, it is clear that crime rates in many population centers of the Northern Tier were considerably higher than those in the areas from which most emigrants came. From the settlers' perspective, the question of crime control was certainly a serious one. The territories were dependent on federal government, which possessed primary responsibility for securing citizens' lives and property. The government, at least on the surface, commanded a formidable number of agencies with police powers, including the U.S. Army, the Customs Service, the Revenue Marine Service, the Office of Indian Affairs, the General Land Office, and the United States Post Office, all with authority to investigate and bring charges in matters related to their primary functions. Central to federal crime control efforts in the territories, as in the states, were the United States attorneys, marshals, and territorial court judges, all of whom reported to the United States attorney general.[31]

Each agency was subject to internal policing by a small army of special agents and inspectors on the lookout for misfeasance and malfeasance by territorial and federal employees. But most of these agencies played only small roles in law enforcement, primarily because of federal parsimony. Land claims accounted for a large number of disputes, both in and out of court, yet Congress not only refused funds for inspectors to investigate such disputes, but it also neglected to supply enough monies to properly survey public lands in the first place. The General Land Office resorted to the implementation of a "Special Deposit" system, by which claimants were permitted to apply up to two hundred dollars of the cost of having the land privately surveyed to the amount owed the government for the property. In Washington Territory, a syndicate that was also active in Oregon and California used its monopoly on survey contracts to file questionable surveys on land it made available, in advance of settlement, to speculators.[32]

There was little that Land Office officials could do in response to land fraud schemes such as the survey contract monopoly; claim jumping in mining areas; the harvest of great tracts of forested public land, without payment, by lumber companies; the free use of federal rangelands by ranchers; illegal settlement on unceded Indian lands; and the apparently widespread tampering with survey markers by both Indians and settlers.[33] There were occasional arrests, as in the case of a surveyor retained by the Washington Mill Company, whose surveys of land along Hood Canal served as the basis for charges of a conspiracy to defraud the government, and that of a Paris, Idaho, mercantile firm accused of large-scale timber trespass.[34] But most frauds went unpunished. When notified by an army officer of timber stealing on Lake Coeur d'Alene, the U.S. attorney in Boise, some six hundred miles from the site, grumbled to his superior that he could not ask the marshal to go, because there were no funds for the trip. Instead of attempting an investigation, he rationalized that the timber probably would be used to build homes for otherwise honest settlers in the area.[35]

The U.S. Postmaster General also had few field investigators in the Northern Tier territories. Investigators could be sent to follow up on reported problems, but postal authorities most often depended on the cooperation of federal prosecutors and marshals for investigations at the scene. The number of postal law violations grew yearly. By 1876, there were 410 cases, 259 of which were for robbery and embezzlement. Meanwhile, despite what the chief of the Post Office's Division of Special Agents termed "outrages upon the mails" in Montana and elsewhere on the Northern Tier, a small budget meant no possibility of any immediate increase of agents.[36]

What cooperation existed was grudging—and for good reason. Tracking suspected mail robbers might involve the already overburdened marshals in long, arduous, even dangerous searches and with little reward. One marshal, having chased three mail robbers through the Blue Mountains and delivered them to jail in Portland, Oregon, returned to his office and a letter from the U.S. attorney general, charging him with neglect of duty. Despite his explanation for his absence, he was removed from his position.[37]

The army's presence in the region was only a little more effective. Although there were some thirty-eight military establishments in the Northern Tier territories during most years before statehood, garrisons were small and their commanders displayed little enthusiasm for undertaking policing duties involving the civilian population.[38] For the most part, frontier duty did little for the army's reputation. Saddled with ill-defined and often conflicting functions, with neither field commanders nor troops properly trained for peace-keeping duties among the Indians, the poorly funded army vacillated between protecting settlers from Indians and protecting Indians from settlers.[39]

During the critical years of the Indian wars in Washington Territory, Pacific Department Commander General John E. Wool took a dim view of efforts to open the area east of the Cascade Mountains to mining and settlement. He was convinced, he wrote the assistant adjutant general of the army, that whites had "banded together to exterminate the peaceable Indians."[40] It was useless, he believed, "even where there are courts, to bring offenders before them, for in such cases they have been uniformly acquitted."[41] Some settlers were sympathetic to the Indians' plight; the army's task, Wool had concluded, was to mediate disputes. Wool was replaced as commander in the spring of 1857, and his successor, Brevet General Newman S. Clarke, was less convinced of the need to provide the Indians with protection.[42] The army's position toward the conflict between the native population and the incoming whites reflected the attitudes and decisions of field officers. In Montana and Dakota territories, for example, men like Brigadier General Regis de Trobriand held the Indians in utter contempt and defined the army's police role as one of aggressively waging war on them.[43]

The lack of manpower, resources, and appropriate training made it difficult for the army to respond efficiently to other police duties, such as protecting wagon trains and those who delivered mail. Post commanders seldom responded to calls for assistance from civilian agencies without orders from their superiors or proof that the requesting agency would pay the costs of any help. When U.S. marshals were available, army officials sometimes investigated allegations of murder, rustling, and smuggling, and tracked down witnesses for important criminal cases.[44] More often, the army was called on to assist or protect Indian agents. There was little affection between the army and the Office of Indian Affairs, and commanders appear to have resented this duty. The Indian agents had even fewer funds than post commanders, and George Wright summed up the position held by most of his military colleagues when he complained that he had always tried to cooperate with Indian agents, but he had found them to be without means or credit. "Most of the duties of Indian Agents are devolved upon the military commanders," he complained.[45]

Beginning in the 1860s, Indian agents sought an alternative to either curtailing their efforts to fit minuscule appropriations or depending on their military colleagues for aid. Nearly twenty years before, Elijah White had attempted to provide the Indians with laws and an enforcement mechanism that he had devised. Now the agents introduced a similar system, with Indian courts and police charged to carry out law codes written by the agents. John Meacham, for example, sought to control the Klamath and Modoc Indians under his supervision with a code that required monogamy and made illegal the tribal practice of men beating their spouses with lodgepoles.[46] Throughout the Northern Tier, as in other parts of the West, the new departure won congressional funding in 1878 and official stature in 1883.[47] Although the new approach imposed the spirit of Anglo-American law on reservation Indians and clarified the lines of authority on the reservations, it was highly destructive of Indian law-ways.[48]

Second only to the Department of Justice in terms of the personnel and resources it committed to the region was the Bureau of Customs. The Department of the Treasury had extended Customs operations north of the forty-ninth parallel with the successful completion of boundary negotiations with Britain. By the early 1850s, a Customs house had been constructed at Port Townsend, Washington Territory, the official port of entry for the Puget Sound District; sub-ports had been established at the principal ports and internal crossroads communities in the area. The Bureau of Customs also maintained small border stations at distant intervals along the international boundary with British North America.[49]

The extension of federal control to the region came on the heels of sixty years of documented American smuggling operations in the North Pacific. Smugglers had developed a brisk, illegal trade with Spanish, Russian, and native settlements on the coast. Hawaii had served as a comfortable wintering location and trans-shipping point for ships carrying liquor, arms and ammunition, and other trade items banned by mercantilist regulations. The heavily forested coastline, with thousands of coves and hundreds of islands, offered almost unlimited protection and opportunity to smugglers, allowing them to take high profits with little risk.[50]

Customs Bureau efforts to contain the illicit trade was ineffectual. As commerce and population grew, Congress agreed to form additional collection districts and Customs houses. But the Bureau's facilities were badly staffed, its regional leadership drawn from patronage lists, and its Revenue Marine Branch represented by vessels too slow to catch the smugglers.[51] Not until the close of the Civil War did the Customs Bureau make a serious effort to enforce federal revenue laws.

The new commissioner of Customs was Nathan Sargent, a former newspaperman and lawyer with more than two decades of experience in the federal government. Sargent believed that it would prove impossible to end all smuggling. Unless Customs inspectors had the authority and were prepared to search every vessel, wagon, and railroad car that entered the United States, some illegal trade would continue. The Bureau's assignment was to make illegal trade difficult and unprofitable, to curtail large-scale smuggling, and to drive professional contraband traders to small-time smuggling. To accomplish these goals, Sargent urged more stringent cording and sealing procedures and recommended hiring honest officers and a force of special agents trained to prevent and investigate smuggling operations.[52]

The most interesting aspect of Sargent's approach to the law enforcement role of the Bureau of Customs was his adoption of both strategy and tactics. Under Sargent's plan, Customs officers would have specialized duties; their resources would be deployed with some forethought; there would be an elite detective force trained to investigate and search for smugglers. Sargent, alone among federal officials, understood the need to think through the overwhelming task of enforcing law in nineteenth century America, particularly in frontier areas such as the Northern Tier territories. But the commissioner was denied the funds needed to recruit and train such a force, and he was unable to implement his plan. Still, some of his approach was adopted by the Bureau of Customs in later years.

Like most other federal agencies, the Department of Justice made no significant adjustments to the conditions of the frontier. United States attorneys and marshals detailed to the frontier were attached to one of three large districts in each territory.[53] Marshals and their deputies were required to travel immense distances, not only in search of fugitives but also to serve writs or attend a session of court. The apparent concentration of criminal activities in the towns, most of which had local law enforcement officers, did not alleviate the department's burden of responsibility. When suspects fled a crime scene, they had thousands of square miles of sparsely settled country in which to hide. The vast distances that slowed the marshals' response time also slowed communication; by the time a marshal reached a crime scene, a month or more of wind and weather could have destroyed even obvious clues.[54]

There is little evidence that such conditions were officially acknowledged as an important aspect of serving federal justice in the West. Department examiner Albert Small displayed a rare understanding among his Department of Justice colleagues when he wrote in defense of an Idaho marshal: "In such a country where frequently there must be miles to travel where there is nothing but a trail, it is impossible to verify every charge for mileage and expenses."[55] The government paid low salaries and meted out expense monies in a dilatory and miserly fashion. Not only were marshals and other court officers treated in this way, but witnesses were also inadequately reimbursed for sometimes gruelling journeys to court hearings. During one year in Washington Territory, federal business was transacted in twenty-seven terms of court in twelve different locations. The hardship created for federal officers, lawyers, and their clients was considerable.[56]

Low salaries may have tempted a few federal marshals to embezzle public funds, but most earned extra money working in other occupations or "moonlighting" as part-time operatives for private detective firms or as hired guns for ranchers or the railroads.[57] U.S. marshals and their deputies on the Northern Tier were no less competent or honest than their colleagues to the east. Like lawmen elsewhere, most were selected on the basis of personal and political associations and they possessed no formal training. But given the natural and governmental environment in which they worked, their record of enforcement was acceptable.[58]

Much the same can be said of the region's United States attorneys. They appear to have been no more venal or ill-prepared than their colleagues in the States. Their conviction rate was similar to that in other parts of the nation, yet they often worked without access to the published statutes of the federal and territorial governments. It was difficult to assemble a jury of educated men, and judges seem to have tolerated and occasionally encouraged informal court behavior. In an 1878 civil case in Moscow, Idaho, for example, the judge reportedly summed up the issue this way:

> Gentlemen of the jury, you have heard both sides of this case. If you believe what the attorney for the plaintiff says, you will have to find for the plaintiff; if you believe what the attorney for the defendant says, you will have to find for the defendant; but if you are like me and don't believe a damned word that either of them says, I don't know what in hell you'll do.[59]

The story may be apocryphal, but the uncertain course of justice and law enforcement was not. Apart from a few bustling towns, most of the Northern Tier frontier was not dramatically more violent or less predictable than towns in the East. Everywhere in the United States during that period, courts were overwhelmed by the rapidly increasing number of laws and caseloads, and the legal profession was ill-equipped for the changes. New concepts of property and new, broadening definitions of crime confused jurists and laymen alike. The extension of the scope of due process and the role of the federal government in its advancement and protection were dramatic results of the ratification of the Fourteenth Amendment. Complicating matters further, powerful, increasingly well-organized interest groups demanded the institutionalization and expansion of the new forms of public law enforcement. The federal government had yet to properly define its law enforcement role or the form it would take.[60]

Only in 1870 did Congress shape a Department of Justice from the semi-autonomous offices of solicitors and federal officers who re-ported to the U.S. attorney general. For many years thereafter, as one writer noted, all of the new department's attorneys "could have met in one room."[61] The actual centralization of the federal role in law enforcement would also take many years. In the meantime, the government's chief law enforcement officers in the Northern Tier territories, as elsewhere, had to struggle with extending their responsibilities as the public substitutes for the ancient reliance on blood feuds and private retribution. To all of these difficulties were added, in the West, the problems of vast distances, inadequate funding, and a myth of frontier violence that, in hindsight, appears to be almost self-fulfilling.

Notes

1. Kermit L. Hall, "The 'Magic Mirror' and the Promise of Western Legal History at the Bicentennial of the Constitution," *Western Historical Quarterly* 18 (October 1987): 429–30.

2. Some writers have made uncritical use of the observations of two early authors with vigilante connections: Nathaniel P. Langford, *Vigilante Days and Ways: The Pioneers of the Rockies; the Makers and Making of Montana, Idaho, Oregon, Washington and Wyoming* (Boston: J. G. Cupplies, 1890); W. J. McConnell, *Frontier Law: A Story of Vigilante Days* (Yonkers, N.Y., 1913). Thomas J. Dimsdale's open espousal of the vigilante cause has not inhibited reliance on his *The Vigilantes of Montana; Or, Popular Justice in the Rocky Mountains* (1865; reprint, Norman: University of Oklahoma Press, 1953). See also Roland L. De Lorme, "Crime and Punishment in the Pacific Northwest Territories: A Bibliographic Essay," *Pacific Northwest Quarterly* 76 (April 1985): 42–51.

3. White attempted to keep order, using as his authority a commission as United States sub-Indian agent, given him by Secretary of War T. Hartley Crawford. The position had dubious legality, since Oregon was not yet U.S. territory. A. J. Allen, *Ten Years in Oregon: Travels and Adventures of Doctor E. White and Lady West of the Rocky Mountains; With Incidents of Two Sea Voyages Via Sandwich Islands Around Cape Horn* (Ithaca, N.Y.: Andrus, Gauntlett & Company, 1850), 200, 340.

4. In recent years, scholars have employed caution in using Langford's work as a primary source. Compare Langford, *Vigilante Days and Ways*, 4–5, 61–64, *et passim*; Robert G. Bailey, *River of No Return* (Lewiston, Ida.: Bailey-Blake Publishing Company, 1935), *passim*; letter, Henry S. Hazlitt, Dixie, Idaho, to Fred Lockley, n.d., in Scrapbook 269, Oregon Historical Society Collections, Portland. The quotation is from W. Eugene Hollon, *Frontier Violence: Another Look* (New York: Oxford University Press, 1974), 148.

5. See R. E. Mather and F. E. Boswell, *Hanging the Sheriff: A Biography of Henry Plummer* (Salt Lake City: University of Utah Press, 1987), 92–118, *et passim*; J. W. Smurr, "Afterthoughts on the Vigilantes," *Montana, the Magazine of Western History* 8 (April 1958): 8–20; Robert E. Wynne, *Reaction to the Chinese in the Pacific Northwest and British Columbia, 1850–1910* (New York: Arno Press, 1978).

6. Mather and Boswell, *Hanging the Sheriff*, 93–95, 111–15.

7. James Stout, United States Land Office, Boise, Idaho, to E. R. Hoar, United States Attorney General, November 25, 1869, General Records of the Department of Justice, RG 60, National Archives, Washington, D.C. [Justice Department Records].

8. Joel Houston, U.S. Attorney for Idaho, to Hoar, December 6, 1870, Justice Department Records.

9. Katherine Johnson to Richard Z. Johnson, July 7, 1883, MS. 14, Box 5, Johnson Papers, Idaho Historical Society and Archives, Boise [IHSA].

10. See, for example, Henry Burdick to Hoar, October 10, 1869, Justice Department Records.

11. A. Akerman to William W. Belknap, Secretary of War, February 13, 1871, Vol. H, RG 107, Records of the Secretary of War, National Archives, Washington, D.C.

12. Granville Stuart, *Forty Years on the Frontier, As Seen in the Journals and Reminiscences of Granville Stuart, Gold-Miner, Trader, Merchant, Rancher and Politician*, ed. Paul C. Phillips, 2 vols. (Cleveland: Arthur H. Clark Company, 1925), 2:175–8, 197–205.

13. A sober analysis of the extent of actual disorder in the Black Hills is Harry H. Anderson, "Deadwood: An Effort at Stability," *Montana, the Magazine of Western History* 20 (January 1970): *passim*.

14. Frank Richard Prassel, *The Western Peace Officer* (Norman: University of Oklahoma Press, 1972); Hollon, *Frontier Violence, passim*. For an excellent summary of the controversy over western violence, see Roger D. McGrath, *Gunfighters, Highwaymen and Vigilantes: Violence on the Frontier* (Berkeley: University of California Press, 1984), 261–72.

15. James M. Poland, "Statistical Characteristics of Criminal Justice Data," *Journal of Police Science and Administration* 11 (1983): 282–9; V. A. C. Gatrell and T. B. Hadden, "Criminal Statistics and Their Interpretation," in *Nineteenth Century Society: Essays in the Use of Quantitative Methods for the Study of Social Data*, ed. E. A. Wrigley (Cambridge, England: Cambridge University Press, 1972), 358, 386; R. N. Davidson, *Crime and Environment* (New York: St. Martin's Press, 1981), 15; Hermann Mannheim, *Comparative Criminology* (Boston: Houghton Mifflin Company, 1965), 203.

16. Demographers, criminologists, and historians specializing in quantification all warn of the dangers, but none more clearly than Francis Walker, in his introduction to statistics of crime in the 1870 census. See U.S. Department

of the Interior, Census Office, *The Statistics of the Population of the United States,
Ninth Census, 1870,* vol. 1 (Washington, D.C.: Government Printing Office,
1872), 566.

17. Gatrell and Hadden, "Criminal Statistics," 338–9, 361.

18. The states and territories selected as the major sources of population for
the Northern Tier region were chosen on the basis of census data reflecting
interstate migrational patterns. A governing assumption is that promulgated
by the nineteenth century demographer, E. G. Ravenstein, who found that
the largest number of emigrants were those who moved the shortest distance.
See Karl E. Taeuber, Leonard Chiazze Jr., and William Haenszel, *Migration in
the United States: An Analysis of Residence Histories,* Public Health Monograph
no. 77, Public Health Service Publication no. 1575 (Washington, D.C.: Government Printing Office, 1968). See also Charles J. Galpin and T. B. Manny,
*Interstate Migrations Among the Native White Population As Indicated by Differences
Between State of Birth and State of Residence: A Series of Maps Based on the Cen-
sus, 1870–1930* (Washington, D.C.: Government Printing Office, 1934), *passim;*
C. Warren Thornthwaite, *Internal Migration in the United States* (Philadelphia:
University of Pennsylvania Press, 1934), *passim.* The author is grateful for the
counsel of Lucky Tedrow, director of the Demography Laboratory, Western
Washington University, Bellingham.

19. Department of the Interior, Census Office, *The Statistics of the Population
of the United States at the Ninth Census,* vol. 1 (Washington, D.C.: Government
Printing Office, 1872), 568–9. I have followed the practice, employed by the
Federal Bureau of Investigation and most historians of crime, of defining the
crime rate in terms of the number per 100,000 persons. Compare, for example,
Roger Lane, *Policing the City: Boston, 1822–1885* (Cambridge, Mass.: Harvard
University Press, 1967). The rates have been computed from census statistics of population and the number of convictions recorded in the year of the
census. The resulting rates are conservative estimates, since there are more
arrests than filed charges and fewer convictions than cases heard. New York
is missing from the 1860 listing because the figure given is unreliable. Dakota
Territory is missing because no total for the number of persons convicted of
crimes was given in the 1860 census. After 1870, the U.S. Census ceased reporting convictions and listed instead the number of prisoners being held in
prisons and jails without giving the dates of incarceration.

20. See Lane, *Policing the City;* James Richardson, *The New York Police: Colonial Times to 1901* (New York: Oxford University Press, 1970); Eric H. Monkkonen, *Police in Urban America, 1860–1920* (New York: Cambridge University
Press, 1981). An excellent comparative study is Wilbur R. Miller, *Cops and
Bobbies: Police Authority in New York and London, 1830–1870* (Chicago: University of Chicago Press, 1976). The reliance on traditional forms of protection,
especially in the West, is noted in Prassel, *Western Peace Officer,* 30.

21. The emergence of justice as an abstract absolute is traced in William J.

Bouwsma, "Lawyers and Early Modern Culture," *American Historical Review* 78 (April 1973): 310–18. See also Michael R. Weisser, *Crime and Punishment in Early Modern Europe* (Hassocks, Sussex: Harvester Press, 1979), chap. 4. The resort to private vengeance by frightened elites is examined in Allan Silver, "The Demand for Order in Civil Society: A Review of Some Themes in the History of Urban Crime, Police and Riot," in *The Police: Six Sociological Essays*, ed. D. J. Bordua (New York: John Wiley & Sons, 1967), 4–15; Adrian Shubert, "Private Initiative in Law Enforcement: Associations for the Prosecution of Felons, 1744–1856," in *Policing and Punishment in Nineteenth Century Britain* (New Brunswick, N.J.: Rutgers University Press, 1981), 25–41; Richard Maxwell Brown, *Strain of Violence: Historical Studies of American Violence and Vigilantism* (New York: Oxford University Press, 1975), vii, 146–7.

22. Compare J. S. Cockburn, *Crime in England, 1500–1800* (London: Metheun, 1977); Miller, *Cops and Bobbies*, 6–7; Lynn McDonald, "Theory and Evidence of Rising Crime in the Nineteenth Century," *British Journal of Sociology* 33 (September 1982): 404; David Jones, *Crime, Protest, Community and Police in Nineteenth-Century Britain* (London: Routledge & Kegan Paul, 1982), 3–4; Rodney F. Allen and Charles H. Adair, eds., *Violence and Riots in Urban America* (Worthington, Ohio: Charles A. Jones Publishing Company, 1969), 32–33.

23. McDonald, "Theory and Evidence of Rising Crime," 405.

24. Monkkonen, *Police*, 74–75; McDonald, "Theory and Evidence of Rising Crime," 405.

25. Monkkonen, *Police*, 74–75. See also Edith Abbott, "The Civil War and the Crime Wave of 1865–1870," *Social Service Review* (June 1927): 212–4.

26. Ray Allen Billington, *Land of Savagery, Land of Promise: The European Image of the American Frontier* (New York: W. W. Norton, 1981), 268. The classic study of such attitudes remains Henry Nash Smith, *Virgin Land: The American West as Symbol and Myth* (Cambridge, Mass.: Harvard University Press, 1950). See also James A. Inciardi, Alan A. Block, and Lyle A. Hallowell, *Historical Approaches to Crime: Research Strategies and Issues* (Beverly Hills, Calif.: Sage Publications, 1977), 59–90.

27. Survey of Ada County Criminal Court Records, 1863–1890, IHSA; Department of the Interior, Census Office, *Compendium of the Eleventh Census: 1890, Part I—Population* (Washington, D.C.: Government Printing Office, 1892), 14; N. B. Willey, Deputy Court Clerk, Idaho County, to Curtis, U.S. Attorney, December 14, 1870, John Dunlop, District Court Clerk, Alturas County, to Curtis, November 24, 1870, and R. G. Evans, Justice of the Peace, Ourida County, to Curtis, November 26, 1870, IHSA. A. S. Mercer, in *The Banditti of the Plains* (Norman: University of Oklahoma Press, 1954), 6–7, has pointed out that outside the towns of that region, on the range, census data suggest exceedingly low incidences of stealing and other forms of lawlessness.

28. Survey of Washington Territorial Court Records, 1853–1889. The author

is indebted to David Hastings of the Washington State Archives staff for this information.

29. Elliott West, "Five Idaho Mining Towns: A Computer Profile," *Pacific Northwest Quarterly* 73 (July 1982): 108–20.

30. James Q. Wilson and Richard J. Herrnstein, *Crime and Human Nature: The Definitive Study of the Causes of Crime* (New York: Simon & Schuster, Inc., 1986), 19.

31. Earl S. Pomeroy, *The Territories and the United States, 1861–1898: Studies in Colonial Administration*, 2d ed. (Seattle: University of Washington Press, 1969), 15–61.

32. Margaret L. Sullivan, "Conflict on the Frontier: The Case of Harney County, Oregon, 1870–1900," *Pacific Northwest Quarterly* 66 (October 1975): 174, 178–9; Thomas G. Alexander, "The Federal Frontier: Interior Department Financial Policy in Idaho, Utah, and Arizona, 1863–1896" (Ph.D. diss., University of California, Berkeley, 1965), 178–80, 302; Frederick J. Yonce, "Public Land Disposal in Washington" (Ph.D. diss., University of Washington, 1969), 135–6, 138.

33. Yonce, "Land Surveys," 2, 53–55; Alexander, "Federal Frontier," 177, 182; Sullivan, "Conflict," 176.

34. Yonce, "Land Surveys," 138; Fremont Wood, U.S. Attorney, to Attorney General, April 12, 1890, Box 472, Justice Department Records.

35. Joel Huston to Charles Devens, Attorney General, April 25, 1878, Box 368, Justice Department Records. See also Huston to Attorney General, August 25, 1874, Box 367, and telegram, Norman Buck, U.S. Attorney, Idaho, to Attorney General, October 3, 1878, Box 368, Justice Department Records.

36. C. Cochran Jr. to Montana Territorial Governor Potts, July 18, 1874, Box 1, File 12, Montana Territorial Executive Office Correspondence, Record Series 40, Montana Historical Society Archives, Helena [MHSA]. See also Fred T. Dubois, U.S. Marshal, Boise, to Attorney General, October 14, 1883, Box 369, Justice Department Records. Even by the 1890s, the number of postal inspectors had risen to only 103. See Marshall Henry Cushing, *The Story of Our Post Office; the Greatest Government Department in all its Phases* (Boston: A. M. Thayer & Company, 1893), 11; Patrick Henry Woodward, *Guarding the Mails; or the Secret Service of the Post Office Department* (Hartford: Dustin, Gilman & Company, 1876), 9.

37. J. H. Alvord, U.S. Marshal, to Attorney General, October 12, 1868, Justice Department Records. Cases of postal theft or embezzlement usually required investigators to travel. One inspector, for example, visited six post offices at scattered locations and traveled more than two thousand miles to investigate mail theft of less than two hundred dollars. Cushing, *Story of Our Post Office*, 324.

38. Robert H. Frazer, *Forts of the West: Military Forts and Presidios and Posts*

Commonly Called Forts West of the Mississippi River to 1898 (Norman: University of Oklahoma, 1965), 43–46, 81–84, 111–16, 135–9, 169–78.

39. Robert M. Utley, *Frontiersmen in Blue: The United States Army and the Indians, 1848–1865* (New York: Macmillan, 1967), 8–11, 40–41, *et passim.*

40. Major General John E. Wool to Lieutenant Colonel L. Thomas, Assistant Adjutant General, February 26, 1855, vol. 12, Letters Sent, Department of the Pacific, Records of U.S. Continental Commands, RG 393, National Archives, Washington, D.C. [Department of the Pacific Letters].

41. Ibid. See also Wool to Colonel George Wright, January 29, 1856, copy in Department of the Pacific Letters.

42. Utley, *Frontiersmen in Blue*, 200–1.

43. See telegram, General Regis de Tobriand, Fort Shaw, to General O. D. Greene, Department of Dakota, January 1, January 28, January 30, 1870, and telegram, de Tobriand to General Alfred Sully, January 30, 1870, Telegram Book, District of Montana, Department of the Pacific Letters.

44. For example, see William T. Sherman, Adjutant, Headquarters, Pacific Division, to Commanding Officer en route for Oregon, April 30, 1849, Colonel George Wright to General Lorenzo Thomas, April 29, 1866, de Tobriand to Major N. W. Osborne, Fort Benton, January 8, 1870, Department of the Pacific Letters. See also Prassel, *Western Peace Officer*, 194.

45. Wight to J. W. P. Huntington, October 9, 1863, Department of the Pacific Letters.

46. William T. Hagan, *Indian Police and Judges: Experiences in Acculturation and Control* (New Haven, Conn.: Yale University Press, 1966), 25–26.

47. Ibid., 1–10; Alexander, "Federal Frontier," 256. See also Department of the Interior, Letters Received by the Office of Indian Affairs, Records of the Tulalip Indian Agency, Box 504, Records of the Yakima Indian Agency, Law Enforcement Records, Box 253, Records of the Colville Indian Agency, Including the Spokane Subagency, Boxes 481–486, RG 75, National Archives and Records Administration, Seattle.

48. See Frederick E. Hoxie, "Toward a 'New' North American Legal History," *American Journal of Legal History* 30 (October 1986): 351–7.

49. Roland L. De Lorme, "The United States Bureau of Customs and Smuggling on Puget Sound, 1853–1913," *Prologue, the Journal of the National Archives* 5 (Summer 1973): 77–88.

50. Roland L. De Lorme, "Policing the Pacific Frontiers: The United States Bureau of Customs in the North Pacific, 1849–1899," *Pacific Northwest Forum* 5–6 (Fall–Winter 1980–1981): 55–56.

51. See Richard H. Dillon, *J. Ross Browne: Confidential Agent in Old California* (Norman: University of Oklahoma Press, 1965), 72–77, 86.

52. William E. Smith, "Nathan Sargent," *Dictionary of American Biography*, ed. Dumas Malone, vol. 16 (New York: Charles Scribner's Sons, 1935), 368;

Nathan Sargent to Hugh McCulloch, Secretary of Treasury, March 1, 1865, January 30, 1866, March 8, 1867, vols. 1 and 2, Department of the Treasury, Bureau of Customs, Letters Sent by the Commissioner of Customs Relating to Smuggling, 1865–1869, RG 217, National Archives, Washington, D.C.

53. Pomeroy, *Territories*, 51.

54. See, for example, Thomas H. Irvine, "Account of Tracking Cattle Rustlers," n.d. [1880], Box 1, File 16, Thomas H. Irvine Papers, MHSA [Irvine Papers].

55. Albert Small, Examiner, to Attorney General, July 31, 1890, RG 60, Justice Department Records.

56. A. J. Chapman, U.S. Attorney, Idaho, to Attorney General, December 28, 1882, Huston to Hoar, April 18, 1870, John S. Crosby, Governor, Montana Territory, to Henry M. Teller, Secretary of the Interior, October 5, 1884, Fred Dubois to Attorney General, January 9, 1883, and Thomas B. Hardin, Examiner, to Attorney General, June 15, 1887, Justice Department Records.

57. For example, Hardin to Attorney General, June 15, 1887, Justice Department Records; W. R. Schnitzer, Deputy U.S. Marshal, Wyoming, to Irvine, November 30, 1881, and W. A. Pinkerton to Irvine, February 19, 1884, Box 11, File 4, Irvine Papers.

58. Compare; Prassel, *Western Peace Officer*, 111; Clark C. Spence, "We Want a Judge: Montana Territorial Justice and Politics," *Journal of the West* 20 (January 1981): 7–13.

59. Eric Bromberg, "Frontier Humor: Plain and Fancy," *Oregon Historical Quarterly* 61 (1960): 293.

60. Henry Robert Glick, "State Court Organization," *Current History* 70 (June 1976): 255; Richard L. Thornburgh, "The Federal Role in Criminal Law Enforcement," *Current History* 70 (June 1976): 250; Sheldon Goldman, "Criminal Justice in the Federal Courts," *Current History* 70 (June 1976): 258.

61. Thornburgh, "Federal Role in Law Enforcement," 249.

7

The First Attempt to Organize Dakota Territory

WILLIAM E. LASS

WRITING FOUR DECADES AFTER THE FACT, EMINENT MINNESOTA jurist Charles E. Flandrau claimed that with the sole exception of the state of Franklin, the first effort to organize Dakota Territory was "the only actual attempt . . . to form a government on the principles of 'squatter sovereignty,' pure and simple, that has ever occurred in the country."[1] Flandrau had been financially interested in the Dakota Land Company, and it is not too surprising that he glorified the firm's efforts during the late 1850s to seize economic and political control of the potentially rich Big Sioux River area in what is now southeastern South Dakota.

The short, futile campaign of the Dakota Land Company to organize Dakota Territory can be adequately understood only in the context of frontier Minnesota. Part of the company's *raison d'etre* was inspired by the circumstances under which Minnesota Territory was formed, and the opportunity to expand into Dakota was created by the formation of the state of Minnesota.

The Dakota Land Company was based in St. Paul. Like many enterprises of its time, it was formed during the mania of a speculative boom in Minnesota Territory. Minnesota's expansive economy was fueled by major Indian land cessions. The opening of the southeastern part of the territory in 1853 precipitated a short-lived land craze in which numerous new towns were started, and speculation was rife. With unbridled faith in continuing inflation, capital was commonly obtained on real estate security at a monthly interest rate of 3 or 4 per cent. During the flush mid-1850s, Minnesota's population increased dramatically. In 1856, the fourth consecutive boom year, it was obvious that Minnesota Territory had the requisite population to apply for statehood.[2]

Late in 1856, Henry Mower Rice, the territory's congressional delegate, proposed a Minnesota Enabling Bill in the House of Representatives.[3] Rice was the leader of the territory's Democratic party and, among other things, was an expansionist. With his roots in St. Paul, he ascribed to the belief that that frontier city was destined to be far more than a territorial or state capital. Rice and some fellow St. Paulites envisioned their community as the metropolis for a vast hinterland, stretching west across the Great Plains and including Rupert's Land north of the international boundary.[4]

This thinking, which soon led to a full-fledged campaign to fulfill Minnesota's Manifest Destiny, affected the shape of the future state of Minnesota. Proponents recognized that the state of Minnesota could include part of the territory, which encompassed a vast area, including what would become the state and those portions of present-day North Dakota and South Dakota east of the Missouri and White Earth rivers. Over a year before Rice proposed the enabling bill, Minnesota's politicians and journalists had initiated serious consideration of the future state's boundaries.[5]

From the beginning there was contention between those who wanted a north-south state and those who sought an east-west state. Originally, the supporters of a north-south state preferred a state stretching between Iowa and Canada, with a western boundary of the Red and Big Sioux rivers. This boundary seemed logical, not only because the rivers provided a natural line but also because the Upper Sioux Indians by the Treaty of Traverse des Sioux had ceded their lands as far west as the Big Sioux. The contemplated east-west state would have extended from the Mississippi to the Missouri rivers, with a northern boundary at approximately the forty-sixth parallel.[6]

The north-south concept, which drew most of its support from the dominant Democratic party, was generally favored by St. Paulites and others who argued that a state so constituted would have a diverse economy of agriculture, lumbering, and mining. As they well knew, opportunities for St. Paul expansion into Rupert's Land also depended on having a boundary abutting Canada. The idea of the east-west state was supported mainly by members of the newly formed Republican party. They believed that an east-west state would not only facilitate wresting the capital from St. Paul but would also help attract a transcontinental railroad to Minnesota and would assure a strictly agricultural base for the future state's economy.

Rice's position as territorial delegate allowed him to specify the north-south state boundaries in Minnesota's enabling legislation. As initially proposed, Minnesota's western boundary would have followed the Red and Big Sioux rivers, thereby placing within the state all land ceded by the Sioux Indians. During congressional deliberations, however, Minnesota's size was restricted by the provision that part of its western boundary would run due south from the foot of Big Stone Lake to the Iowa line. This change left the tract of ceded land between that line and the Big Sioux River outside the proposed state of Minnesota.[7]

Why would the representative of an aspiring state consent to such a reduction? Circumstantial evidence suggests that Rice was influenced by men of his own party and city who wanted to lay the groundwork for the rapid creation of a new political entity west of Minnesota. Within several months after the Minnesota Enabling Act was passed, a clique dominated by influential St. Paul Democrats organized the Dakota Land Company.

The incorporation of the company on May 21, 1857, occurred during a special session of the Minnesota territorial legislature. The session, which had been convened in late April primarily to assign Minnesota's liberal railroad land grant to particular routes and companies, became a party to expansionist zeal. During the session, the legislature incorporated not only the Dakota Land Company but the Minnesota and Dakota Land Company and the Big Sioux Land Company as well.[8] Obviously, more than one group of investors coveted the lands beyond Minnesota's likely western boundary.

The Dakota Land Company was better prepared than its rivals. Two days after incorporating the Dakota Land Company, the legislature passed a company-inspired act that created and named counties in the unoccupied southwestern portion of the future state as well as adjacent areas in the Big Sioux Valley. The legislators created Martin, Jackson, Nobles, Cottonwood, and Murray counties, all of which would be entirely within the state of Minnesota; Pipestone and Rock counties, which would be partially in the state and partially out of it; and Big Sioux and Midway counties, which would be outside the proposed state in the Big Sioux Valley. The act was specific to the point of naming some county seats, including Medary as the seat of Midway County, and authorizing the territorial governor to appoint county commissioners, who were to appoint other necessary county officials.[9] By any assessment, the act creating these counties was extraordinary because it applied to a vast grassland beyond the pale of settlement. Through the expedient of naming specific county seats, the act's promoters naturally left the impression that the area had been previously settled and that county government was needed immediately to serve actual rather than contemplated pioneers.

The initial successes of the Dakota Land Company reveal both something about the nature of the company and the times during which it was formed. The incorporators included some of the most powerful Democrats in the territory. Of the nine incorporators named in the act, Joseph Renshaw Brown was the most prominent public figure. By the time the company was established, Brown had lived in the Minnesota region for some thirty-five years as a soldier, fur trader, townsite developer, and politician. While engaged in the fur trade, Brown had spearheaded the original political organization of the St. Croix River area during the early 1840s. Since then, Brown had been recognized as a major figure in the region's Democratic party, and he played a prominent role in the formation of Minnesota Territory. After the territory was formed in 1849, he remained active as a fur trader, developer, journalist, and politician.[10]

William H. Nobles, another incorporator, described himself as an "old line Whig" even after the Republican party was formed.[11] Despite his adherence to that lost cause, he easily associated with St. Paul's Democrats and shared their expansionist goals. At the time when the Dakota Land Company was formed, Nobles was a regional hero. One of the pioneers in the St. Croix Valley, he had left Minnesota to participate in the California gold rush. While there he had found a new route through the Sierra Nevada. The discovery of Nobles' Pass had helped involve Nobles in California's scheming for government-improved wagon roads that would connect its gold region with the rest of the nation.[12]

Nobles took advantage of the situation and proposed a wagon road from Minnesota to the South Pass, which would enable emigrants to travel from the Mississippi Valley to the main overland trail by a northerly route. After extensive lobbying in Washington, D.C., Nobles obtained congressional funding in 1857 to locate and improve the route. This plan, which promised to make Minnesota a significant departure point for California, made Nobles an immediate regional celebrity. In an area that was hungry for development of any kind, the highly proclaimed Pacific Wagon Road dovetailed nicely with St. Paul's desire to become another gateway to the West. Mainly because of Nobles' prominence, one of the new counties in southwestern Minnesota, created at the behest of the Dakota Land Company, was named in his honor.

Brown and Nobles had been working together for some time in scheming the development of the area west of Minnesota. Not only did they realize the interdependence of a wagon road and land development in the same area but they also planned to control mail service. Brown and Nobles were two of the creators of the Minnesota, Nebraska and Pacific Mail Transportation Company, which the Minnesota territorial legislature incorporated on March 6, 1857. The company's purpose was to transport "United States Mail, passengers, or other matters, between the eastern boundary of the Territory of Minnesota and the Pacific. . . ."[13] Perhaps significantly, another of the incorporators was Edmund Rice, the brother of Henry Mower Rice.

Another prestigious member of the Dakota Land Company was Samuel Adams Medary, the son of Samuel Medary, Minnesota's territorial governor when the company was incorporated. At the least, young Medary's association with the company implied that the firm had the governor's blessing—a belief that was underscored when the Midway County seat was named Medary in honor of the executive. Samuel Adams Medary provided yet another link between the Dakota Land Company and the Nobles' Wagon Road survey when he worked as Nobles' chief engineer during the 1857 season.[14]

The Dakota Land Company actually began operating before its incorporation. The company's initial expedition to the Big Sioux Valley left St. Paul on May 21, 1857, the very day it was incorporated, so it was obvious that the firm had been raising capital and supplies for some time. Alpheus G. Fuller, the proprietor of the Fuller House, a St. Paul hotel, was in charge of the party that claimed townsites in the Big Sioux Valley. His forty-man expedition, outfitted with animals, wagons, building materials, and a year's worth of provisions, proceeded up the Minnesota River by chartered steamboat. Then, from a point near Fort Ridgely, it traveled overland to the Big Sioux River by way of the Redwood River, Lake Benton, and Hole-in-the-Mountain, a natural opening in Coteau des Prairies, the ridge separating the watersheds of the Minnesota and Missouri rivers.[15]

From Hole-in-the-Mountain, Fuller led his party southwest to the land company's most prized site—the Falls of the Big Sioux River. The Dakota Land Company believed that the falls, with their potential water power, were the key to the development of the region. With their Minnesota backgrounds, company officials naturally made favorable comparisons between the Falls of the Big Sioux and St. Anthony Falls in the Mississippi at Minneapolis.

Having beaten its Minnesota rivals into the field, the Dakota Land Company apparently anticipated no difficulty in staking a claim to the land adjoining the Falls of the Big Sioux. Much to Fuller's amazement, however, he found five white men living at the falls when he arrived on June 6. As he soon determined, the pioneers were employed by the Western Town Company of Dubuque, Iowa, which was formed in 1856 by Dubuque businessmen who had learned about the falls from a report by explorer Joseph N. Nicollet. Lured by the prospects of land speculation in the falls area, the Western Town Company first claimed the site during the fall of 1856 by sending a small party up the Big Sioux River from Sioux City, Iowa.[16]

Undaunted by this unexpected development, Fuller claimed a half section of land adjoining the Western Town Company claim as "Sioux Falls City" for the Dakota Land Company. Leaving only a token representation at the falls, Fuller located three other townsites on the Big Sioux, Emenija, Flandrau, and Medary. Emenija, about twelve miles downstream from the falls, was promoted as the head of steamboat navigation on the Big Sioux. In its ballyhooing of Emenija, the Dakota Land Company was never inhibited by the fact that the Big Sioux was a relatively narrow, unnavigable stream. Prospective emigrants wanted navigable streams, and the company merely proclaimed that there was one. About thirty miles northeast of Sioux Falls was Flandrau, named in honor of Charles E. Flandrau, then an associate supreme court justice for Minnesota Territory and a shareholder in the Dakota Land Company. Medary was platted about twenty miles farther upstream at the site of Joseph R. Brown's trading post.[17]

During the summer of 1857, the Dakota Land Company strived to solidify its hold on southwestern Minnesota. A number of company officials, including incorporators Joseph R. Brown, Alpheus G. Fuller, Franklin J. DeWitt, and Samuel Wigfall, spent time in the field. Wigfall, Nobles' partner in a St. Paul lumber and wood business and later secretary of the Dakota Land Company, was particularly active in leading work crews. The townsites platted east of the proposed Minnesota state line were Saratoga, about sixty miles west of New Ulm on a branch of the Cottonwood River; Grand Oasis, about fifteen miles south of Saratoga; and Mountain Pass at Hole-in-the-Mountain. Saratoga and Grand Oasis were pronounced to be seats of two counties that had been created on May 23.[18]

In part because of its own propaganda campaign, the Dakota Land Company attracted a lot of public attention. Company spokesmen, cryptically identified by such pseudonyms as "Veritas" and "Cosmopolite," regularly sent letters to the leading St. Paul newspapers— the *Pioneer & Democrat*, the *Advertiser*, and the *Minnesotian*. In addition to reporting company activities, the writers extolled the fertility and verdancy of the land and its general attractiveness to prospective settlers.[19]

Throughout much of the summer and early fall, Dakota Land Company employees worked in close proximity to the seventy-five-man Nobles' Road Expedition. Because the first phase of the Pacific Wagon Road ran from Fort Ridgely on the Minnesota River southwestward through Hole-in-the-Mountain and then westward across the Big Sioux at Medary, Nobles' men were often working in the same region being claimed by the Dakota Land Company. Work parties from both groups joined together for social festivities, such as a Fourth of July picnic at Hole-in-the-Mountain, which involved Joseph R. Brown. The enterprising Brown was then augmenting his company and newspaper activities by serving as the contractor for government mail on a route running from his hometown of Henderson, Minnesota, to Medary.[20]

Concern about possible Indian attacks contributed to the desire of the two groups to work closely together. Apprehension and fear were prevalent in the area, which was still reacting to the Spirit Lake massacre of March 1857. Although Inkpaduta, a renegade Sioux leader and the perpetrator of the Spirit Lake incident, had fled with his followers across the Big Sioux and James rivers, area settlers were generally fearful of other Indians. The Santee Sioux, then living on upper Minnesota River reservations, and the nontreaty Yankton and Yanktonai Sioux of the Dakota plains were all suspect. Concern over the possible Indian menace was heightened when some of Fort Ridgely's garrison were reassigned to the troops that were being sent to occupy Utah Territory.[21]

The Indian problem had ramifications for both the Dakota Land Company and the Nobles' Road Expedition. The company had great difficulty attracting settlers to its isolated and seemingly vulnerable townsites in southwestern Minnesota and the Big Sioux Valley. Even those who only casually followed the Minnesota news in 1857 would have had the impression that these were very hazardous regions. Nobles' party, although relatively large and well-armed, was hindered by the nontreaty Yanktonai Sioux, who believed that they owned some of the lands the government had obtained from the Sisseton and Wahpeton Sioux and resented any white incursions into the Big Sioux country.

The Yanktonais halted Nobles' advance on July 8. After a stalemate of a week and a half, Nobles withdrew his entire party eastward to a camp on the Cottonwood River, where it was joined by some Dakota Land Company employees. After a delay of nearly three weeks, Nobles renewed his march to the Missouri River. By season's end, his party had surveyed, marked, and partially improved the 250-mile route from Fort Ridgely to a point on the Missouri opposite the site of the Old Fort Lookout fur-trading post. By then, Nobles had expended his season's funds and had fallen far short of his intention to locate a road to South Pass. The failure of the Nobles' Road Expedition to develop the road as a grand thoroughfare to California was well publicized, and the anticipated flood of emigrants through the company's lands never came.[22]

The obvious relationship between the Dakota Land Company and the Nobles' Road Expedition evoked criticism in St. Paul from the *Minnesotian*, a strident Republican newspaper. While Nobles was in the field, the *Minnesotian* and its Democratic arch rival, the St. Paul *Pioneer & Democrat*, regularly denounced each other during Minnesota's contentious constitutional convention. The ferocity of this partisan campaign soon affected other matters, including the intentions of the Dakota Land Company. The *Pioneer & Democrat* depicted the company as an almost benevolent developer that would benefit the entire state, but the *Minnesotian* regarded the firm as a group of manipulative speculators who wanted only to extend Democratic control.

Other Republican newspapers, including the *Free Press* of St. Peter, Minnesota, joined in denouncing Nobles and the Dakota Land Company. In reacting to one *Free Press* attack, Nobles wrote: "I have nothing to do with the Dakota Land Company" and explained that "if the Company sees fit to build cities along my road, I judge it to be a compliment to my judgment in selection of a route, and certainly no evidence of my being a manager of the Company."[23] Because Nobles was an incorporator of the Dakota Land Company, his denial was hardly plausible. Significantly, the journalistic bickering highlighted the Democratic dominance of the company, which would later work to its detriment.

During the fall of 1857, the Dakota Land Company moved to consolidate its political control over the Big Sioux Valley. On September 18, Governor Samuel Medary appointed three commissioners for Midway County. For the county seat of Medary, he appointed three trustees, a president of the board of trustees, and a recorder. The Midway County and Medary officials included Franklin J. DeWitt, one of the Dakota Land Company's incorporators, and Daniel F. Brawley, one of the company's field managers. The governor appointed three county court justices for Big Sioux County, and three trustees, a president of the board of trustees, and a recorder for its county seat, Sioux Falls City. The appointments for the Big Sioux and Sioux Falls City positions included employees of both the Dakota Land Company and the Western Town Company.[24] The St. Paul and Dubuque speculators apparently had no difficulty accommodating each other and putting aside their differences so they could develop their settlement, economically and politically.

The nature of these political appointments suggests that the Big Sioux area was hardly over-run with settlers. The eight positions in Big Sioux County were held by only five men, with three of them appointed to two positions each. In Midway County, where DeWitt and Brawley held two positions each, the eight positions were filled by six men. Despite its braggadocio about occupying the Big Sioux Valley, the combined strength of the St. Paul and Dubuque groups during their first winter at Sioux Falls was only sixteen or seventeen men.[25]

But the paucity of settlers did not deter the speculators from political scheming. If anything, they were helped by the lack of local opposition. Years later, Flandrau suggested that the Dakota Land Company's original intention was to create a situation where some of its holdings were left outside the state of Minnesota, which would give its leaders an opportunity to organize a new territory and state with such significant institutions as a capitol, a university, and a penitentiary.[26]

The political aims of the St. Paul and Dubuque groups became apparent soon after the election of October 13, 1857, in which voters of the proposed state of Minnesota approved a constitution and elected state officers. Although Congress still had to approve Minnesota's statehood and Minnesota was not admitted to the Union until May 11, 1858, the Big Sioux promoters evidently already thought of themselves as being left out of the state. From election day on, they presumptuously referred to themselves as "the people of Dakota Territory."

David McBride and James L. Fisk, the two Dakota Land Company employees that Fuller had left at Sioux Falls, assumed the early political leadership of "Dakota Territory." They dominated a meeting held in Sioux Falls on October 24 to consider "the proper course to be pursued by the inhabitants of the former Territory of Minnesota, residing west of the line of the State of Minnesota, who, in consequence of the State organization, are left without all civil government whatever."[27] The group's first action was to appoint a committee of nine men to draft "a plan of operations to be pursued by the people of Dakota Territory to secure an early organization of the Territorial Government of said Territory."[28]

Reporting for the committee, Fisk deplored the plight of the people who had been left outside Minnesota. Without specifying a figure, he claimed that the combined population of the Big Sioux and Red River areas was "greater than that of Minnesota at the time of the organization of that Territory; and is increasing, with a rapidity unprecedented in the settlement of the West." This "energetic and prosperous population," which was "daily increasing," said Fisk, would "undoubtedly exceed ten thousand souls" by May 1, 1858. Speaking for the committee, Fisk recommended that a convention be held in Medary on November 16 "for the purpose of considering the important subject of an early Territorial organization of Dakota Territory, and making known to the proper authorities of the General Government the wants and wishes of the people therein." Each county and settlement west of Minnesota was to elect one convention delegate for every five voters.[29]

According to a newspaper story that was probably prepared by officials of the Dakota Land Company, the Medary convention was held as planned. The eighty-three delegates who purportedly met at the "Dakota House" chose Fisk as convention president and Dr. J. L. Phillips of the Dubuque group as vice-president. All of the delegates were from the Big Sioux area. Pembina County in the Red River Valley was not represented, but the delegates graciously appointed three men from the Medary area to represent that county.[30]

The convention's greatest revelation was that Alpheus G. Fuller had been previously "selected by the voters of Dakota Territory, as Delegate to represent her interests at Washington." With Fuller recognized as the elected delegate of Dakota Territory, the convention passed a resolution urging him to obtain official territorial status from Congress for the people who had been left outside the state of Minnesota. Other resolutions urged Fuller to exert his influence to obtain a land cession from the Yankton Indians, gain appropriate fortification of the ceded lands, survey them rapidly, and name a temporary capital.[31]

Because Minnesota Territory, which included the Big Sioux area, still existed, Fuller did not attempt to take his seat as the delegate from Dakota Territory until after Minnesota was admitted to the Union. In the meantime, the prospects of Minnesota's economy in general and the Dakota Land Company in particular were dashed by the Panic of 1857.

The crash was precipitated in late August by the failure of the Ohio Life Insurance and Trust Company. Leading New York City banks soon suspended specie payments, and some major railroads made assignments. As the panic spread west, affecting the entire frontier, numerous Minnesota businesses curtailed or suspended operations. By late fall, the Minnesota economy, which had been based on over-speculation, was shattered. The panic ushered in a depression that would not ease in Minnesota until the Civil War years.[32] As capital dwindled, there was little opportunity for the Dakota Land Company to lure new investors and settlers. Thousands of Minnesotans left the state during the depression years for the goldfields of Colorado and British Columbia and the farmlands of Nebraska and Kansas.

Throughout the bad times, the Dakota Land Company continued to promote "Dakota Territory." An article in the St. Paul *Pioneer & Democrat*, which was probably planted by company officials, described the "principal settlement" of Sioux Falls as having "thirty houses, a steam saw mill, and several stone buildings." Medary was said to be "a thriving settlement, boasting upwards of twenty houses, and probably as many families."[33] While conceding that "no very definite information can be procured," the article's writer placed the population of the Big Sioux area at about twenty-five hundred. Throughout the company's effort to organize Dakota Territory, the *Pioneer & Democrat* was its most consistent publicist. But during the spring of 1858, the *Henderson Democrat*, then owned and edited by Brown's compatriot James W. Lynd, tried to boost Dakota's development with reports that "the territory of Dakota is receiving a fair share of immigration" and a prophecy that the area "will undoubtedly fill up rapidly this summer, notwithstanding the hard times."[34] For those dubious Minnesotans who had witnessed no overland movement to Dakota, Lynd offered the assurance that most settlers were traveling by way of the Missouri and Big Sioux rivers.

As the Dakota Land Company kept Dakota Territory in the news, Fuller moved to Washington, D.C., to await the fate of Minnesota's statehood bill. Minnesota's bill had become embroiled in the congressional debate over admitting Kansas, and statehood was delayed until May 11, 1858. In the meantime, Fuller had been bolstered by petitions from the alleged settlers of the Big Sioux area. A memorial to Congress from the "citizens of Big Sioux and Midway Counties, in Dakota Territory" bearing 117 signatures urged that "Alpheus G. Fuller be recognized as our Representative, and So Soon as the Territory of Dakota may be organized he be admitted to a Seat in the House of Representatives as the Delegate for Said Territory." The petitioners claimed that some four hundred and fifty families were living in the ceded lands between the state of Minnesota and the Big Sioux River. With respect to Fuller, they assured Congress that he was "the almost unanimous choice" in an election of October 13, 1857, which had been "conducted fairly . . . pursuant to public notice." Congress received a similar petition with 131 signatures from "the citizens of the town of Medary in the territory of Dakota."[35]

Both petitions were referred to the House Committee on Territories on March 31, 1858, but many congressmen may have been dubious of their authenticity. The promotional efforts of the Dakota Land Company had been regularly denounced by the *Minnesotian*, which claimed that "there are not a dozen of white men" in the Big Sioux area.[36] While the *Minnesotian* went to its own extreme, the estimate of fewer than a dozen was undoubtedly closer to the truth than the ten to fifteen thousand that Fuller claimed when he sought a House seat.[37] It is not possible to determine the precise population of the Big Sioux area in 1857–1858, but those who later wrote accounts generally agreed that there were only sixteen or seventeen men at Sioux Falls during the winter. Samuel J. Albright, the editor of Dakota's first newspaper, placed the 1859 population at fewer than forty within a radius of seventy-five miles of Sioux Falls.[38]

In his quest to be seated as delegate from Dakota Territory, Fuller presented a logical but unpersuasive case to the House Committee on Territories. The people of Dakota, he argued, were entitled to representation, which Congress could accomplish by seating him and then formally organizing the territory. As for his right to speak for the people of Dakota, Fuller presented a document showing that he had received 612 votes from ten precincts in five Big Sioux counties in the October 13, 1857, election. He also submitted an election certificate signed by William E. Brown, the register of deeds for Midway County;

A. J. Whitney, the county sheriff; and Daniel F. Brawley, the chairman of Medary's board of trustees. All three claimed to have issued the certificate only after canvassing the election results.[39]

Fuller also argued that he should be seated because of the precedent established by the seating of Henry Hastings Sibley after Wisconsin had been admitted as a state in 1848. His position was identical to Sibley's, Fuller claimed, who had been seated as the delegate from the territory of Wisconsin after the state of Wisconsin had been formed. In this respect, Fuller was merely parroting the Dakota Land Company's position. The company not only chose to see the Wisconsin-Minnesota and the Minnesota-Dakota situations as identical, but it may also have been inspired by the precedent in creating a territory that would be left outside of Minnesota. Joseph R. Brown had connived to get Sibley seated, and other Dakota Land Company officials were certainly familiar with the Sibley case, which was still fresh in the minds of many Minnesotans.

Fuller could hardly concede that his position was only analogous and not identical to Sibley's. After Wisconsin had been admitted as a state, the last secretary of Wisconsin Territory, John Catlin, had assumed the position of acting governor of the Territory of Wisconsin, the residuum of the old territory in present-day Minnesota. Catlin had established his headquarters in the proclaimed territory, persuaded the incumbent delegate of Wisconsin Territory to resign, and issued an election proclamation. After Catlin had carefully established precincts according to the laws of Wisconsin Territory, Sibley was elected delegate on October 30, 1848. The House of Representatives, on that occasion, had never really recognized Wisconsin Territory but had seated Sibley because he did represent at least several thousand people. He had been elected, as Catlin stated, by the "color of law," and the House anticipated that Congress would soon organize Minnesota Territory at Sibley's behest.[40]

If Fuller hoped to use the Sibley precedent, why did he not insist that the Territory of Minnesota still existed rather than contend that he represented Dakota Territory? As Fuller must have realized, one important difference between his status and Sibley's was that the old territorial delegate had resigned. Unfortunately for Fuller and the Dakota Land Company, William Wallace Kingsbury, the last regularly elected delegate of Minnesota Territory, insisted that the territory still existed in rump form after Minnesota statehood was achieved and that he should be continued as delegate. Whatever influence the Dakota Land Company had on the Minnesota Democratic party did not extend to Kingsbury, who had been elected as the party's candidate.[41]

The presence of both Fuller and Kingsbury presented the House of Representatives with an awkward situation. On May 27, 1858, James M. Cavanaugh, a Democrat and one of Minnesota's two representatives, challenged Kingsbury's right "to a seat upon the floor as Delegate from that part of the Territory of Minnesota outside the State limits." [42] Cavanaugh's action caused considerable bickering from the floor about whether there was or was not a Dakota Territory and whether Fuller had a right to represent a territory that Congress had not created. Seeking a resolution, the House members referred the matter to the Committee on Territories.

The Committee on Territories had already received petitions from the Medary residents and the men of Big Sioux and Midway counties. But whatever influence these petitions may have had was undoubtedly minimized by a petition "of the citizens of Pembina County asking for the organization of Dakota Territory with its capital at Saint Joseph." [43] This memorial, written in French and bearing 219 signatures, emphasized the economic advantages of St. Joseph, a small community located about thirty miles west of the Red River and just south of the Canadian boundary. If nothing else, it indicated to Congress that the people who had been left outside of Minnesota were not in accord.

On June 2, the committee presented both a majority report favoring Kingsbury and a minority report recommending that Fuller replace him. In a debate extended over two days, the majority held that there was no Dakota Territory and that the Midway County officials who attested to Fuller's supposed election had no authority because they were only county officers and not officials of a duly created territory. The vociferous minority, dominated by Free Soilers who were sympathetic to squatter sovereignty, accepted all of Fuller's main contentions. They took his questionable election certificate at face value and even accepted his statement that he represented ten to fifteen thousand people.[44]

One of the factors that influenced the majority was a letter from John Blair Smith Todd, who appeared in Washington to oppose Fuller. Todd argued that Kingsbury not only had been properly elected in Minnesota but he had also received votes in the October 13, 1857, election as territorial delegate in some precincts outside the state. Todd's appearance did not bode well for the Dakota Land Company. Todd, a former army officer, and his partner, David M. Frost, a St. Louis businessman, operated an Upper Missouri River trading firm. The two partners aspired to engineer a land cession from the Yankton Sioux and to open Dakota Territory under their own aegis. In his letter to the Committee on Territories, Todd did not mention the sparse population in the Dakota Land Company's realm, but he certainly did not withhold that information from his congressional acquaintances.[45]

After the majority report was issued, Fuller's case was doomed. Most House members were generally critical of Midway County officials for contending that there was a Dakota Territory. One congressman labeled their posture "a piece of presumption and a piece of impertinence." On June 3, the House decided that the part of Minnesota Territory left outside the state was not entitled to representation.[46]

The failure of Fuller's mission was soon followed by another blow to the Dakota Land Company. On June 10, marauding bands of Yanktonai Sioux forced the evacuation of Medary and Flandrau. After the whites withdrew, the Indians destroyed both places. Sioux Falls was menaced but not attacked; its residents had enough warning to fortify their few buildings with a sod stockade.[47]

As the only remaining site in the Big Sioux area, Sioux Falls was the center of subsequent political activity. Failing to achieve congressional recognition for Dakota Territory, Sioux Falls schemers resorted to a squatter government. On September 18, 1858, at a "mass convention," they set the election of a legislative assembly for Dakota Territory for October 4. Election notices were printed by Samuel J. Albright, who, assisted by Fuller and DeWitt, had recently moved an old printing press from St. Paul.[48]

Concerned about their lack of numbers, the plotters created a bogus vote. Years later, two men who were well-acquainted with some of the participants, described the tactics used. On the morning of October 4, the Sioux Falls men reportedly divided themselves into parties of three or four, elected each other judges and clerks of election, and then each party, with a team and wagon, started off in whatever direction best pleased them; but all going in different ways. Every few miles they would stop to rest. An election precinct would be established, and an election held.

At every precinct, each man not only cast his vote "but also the votes of as many uncles, cousins, and other relatives, as he could think of, until the total vote ran up into the hundreds, all properly tallied and certified to." According to the report, "the whole number of voters in the Territory at that time did not exceed fifty."[49] Whether it was necessary to create a fraudulent vote in such a laborious fashion is questionable, but the subsequent actions of the Sioux Falls group clearly show that they rigged election results in some manner.

On October 12, the elected legislators organized themselves into a House of Representatives and a Council and proclaimed Henry Masters to be the "Governor of Dakota Territory." Masters, who had moved to Sioux Falls by way of Dubuque, was evidently the most prestigious man in the community before the election.[50] On October 13, the legislators enacted a "Code of Laws for the temporary government of the Territory of Dakota," which accepted the Minnesota territorial code, recognized the old counties of Big Sioux, Midway, Rock, and Pipestone, and created new counties of Yancton, Vermillion, and Stephens.[51] Interestingly, even though the act declared that Dakota Territory consisted of all of Minnesota Territory that had been excluded from the state, there was no mention of Pembina County.

Following the politicking in Sioux Falls, the Dakota Land Company renewed its propaganda campaign to assure Minnesotans that all was well in Dakota Territory. One of its reports in the St. Paul *Pioneer & Democrat* reviewed the company's original expedition to the Big Sioux area and stated that "hundreds have followed in the wake of those pioneers, and now boast their choice homesteads."[52] The writer apparently believed that if one lie was good then two would be even better, and readers were informed about Medary as if it still existed.

The action of the Sioux Falls squatter government was sent to Henry Mower Rice and James M. Cavanaugh. On December 20, 1858, Rice, who was serving as a United States senator from Minnesota, introduced a bill calling for the organization of the "Territory of Dacotah."

Cavanaugh, who earlier had supported Fuller, introduced a companion bill in the House the next day.[53]

During the deliberations of the Senate Committee on Territories, two versions of a Dakota Territory bill were drafted. The Rice bill, which applied only to Dakota Territory, would have restricted the territory to that part of the old Minnesota Territory excluded from the state. The other bill, which called for establishing temporary governments for both Dakota and Arizona territories, provided for an enormous Dakota Territory stretching from Minnesota on the east to Oregon and Washington territories on the west. The Committee on Territories adversely reported the Rice Bill on February 8, 1859; the other bill languished after being passed to a second reading. The next week, the House tabled Cavanaugh's bill as well as bills for the creation of Arizona and Jefferson (present-day Colorado) territories.[54] Congress, embroiled in the slavery question and the continuing debate over Kansas statehood, was not in a mood to form any new territories.

As the Dakota Land Company suffered setbacks, its principal rival, the trading firm of Frost, Todd and Company, led the way in effecting a land cession by the Yankton Sioux. In February 1858, Frost and Todd were the key organizers of the Upper Missouri Land Company. Acting in the interests of their new firm, they persuaded Yankton leaders to negotiate a formal treaty with the United States under which they ceded a large tract comprising approximately the southeastern quarter of present-day South Dakota. After the land was officially opened on July 10, 1859, perhaps as many as a thousand settlers soon moved into the Missouri River Valley near the newly established towns of Yankton and Vermillion.[55]

The developments along the Missouri led the Sioux Falls squatters to renew their efforts to organize Dakota Territory. Under a notice dated August 6, 1859, James M. Allen, the clerk of Big Sioux County's board of commissioners, advised the settlers that an election was scheduled for September 12 to choose "a Governor, a Secretary of the Territory, a Delegate to Congress, four members of the House of Representatives, two members of the Territorial Council, a Judge of Probate, a District Attorney, three Co. [County] Commissioners, a Sheriff, a Register of

Deeds, a County Treasurer, a Coroner, two Justices of the Peace, two county Assessors and two Constables."[56]

Allen of the Dakota Land Company tried to leave the impression that Sioux Falls had a considerable population. In the notice, he specified polling places for three precincts—a generous reckoning, considering that a Minnesotan who traveled through Sioux Falls shortly thereafter described the settlement as consisting of "five cabins, one saw mill, blacksmith shop, two white women and twenty-three white men."[57] For the entire Big Sioux area, including Sioux Falls and as far downstream as the mouth of the Rock River about forty miles below, the *Minnesotian* estimated that there were fewer than a hundred residents.

Although few in number, the Sioux Falls squatters managed to create a different impression. Much of their promotion was accomplished through Albright's *Dakota Democrat*, Dakota's first newspaper. Albright, who had been the owner of the *Daily Free Press* in St. Paul before his association with the Dakota Land Company, published the *Democrat* intermittently from July 1859 to February 1860. As editor, Albright not only publicized the acclaimed "Dakota Territory" but he became a political participant as well.[58]

In keeping with their characteristic disregard for the truth, the Sioux Falls settlers reported a great turnout for the September 12 election. Jefferson P. Kidder, the settlement's nominee for territorial delegate, out-polled Alpheus G. Fuller by 1,938 to 147 votes, according to James M. Allen, who was elected territorial secretary. Somehow Kidder garnered 485 votes from Big Sioux County, an amazing 973 from the vacated area of Midway County, and 359 from distant Pembina County. Information of the fraud was soon circulated by Moses K. Armstrong, whose sympathies lay with the Missouri slope settlements of Yankton and Vermillion. Armstrong wrote to the editor of the *Winona Democrat* that the twenty-three men in Sioux Falls had somehow cast 187 votes in one precinct.[59]

Despite their frauds, the Sioux Falls men satisfied themselves that they stood for frontier democracy. Earlier, Albright had joyously reported that the "people of Dacotah Territory" had effected "a genuine, simon pure 'squatter sovereignty' organization . . . without even doing the 'great father' at Washington the grace of saying 'by your leave sire.' A new star has been born into the milky-way of Territories. . . ."[60]

For some reason, the elected legislative assembly, composed of a six-man Council and an eleven-man House, was not convened until nearly two months after the September 12 election. When it was organized, Wilmot W. Brookings, who had moved to Sioux Falls in 1857 as the director of the Western Town Company's interests, was chosen president of the Council and Albright was made speaker of the House. Because Governor Masters had died shortly before, the position was tendered to Albright. When he declined the honor, Brookings was named acting governor.[61]

During their November session, which lasted a week and a half, the legislators confined themselves primarily to routine matters. They chartered more paper towns, redefined county boundaries, and prepared memorials for Congress requesting improved mail service, a land office in Sioux Falls, and the organization of Dakota Territory. Perhaps their most important action was approving a memorial requesting the House of Representatives to seat Kidder "as the representative of the people of Dakota."[62]

The next spring, when Kidder appeared before the House Committee of Elections, he presented an election certificate signed by Brookings and was allowed to state his case. Unlike Fuller, Kidder had some political credentials. A lawyer, he had served as lieutenant governor of Vermont before moving to St. Paul and becoming associated with the Dakota Land Company. His election was apparently concocted to enable the Sioux Falls groups to send its most prominent member to Washington. He even had the unqualified support of Fuller, who insisted that he had opposed Kidder merely to preclude possible competition from a Missouri Slope candidate.[63]

Rather than imitate Fuller's insistence that there was a Dakota Territory, Kidder merely presented himself as the representative of the people "in that portion of the Territory of Minnesota not included within the limits of the State of Minnesota, (now by common consent called Dakota). . . ." After arguing that Minnesota Territory still existed, he reiterated familiar popular sovereignty claims about the people who had been denied the benefits of law and government. The population of his area, which numbered "several thousand" in

1858, he claimed, "has since increased to many thousands and is still increasing." Most of Kidder's presentation consisted of a carefully prepared brief detailing instances of House precedent, which he believed should dictate his seating. In this connection, like Fuller and some other Dakota Land Company men, he made a point of Sibley's acceptance as the delegate from Wisconsin Territory.[64]

Although Kidder's appeal was more cogent than Fuller's, it had little impact. By April 1860, the battle had been lost to Sioux Falls' Missouri Slope opponents. Todd and his supporters had organized mass meetings in the Yankton-Vermillion area, and Todd used his considerable influence in Washington to block the Dakota Land Company's scheme. Ironically, the company's men, who had counted on support from the Buchanan administration, had to witness their principal rivals successfully organize Dakota Territory with Yankton as its capital during Buchanan's days in the White House.[65]

The Dakota Land Company's futile effort to organize Dakota Territory failed for a variety of reasons. The first time the Dakota issue was introduced in Congress, the slavery question, which focused attention on troubles in Kansas, cooled congressional desires to consider new territories. Later, the company miscalculated the degree of support it would get from the Buchanan administration. Some company officials believed that Buchanan would personally support their organization of Dakota Territory, but they were ignorant of some territorial history.[66] In 1848, when Buchanan was serving as Polk's secretary of state, he was asked for an opinion about the co-existence of the state of Wisconsin and the territory of Wisconsin. On that occasion, he held that local officials left outside of the state retained their authority, but on the vital question of territorial officers he offered only "no opinion." [67] Men such as Albright and Flandrau construed Buchanan's words to mean that he recognized the continued existence of a territory after a state had been formed out of part of it. This helps to explain the perception by the Dakota Land Company that their Dakota venture was identical to the Wisconsin-Minnesota experience of a decade earlier.

The Dakota Land Company was also frustrated by regional circumstances. It never recovered from the Panic of 1857 and never achieved its incorporation goal of a $400,000 capitalization. In August 1859, at the company's third annual meeting, its secretary, Samuel Wigfall, reported that the company's balance was a paltry $25.10 and that its receipts for the past year were only $888.[68] Without adequate capital the company tried to develop an area far removed from the edge of settlement in Minnesota. In the late 1850s, the land was occupied for only a few miles west of New Ulm. With good land available close to established Minnesota settlements, there was little inducement for pioneers to venture into the Big Sioux country.

In Minnesota, and ultimately outside of it, the close identification of the Dakota Land Company with the Democratic party worked to the company's detriment. Minnesota Republicans were prompted, in part, to oppose the company's Dakota plans because they saw it as a Democratic scheme to benefit land speculators. Adverse publicity in Minnesota's Republican newspapers undercut the company's exaggerated claims about Dakota's population.

The company's lack of integrity, which contributed to its political failure, was of its own doing. In Minnesota's first state election, the Dakota Land Company organized precincts in mythical towns on its lands in the southwestern part of the state and peopled the towns with mythical voters, who voted almost unanimously for Democratic candidates.[69] This manipulation, which was well known in Minnesota, hardly enhanced the company's reputation. The company's use of the same tactics in the Fuller and Kidder elections made it an easy target for critics, who were well aware of the scant population in the Big Sioux area. The company's expressed interest in helping people achieve territorial status was rather hollow considering the lack of settlers on its holdings.

Even though it failed to realize its own ends, the Dakota Land Company did help promote the cause of organizing Dakota Territory. It publicized the area regionally and, through men such as Rice and Cavanaugh, made the name "Dakota" familiar in the halls of Congress. The company's congressional efforts also introduced the concept of the massive Dakota Territory, which was created in 1861. Furthermore, its activities doubtless stimulated its Missouri Slope rivals to press for a rapid organization of Dakota Territory. If nothing else, the premature effort to organize Dakota Territory is an interesting example of the type of boosterism that typified many American frontiers.

Notes

1. Charles E. Flandrau, "The First Organized Government of Dakota," *Minnesota Historical Collections*, vol. 8 (St. Paul, 1898), 129.

2. Alice H. Felt, "Minnesota and the Financial Situation, 1857–1873" (M.A. thesis, University of Minnesota, Minneapolis, 1918), 10.

3. William E. Lass, *Minnesota: A Bicentennial History* (New York: W. W. Norton, 1977), 100.

4. Alvin C. Gluek Jr., *Minnesota and the Manifest Destiny of the Canadian Northwest: A Study in Canadian-American Relations* (Toronto: University of Toronto Press, 1965), 105–85 *passim*.

5. See, for example, the *Shakopee Independent* (Shakopee, Minnesota), December 1, 1855. In a lengthy article, "Hail the Future State of Dacotah," the newspaper's editor suggested that the state of Dakota would be developed "west of the Big Sioux and the Red River of the North."

6. William Anderson and Albert J. Lobb, *A History of the Constitution of Minnesota* (Minneapolis: University of Minnesota, 1921), 44–53.

7. William Watts Folwell, *A History of Minnesota*, 4 vols. (1921–1930; reprint, St. Paul: Minnesota Historical Society, 1956), 1:393.

8. Minnesota Territory, *Session Laws*, extra session, 1857, 54–55, 146–7, 336–9.

9. Ibid., 66–69.

10. Warren Upham and Rose Barteau Dunlap, comps., *Minnesota Biographies 1655–1912*, vol. 14 of *Minnesota Historical Collections* (St. Paul, 1912), 84.

11. *Daily Pioneer & Democrat* (St. Paul), October 7, 1858.

12. See Upham and Dunlap, *Minnesota Biographies*, 551; W. Turrentine Jackson, *Wagon Roads West: A Study of Federal Road Surveys and Construction in the Trans-Mississippi West, 1846–1869* (Berkeley: University of California Press, 1952), 168; *Daily Pioneer & Democrat*, February 11, March 5, 1857; *Daily Minnesotian* (St. Paul), March 28, 1857.

13. Minnesota Territory, *Session Laws*, 1857, 224.

14. *St. Paul Advertiser*, May 16, 1857; "The Nobles' Trail," South Dakota Historical Collections, 41 vols. (Pierre, 1912), 6:192–201.

15. *St. Peter Courier* (Minnesota), July 10, 1857; *Daily Pioneer & Democrat*, November 17, 1858.

16. *Daily Express and Herald* (Dubuque), May 27, July 19, 1857.

17. *Daily Minnesotian*, August 13, 1857; *St. Paul Advertiser*, September 26, 1857; *Daily Pioneer & Democrat*, August 6, 1859; Certificate of Dakota Land Company issued to Charles E. Flandrau, October 27, 1857, in Charles E. Flandrau and Family Papers, Minnesota Historical Society, St. Paul.

18. *Daily Pioneer & Democrat*, June 11, October 2, 1857.

19. See, for example, *St. Paul Advertiser*, July 18, August 8, August 15, 1857; *Daily Minnesotian*, August 13, 1857; *Daily Pioneer & Democrat*, July 16, 1857.

20. *Weekly Minnesotian*, July 4, 1857; *Daily Pioneer & Democrat*, July 12, 1857; *St. Paul Advertiser*, July 18, 1857.

21. See *Daily Pioneer & Democrat*, July 29, 1857; *St. Paul Advertiser*, August 8, 1857.

22. *St. Paul Advertiser*, August 13, October 3, 1857; *Daily Pioneer & Democrat*, September 26, 1857.

23. *Daily Pioneer & Democrat*, December 4, 1857.

24. Minnesota Territorial Archives, Records, "Civil Appointments" volume, Minnesota Historical Society, St. Paul.

25. Dana R. Bailey, *History of Minnehaha County, South Dakota* (Sioux Falls, 1899), 13; *History of Southeastern Dakota* (Sioux City, Iowa: Western Publishing Company, 1881), 45.

26. Flandrau, in *Minnesota Historical Collections*, 8:131.

27. *Daily Pioneer & Democrat*, November 10, 1857.

28. *Daily Pioneer & Democrat*, November 10, 1857.

29. Quoted in *Daily Pioneer & Democrat*, November 10, 1857.

30. *Daily Pioneer & Democrat*, December 1, 1857.

31. Quoted in *Daily Pioneer & Democrat*, December 1, 1857.

32. Here and below, see William E. Lass, "Ginseng Rush in Minnesota," *Minnesota History* 41 (Summer 1969): 251.

33. *Daily Pioneer & Democrat*, November 29, 1857.

34. *Henderson Democrat*, May 12, 1858.

35. U.S. Senate, Territorial Papers of the United States Senate, 1789–1873, Roll 18, Dakota, March 31, 1858-February 5, 1873, Microcopy 200, National Archives and Records Service, 1951.

36. Quoted in *Daily Democrat & Pioneer*, December 30, 1857.

37. *Congressional Globe*, 35th Cong., 1st sess., June 2, 1858, 2660.

38. Samuel J. Albright, "The First Organized Government of Dakota," *Minnesota Historical Collections*, 8:138.

39. Here and below, see *Congressional Globe*, June 2, 1858, 2661–4.

40. John Catlin to William Holcombe, August 22, 1848, in "Organization of Minnesota Territory," *Minnesota Historical Collections* (1872; reprint, St. Paul, 1902), 33–34; Holcombe to Catlin, September 6, 1848, Catlin Papers, State Historical Society of Wisconsin, Madison; Robert Malcolm Brown, "Office of Delegate for Minnesota Territory" (M.A. thesis, University of Minnesota, Minneapolis, 1942), 23–24.

41. *Congressional Globe*, May 27, 1858, 2428–9.

42. Ibid., 2428.

43. U.S. Senate, Territorial Papers, Roll 18.

44. *Congressional Globe*, June 2, 1858, 2662–4.

45. Ibid.

46. Ibid., 2678. At that time, the House decided that Kingsbury was entitled

to retain his seat but only until the end of the session on June 14, 1858. See ibid., 2579; *Biographical Directory of the American Congress, 1774–1971* (Washington, D.C.: Government Printing Office, 1971), 167, 170n; *House Journal,* 35th Cong., 2d sess. (995).

47. Herbert S. Schell, *Dakota Territory During the Eighteen Sixties* (Vermillion: Governmental Research Bureau, University of South Dakota, 1954), 12; Bailey, *Minnehaha County,* 14–15; *Daily Pioneer & Democrat,* June 24, 1858.

48. "The Settlement of Sioux Falls," *South Dakota Historical Collections* (Pierre, 1912), 6:144; *Daily Pioneer & Democrat,* August 28, 1858.

49. Bartlett Tripp and John Henry Worst, "Territory of Dakota," in *The Province and the States,* ed. Weston Arthur Goodspeed, vol. 6 (Madison, Wisc.: Western Historical Association, 1904), 214.

50. "Act of Dakota Territory, October 13, 1858," in U.S. Senate Territorial Papers, Roll 18; *Dubuque Express & Herald,* November 5, 1858; Albright, in *Minnesota Historical Collections,* 8:144–5.

51. "Act of Dakota Territory, October 3, 1858," in U.S. Senate, Territorial Papers, Roll 18.

52. *Daily Pioneer & Democrat,* November 17, 1858.

53. *Congressional Globe,* 35th Cong., 2d sess., December 20–21, 1858, 138, 159.

54. Ibid., 876–7, 1065. Verbatim copies of both bills are in U.S. Senate, Territorial Papers, Roll 18.

55. Schell, *Dakota Territory,* 7–9.

56. *Dakota Democrat* (Sioux Falls), August 26, 1859.

57. *Winona Democrat* (Minnesota), December 3, 1859.

58. *Daily Free Press,* October 11-November 3, 1855. The South Dakota Historical Society has five issues (vol. 1, nos. 2, 3, 4, 6, 9) of the *Dakota Democrat,* which were published from August 5, 1859, to February 18, 1860. A portion of issue no. 1 was printed in the *Daily Pioneer & Democrat,* August 11, 1859.

59. "Settlement at Sioux Falls," *South Dakota Historical Collections,* 6:147; *Winona Democrat,* December 3, 1859.

60. *Daily Pioneer & Democrat,* October 29, 1858.

61. *Dakota Democrat,* August 26, November 8, 1859; Albright in *Minnesota Historical Collections,* 8:145–6.

62. *Dakota Democrat,* November 8, December 15, 1859; "Claiming Seat in House of Representatives as delegate from Dakota," H. Misc. Doc. 73, 36th Cong., 1st sess. (Serial 1065), 1.

63. Upham and Dunlap, *Minnesota Biographies,* 400; *Daily Democrat & Pioneer,* July 12, 1859; "Settlement at Sioux Falls," *South Dakota Historical Collections,* 6:146.

64. "Claiming Seat in House of Representatives," 2–8.

65. Schell, *Dakota Territory,* 15–16.

66. "Claiming Seat in House of Representatives," 6.

67. James Buchanan to Henry Dodge, July 18, 1848, in *The Works of James Buchanan*, ed. John Bassett Moore, 12 vols. (reprint, New York, 1960), 8:126.

68. *Daily Pioneer & Democrat*, August 6, 1859; *Dakota Democrat*, November 8, 1859. The detailed report submitted to the company's third annual meeting of stockholders was prepared by James L. Fisk. James L. Fisk Record Book, 1856–1860, 4–5, in James Liberty Fisk and Family Papers, Minnesota Historical Society, St. Paul. For Fisk's later activities as a leader of Minnesota-to-Montana wagon trains, see Helen McCann White, ed., *Ho! For the Gold Fields: Northern Overland Wagon Trains of the 1860s* (St. Paul: Minnesota Historical Society, 1966).

69. Robert J. Forrest, "Mythical Cities of Southwestern Minnesota," *Minnesota History* 14 (September 1933): 246–50.

8

Railroads and Urbanization in the Northwestern States

JOHN C. HUDSON

THE ECONOMIC HISTORY OF THE NORTHWESTERN STATES HAS GEN-
erally been approached from one of two perspectives on the role of
capital in regional development. In one view, railroad builders and
other men of wealth and influence were foresighted investors who assumed the risks that were necessary to bring such a large but sparsely
populated territory into the national economic sphere. Their bold
actions laid an enduring framework for regional prosperity. In the
more critical view, capitalists were reckless predators who risked little
when compared to the virtually certain torrent of benefits that would
pour from a region with so rich an endowment of natural resources.
Outsiders had the money and the power, and they used it to their own
advantage by expropriating the region's wealth. They left a plundered
landscape and little more than broken dreams for the nourishment of
those who actually lived there.

A tacit assumption of both sides in this continuing debate is that
the various agents of capital were truly influential, whether for good
or for ill, in determining the course of development. It is commonly
acknowledged, for example, that railroad companies had a great deal
to do with determining the patterns of urban development in the six
northwestern states admitted to the Union in 1889–1890. To what extent is this view justifiable? How important and how lasting was the
role of railroads in creating the fabric of settlement? And what blame
or credit is due those who did the most to shape the course of events? I
will examine these questions at a regional level by studying the broad-
scale geographic patterns resulting from railroad-influenced development and assess the railroads' role in the formation of the system of
cities and towns.

The maps used to illustrate this discussion show features of the natural environment as well as the location of towns and railroads. The logic of urban development in the Northern Tier states can only be understood in its relevant environmental context. Rugged mountains demanded detours to avoid, good agricultural land was worth detouring to capture, and other broad sections of territory were simply there to be crossed.

The Northern Transcontinental Railroads

In the minds of mid-nineteenth century Americans, the building of the West, including the founding of towns and cities, was closely linked to the construction of railroads. Although the federal government stood ready to assist in such construction, the actual work was to be undertaken by private companies. Part of the necessary reconnaissance work in locating the lines was undertaken by the Pacific Railroad Survey of 1854. An extensive mapping project by the U.S. Army's topographical engineers, the survey was authorized by Congress to examine six routes for a possible railroad line from the Mississippi Valley to the West Coast.[1] Following various parallels of latitude, two of the routes (along 32 degrees and 35 degrees) were championed by the southern states in the growing sectional conflict. Two mid-continent routes, following the 38th and 41st parallels, diverged westward from the Great Bend of the Missouri at Independence or St. Joseph along alignments suggested by the Oregon, California, and Santa Fe trails. Two other possible routes crossed the northern interior and terminated either at Fort Vancouver (47 degrees) or Seattle (49 degrees) in Washington Territory.[2]

National economic and political motives demanded the linking of East and West, while sectional rivalries between the northern and southern states led to disputes over the route that would be chosen. Secretary of War Jefferson Davis favored a southern route along the 35th parallel; but Los Angeles, the port city at that latitude, would have decades to wait before it became the major center of West Coast development. California's focus in the 1850s was San Francisco and the lower Sacramento Valley. That, plus a logical choice of line midway across the nation, north to south, favored a route west from

Iowa or Missouri, then on to the frontiers of settlement. The arts of geopolitical compromise might have been employed to secure an east-west route to San Francisco in the 1850s, but no actual construction was possible until southern advocacy of a 35th parallel route was removed through the circumstances of secession. The Pacific Railroad Act, signed by President Lincoln in 1862, specified westward construction from Council Bluffs, a point that was still waiting for a railroad connection to the east as competing lines built west across Iowa.

The Union Pacific Railroad

The Platte River Valley of Nebraska, which had guided westward-moving settlers for more than a generation, was an inevitable alignment for the Union Pacific Railroad west from Council Bluffs. Beyond the forks of the Platte (at present-day North Platte, Nebraska) the Pacific Railroad Survey map of 1855 specified two alternative routes. One survey followed the north fork of the Platte into Wyoming along the route of the Oregon Trail via the Sweetwater River and took the South Pass route across the Continental Divide (Map 1). A shorter route was to strike directly west from the forks of the Platte through the Laramie Range and the Great Divide Basin and to join the more northern route in the vicinity of Fort Bridger, Wyoming, before threading the Wasatch Mountains to reach the Salt Lake Basin.

In a masterful synthesis of physical and economic geography, James Vance has shown why the Union Pacific avoided the old Oregon Trail alignment in favor of a direct assault on the Laramie Range and a more southerly route across Wyoming.[3] The Oregon Trail was an emigrant's track, a one-way route to the Willamette Valley that had to provide for the food needs of animals as well as offer a passable route for wagons. Great Plains grasses swept westward along its uniquely favorable route. Stretches of even fifty miles without such vegetation were a problem, as were timbered mountain passes that impeded progress. Undulations in terrain were far less important for the wagon road than they were for the railroad that followed.

What the Union Pacific needed was a short, easy climb from the High Plains across the Rocky Mountains. Surveyors soon found such a site at the western edge of the "Cheyenne Gangplank," a section of plains land over seven thousand feet in elevation that bridged the

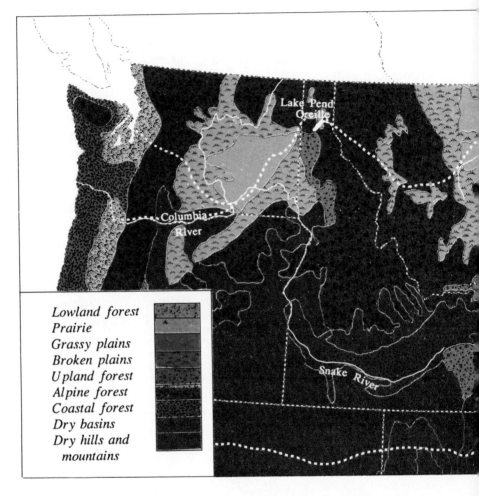

Map 1. Environmental regions of the northwestern states. Dashed lines show the approximate alignment of the Pacific Railroad Surveys of 1855.

knick-point between the soft sedimentary rocks of the plains and the hard granites of the Laramie Mountains. Less than a thousand feet of additional climb was required to attain the mountain pass, on a grade the railroad called Sherman Hill to emphasize the low-level crossing. The Union Pacific then built in a broad arc across the grassy Laramie Basin (Map 2) and headed due west to make the easiest of all the crossings of the Continental Divide, the low rims of the Great Divide Basin

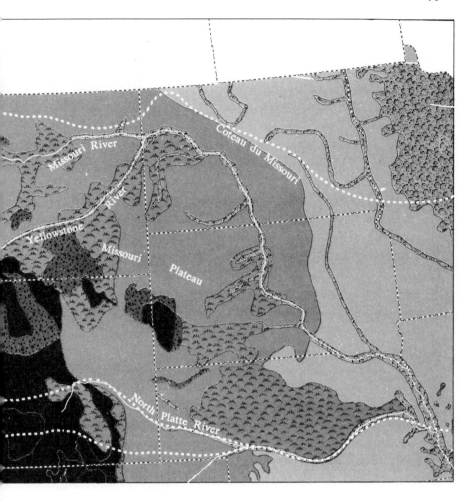

of interior drainage between Rawlins and Rock Springs in Wyoming Territory.

The Union Pacific line, joined in 1869 with the eastward-building Central Pacific at Promontory Point, Utah, was the nation's first transcontinental railroad. The Union Pacific was not among the first railroads built with the assistance of a land grant nor was it a pioneer in the railroad townsite business, but its experience with town-founding in Wyoming is instructive because it foreshadowed many similar developments that would follow in the northwestern states during the latter part of the nineteenth century. A combination of political and

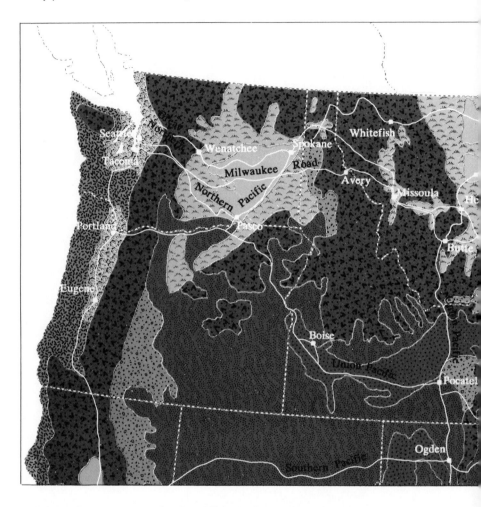

Map 2. Transcontinental railroad lines in the northwestern states.

economic forces had dictated the line's general location, while the limitations of technology and features of topography had determined most of the rest of its route. But selling the alternate sections (square miles) of a land grant in the arid interior of Wyoming, to say nothing of booming townsites where only military camps had existed before, posed problems that the railroad had to overcome if it was to realize any of the benefits bestowed in the land grant.

In 1867, the Union Pacific made General Grenville M. Dodge its chief

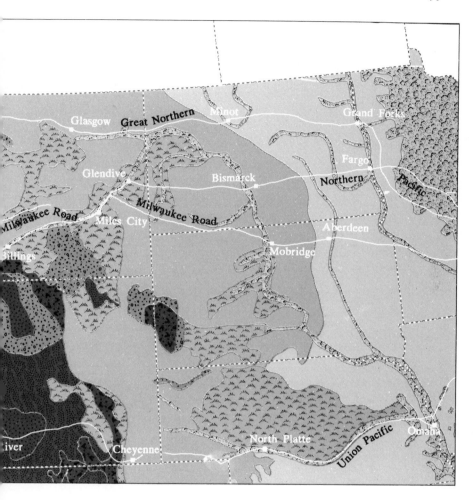

engineer and gave him responsibility for supervising construction, townsites, and land matters in Wyoming Territory. One of Dodge's first problems was to unravel the complications already plaguing the newly surveyed city of Cheyenne. The railroad selected its townsites before the tracks were laid in order to squeeze out the speculators who inevitably appeared wherever railroads were built. The law forbade anyone else to lay out a townsite within the limits of the Union Pacific's grant before the survey was made, guaranteeing the railroad a short-term but nonetheless total monopoly.

Lot sales were brisk in Cheyenne by October 1867, but because the site had been platted ahead of the surveyors it had been impossible to know that part of the town fell on an even-numbered section of public land rather than on one of the odd-numbered sections that would be awarded to the railroad. Cheyenne was swarming with men the railroad called "claim jumpers," led by a former justice of the peace from Omaha who organized a meeting that resolved that "the R. R. Co. have no authority to sell and transfer any property in Cheyenne that is not on a section of land that will fall to them by survey." There were other bad feelings as well, such as the complaint lodged by one man who bought a town lot from the railroad for $1,000, sold it immediately, and then was astonished to discover that his purchaser had resold it again at a $1,400 profit.[4]

The railroad had a rigid scheme of predetermined prices on its lots; and even though there were various strategies to bring a greater return, the Union Pacific scarcely reaped the profits they have been credited with taking. And despite their efforts to keep speculators from driving up prices, there was not a chance of doing so once a parcel had been sold. It surely was not the railroad's fault that some speculators found themselves bested by others playing the same game, yet it is plain from the record that the railroad had no title to the Cheyenne townsite land it was selling.

Other problems were encountered in subsequent townsites along the Union Pacific in Wyoming. Laramie's plat was staked out on a United States military reservation (Fort Sanders), and Dodge had to persuade the government to relinquish it so that the town could be developed.[5] Plans for Rawlins and Rock Springs were late in coming and suffered from uncoordinated attempts at promotion. Despite the difficulties, Dodge remained optimistic as to what the railroad could accomplish:

> All inland Towns, Cities, Mining Camps, Herding Camps &c in this latitude must for all time be supplied from our Rail Road Line, and there can be no competition: the Company controls all lands suitable for use or to even be used for Town Sites and the location of stations is exclusively in the Companys hands.[6]

Like other railroad development promoters, Dodge encouraged liberal terms to get groups of settlers onto railroad lands: "these colonies all have a *leader* or *leaders* and a few 'corner lots' to *them* would not fail to *interest* them in the Town and surrounding country."[7]

Wyoming's low mountain passes and broad basins offered a natural route for a transcontinental railroad, but any hope of creating some semblance of what had been done in terms of agricultural settlement and town-building in the more humid eastern parts of the nation was not to be realized. Dodge proposed the planting of one hundred thousand "shade or Forest trees" around the Union Pacific's depots (which he believed would make his line as attractive to settlers as the Kansas Pacific), and he urged his company to run excursion trains for the "hundreds of old farmers in Penna., Ohio, Ind., and Ill. [who] are anxious to locate their boys on new farms."[8] Such schemes were to be repeated many times in subsequent years, sometimes with considerable short-term success, but promotional pipedreams eventually had to face environmental reality.

The "Overland Route" of the Union Pacific did not reach California because the Central Pacific (later, the Southern Pacific) owned the route west of Ogden; but under the auspices of a subsidiary, the Oregon Short Line, the Union Pacific did build to Portland in 1885. The Oregon route diverged west of Green River, Wyoming, and followed the drainage of the Bear River into Idaho to reach the Snake River plain. The railroad platted a small townsite at Pocatello in 1882.[9] Boise, which had originated as a civilian counterpart of the army's Fort Boise in the 1860s, predated the railroad. The Snake River country was still awaiting development when Idaho became a state and the urban frontier lay far distant.

The Northern Pacific Railroad

The first popular plan for a railroad to the Pacific Coast was not the Union Pacific-Central Pacific line that was built. Asa Whitney, a New York dry-goods merchant and Orient trader, had recognized early the importance of an overland route toward the Far East. In 1849, he published a map showing a railroad projected west from Prairie du Chien, an old fur-trade and military fort on the Mississippi River in southwestern Wisconsin, to Puget Sound. Whitney had little knowledge of what lay between Prairie du Chien and Fort Walla Walla on the Columbia, but his map and calculations clearly demonstrated that the closest route to the Orient lay along the northernmost alignment that could be constructed.[10]

Whitney's plan was redrawn in a more realistic fashion in the Pacific Railroad survey reconnaissance of the northern route under the direction of Isaac I. Stevens, governor of Washington Territory. The Stevens route began at St. Paul and reached nearly to the Canadian border in what is now western North Dakota before striking southwest toward a Rocky Mountain crossing at either Lewis and Clark's Pass or Cadotte's Pass in Montana (Map 1).[11] West of the Continental Divide, Stevens proposed two alternate routes. One followed the Clark Fork River north via Lake Pend Oreille and then struck south to the confluence of the Columbia and the Snake before turning northwest once more to cross the Cascades. This route was very similar to the one actually constructed by the Northern Pacific Railroad in 1882–1883, nearly thirty years after Stevens' map was drawn.

The Stevens proposal for a northern transcontinental railroad illustrates two purposes of railroad construction. In North Dakota, the route followed the western limit of tall and medium grass vegetation, traversing lands that were sure to be better for farming and avoiding the poorer land west of the Coteau du Missouri, and reached close to the Canadian border before turning west into Montana. Stevens added miles to the straight-line route for the sake of traversing as much good agricultural land as possible. West of the Divide, the objective was to avoid the Bitterroot Mountains along the Idaho-Montana line, and mileage was added for the sake of gaining a low-level mountain crossing. Nearly all of Stevens' route was occupied in later years by one or another railroad.

The Northern Pacific Railroad was chartered and awarded a land grant by Congress in 1864 for the construction of a line from Lake Superior to Puget Sound. The tracks reached the Red River at Fargo in 1871 and the Missouri River at Bismarck in 1873. But the financial crises that would plague the Northern Pacific for the remainder of its corporate life intervened, and in 1882 the end of track stood at Glendive, in Montana's Yellowstone Valley, only two hundred miles beyond Bismarck (Map 2).

In the meantime, the western end of the Northern Pacific was commandeered by German investors working through Henry Villard of the Portland-based Oregon Railway & Navigation Company. Villard sought to preserve his monopoly over transportation in the interior Northwest by diverting the Northern Pacific down the Columbia River Valley, away from its Puget Sound destination.[12] The Northern Pacific leaped to life, stimulated by the financial intrigues of its various would-be leaders, and under Villard managed to complete the entire balance of its line, from the Columbia Basin to Glendive, in 1882–1883. A direct line from Pasco to Puget Sound over the stiff grades of Stampede Pass was completed in 1887.

Tacoma, the Northern Pacific's port on Commencement Bay, had been platted by railroad officials in 1873. They hired the renowned Frederick Law Olmsted to design the plat, but Olmsted's design for Tacoma, like his other urban plans, was better suited to a cemetery than a city. The graceful, curving residential streets that Olmsted drew on Tacoma's hilly contours left little room for a commercial core and virtually ignored the port function.[13] The Northern Pacific turned instead to the standard urban grid, itself a poor choice for the site, but Tacoma boomed nonetheless. It remains as probably the most successful railroad-inspired city in the nation, and on the continent it is surpassed only by the Canadian Pacific's Vancouver, British Columbia, which is similar in age as well as function.

Conventional wisdom holds that the western railroad companies, especially those built with a land grant, platted towns at seven- to ten-mile intervals along their lines and then made a fortune selling town lots to people once settlement got underway. The Northern Pacific laid more than eighteen hundred miles of track between Lake Superior and Puget Sound. Such a stretch of territory might have offered two hundred or more sites where towns could be started, since there were relatively few cities in place before the railroad arrived. From such a base it is not difficult to project that the railroad earned many millions of dollars from its townsite operations. But a closer examination of the actual record reveals that town-founding was seldom a money-making venture.

The list of towns launched by the Northern Pacific numbers in the dozens, not the hundreds, because the company was in financial difficulty much of the time, nearly always plagued by managerial confusion, and as a result lacked the coordination necessary to produce a coherent townsite strategy. In the Yellowstone Valley, where there was little competition from other parties in founding towns along three hundred miles of river—in bottomland that ought to have offered many inducements for settlement—the company managed to earn $330,000 on townsites in the boom year of 1883 when the line was constructed. The railroad earned $3.4 million from its land sales that same year, however, which suggests how minor a source of revenue townsites were, compared with resource lands, even when townsite activity was at a peak.[14]

Many of the towns launched by the Northern Pacific were joint ventures, usually with local businesspeople, and the company often left its own interests in the care of agents who would, in the course of their own promotion, do at least some good for the railroad as well. When the company was in bankruptcy again in 1897 it sold to local parties, at less than one dollar each, many thousands of unsold lots in the various towns. Some of the Northern Pacific towns, including Jamestown, Bismarck, Billings, Livingston, Yakima, and Ellensburg, became important urban centers, but places that saw little growth beyond their early boom years far outnumbered those we can now call successful.

The Northern Pacific actually may have done a better job connecting the few centers of urban activity that already existed in the Northwest. In Montana, Bozeman (founded in 1864), Helena (1864), and Missoula (1865) had been settled as the result of mining and trading activity prior to the railroad's arrival. The Northern Pacific's path up the grassy lowlands of the Yellowstone required a mountain crossing east of Bozeman in order to reach the Missouri drainage for another transit of fairly level grassland to Helena. The Continental Divide was then crossed in a relatively short but steep climb over Mullan Pass, the route of an early wagon road, before dropping into the Columbia drainage (Clark Fork River) through Missoula to reach the existing city of Spokane. Steep sections around the two passes were isolated by much longer stretches of low-profile running, and it was in these relatively settled valleys, which struck in various directions of the compass, that the railroad chose to lay its tracks.

The Great Northern Railway

The most successful of the transcontinental routes was the Great Northern Railway from Grand Forks through Minot (1886) to Seattle (first settled in 1852, reached by the Great Northern in 1893). Although the Northern Pacific was the first line across the Northern Tier of states and has often been identified as the route that followed the Stevens survey, it was the Great Northern that eventually built across the Northern Plains much as Stevens had suggested. As a result, it was the Great Northern that was to become the major hauler of Northern Plains grain, because of its early strategy of occupying the best agricultural lands and, later, constructing branch lines of track into adjoining areas where grain farming was profitable.

The Great Northern followed an almost perfect latitudinal alignment just north of 48 degrees from the Red River Valley to Lake Pend Oreille. The route required only a single mountain crossing, and an easy one at that (Map 2). Marias Pass, with an elevation of only 5,213 feet, was a low crossing of the Continental Divide that had been little known to earlier surveying parties due to the fierce opposition of the Blackfeet Indians who occupied its eastern approach. The Great Northern's locating engineer, John F. Stevens, made a belated "discovery" of Marias for the railroad in 1889, and in 1892 he secured a relatively favorable route through the Cascades at the headwaters of the Wenatchee River (Stevens Pass). Only fifty-five miles of the entire line lay above 4,000 feet elevation, an especially fortunate condition for winter operation in this northern latitude. The route had a low profile and was shorter than the Northern Pacific's as well. Added to the list of favorable circumstances was the spectacular scenery of the Rocky Mountains north of Marias Pass. The Great Northern promoted tourism, and the area was later set aside as Glacier National Park.

What the Great Northern's territory lacked was on-line population. Its straight-line route, unlike the routes of the transcontinentals to the south, had no string of outposts along major water courses or wagon roads, because virtually no one had ever traversed the country along the line of 48 degrees. Here was a *tabula rasa* for urbanization: good agricultural land that was sure to be occupied yet was totally lacking in the infrastructure that would organize local trade and commerce. But this condition was not what James J. Hill had in mind when he projected his Great Northern west from Devils Lake, North Dakota, a town he and several associates platted in 1883. At the time of construction, only four townsites were even planned for the first 120 miles, and only three of them (Rugby, Towner, and Minot) were actually launched by the railroad.[15]

Hill's objective was long distance, not local. His line was extended rapidly across North Dakota and Montana in order to reach Great Falls, the town developed at a natural water-power site on the Missouri, where the Boston & Montana Company would locate its copper and silver smelter and refining works. Hill also extended his line on via Helena to link the copper mines at Butte with the Great Falls operation before the transcontinental route west from Havre through Marias was laid out in 1889. Hill's line across the Northern Plains in its early years was simply that: a line of track heading for the distant horizon that had little to do with the locale through which it passed. The Great Northern's completion in 1893 coincided with the beginning of a nationwide economic depression, which further dampened efforts to build up on-line communities.

The Milwaukee Road

The Great Northern should have been the last transcontinental built across the Northern Tier, but the euphoria of economic prosperity that seized the nation after 1900 led William Rockefeller and other influential stockholders of the Chicago, Milwaukee & St. Paul Railroad (Milwaukee Road) to plan an extension of that Middle Western-based company to the Pacific. In 1907–1908, the company extended its tracks from Mobridge, South Dakota, nearly fourteen hundred miles to Seattle and Tacoma. Its route generally followed that of the Northern Pacific, and although the route was more than one hundred miles shorter than the Northern Pacific's, it required stiffer grades. The Milwaukee Road gained access to Butte by crossing the Continental Divide on Pipestone Pass (6,418 feet) and was forced to cross the Bitterroot Mountains on a 1.7 per cent grade to reach the desolate St. Joe River Valley at Avery, Idaho. The company electrified its mountainous sections, between Harlowton, Montana, and Avery and across the Cascades in Washington, and it captured national attention for its engineering prowess; but the need for powerful electric locomotives simply underscored its problems with grade and profile.

The Milwaukee Road connected urban places such as Miles City, Butte, Missoula, Spokane, and Ellensburg, not to mention Seattle and Tacoma, that were already served by the Northern Pacific or other lines. But the company's role in building new urban centers was almost absurdly minor. By 1980, when the company entered bankruptcy, the only places it had created on the Puget Sound extension that had reached and sustained a population of twenty-five hundred or more were Mobridge; Othello, Washington; Baker, Montana; and St. Maries, Idaho—with a combined urban population of under fourteen thousand people. Most of the Milwaukee Road's western lines were abandoned during the 1980s. Financially the weakest of the northern lines, it had proven to be one more transcontinental than was needed.

The Pacific Railroad Surveys and the Pattern of Urbanization

Although none of the routes outlined by the Pacific Railroad Survey of the 1850s was followed in its entirety by any of the companies that built across the northwestern states, the survey nonetheless had a profound effect—not so much for what it proposed but for what is ignored. No route was proposed to cross the plains between the mouth of the Yellowstone and the headwaters of the North Platte (Map 1). This situation was due in part to a lack of Pacific Coast cities to serve as long-distance objectives between San Francisco and the mouth of the Columbia, partly because of difficult terrain in the central Rockies, and probably even more because the unglaciated Missouri Plateau was considered unfit for settlement.

Western South Dakota and central Wyoming became graveyards for the frustrated expansion dreams of Middle Western railroads. The Pacific Railroad Survey did indicate an alternative route roughly paralleling the Niobrara River in northern Nebraska, but it lacked a separate westward projection to the Pacific. The Chicago and Northwestern Railroad built west from Fremont, Nebraska, south of the Niobrara route, through the Sand Hills, to reach the gold-mining frontier of the Black Hills region in 1886.[16] The connection to eastern markets helped stimulate the Dakota range livestock frontier as well. Belle Fourche, which was platted by the railroad in 1890, soon achieved prominence as the nation's largest livestock shipping point. The Chicago and Northwestern also reached into the North Platte River Valley in Wyoming, where it platted Casper in 1888.[17] Although the railroad was later extended another 150 miles west, to the slopes of the Wind River Mountains at Lander, central Wyoming was as close to the Pacific as the Chicago and Northwestern Railroad ever got.

The boom year of 1907 witnessed a short-lived upsurge of interest in agriculture, railroads, and townsites in West River South Dakota.[18] Two railroads, the Chicago and Northwestern and the Milwaukee Road, raced to complete lines from the Missouri River (at Pierre and Chamberlain) to Rapid City. Other companies, including the Illinois Central, Minneapolis & St. Louis, and Soo Line, also contemplated westward extensions across the Missouri to tap the rising tide of commerce in the West. Plans for transcontinental construction lingered there until World War I, and even the Great Northern Railway considered laying another long-distance line across the Missouri Plateau, but none of these lines was built. The Milwaukee Road remained the only latter-day entrant to fulfill such ambitions.

The only remaining links in the transcontinental system that would be built were two north-south lines in Wyoming, one across the Missouri Plateau via Sheridan and the other through Worland and the Big Horn Basin. The lines were constructed by the Chicago, Burlington and Quincy Railroad to link Colorado and Nebraska with the Great Northern and Northern Pacific lines at Laurel, Montana. This arrangement was part of James J. Hill's strategy to create a single railroad under his control, however, rather than a separate effort to build a transcontinental.

The territory between the 42nd and 45th parallels was not to become a corridor of expansion from the Middle West to the Pacific. The Black Hills remained an inlier of urban settlement, linked more closely to the agricultural Middle West than to the cluster of western mining regions to which it belonged. North Dakota straddled the transcontinental flow, but South Dakota was to remain a *cul de sac*.

Patterns of Development

Although it was the building of transcontinental railroads that was supposed to stimulate urban and economic growth in the West, one must look beneath this grand scale of planned expansion to find the real associations between railroads, urbanization, environment, and land use that actually did develop over time. Two snapshots of this continually unfolding pageant can serve to summarize the overall process (Maps 3 and 4). In 1890, when statehood was achieved, there remained large gaps that the railroads would fill. By 1940, the railroads had accomplished most of what they would ever achieve in terms of influencing the settlement pattern; after that time, highways, air transportation, and the associated growth of tourism and other forms of exurban expansion shaped the system.

The Northern Tier in 1980

The year 1890—associated with the supposed "closing" of the frontier and the coming of age of Washington, Idaho, Wyoming, and the Dakotas—saw two frontiers of settlement a thousand miles apart. Agriculture in the Pacific Northwest had begun in the Willamette Valley, but by 1870 settlers moving west to Oregon were being lured to the bottoms and bench lands of the Columbia Basin around Walla Walla, Washington.[19] By 1890, the outlines of the "Inland Empire" had taken shape. Grain production had spread into the rolling Palouse Hills of Washington and Idaho to form a nearly continuous agricultural region from Spokane to the high plateau south of the Columbia River in Oregon. Between there and the eastern Dakotas, however, there was little settlement outside the Idaho, Montana, and Black Hills mining districts. Improved farmland was rare west of the Coteau du Missouri, except in the newly opened lands of central South Dakota. Among the state capitals, Cheyenne and Pierre (both railroad towns) had achieved urban status and so had the older cities of Helena and Olympia, but Bismarck and Boise were not in the urban category in 1890.

Eastern North Dakota and South Dakota had assumed the pattern of the Middle West, with a dense network of railroad branch lines and a fairly widespread pattern of crop and livestock farming, yet urbanization had not developed there to the extent that it had in Iowa, Min-

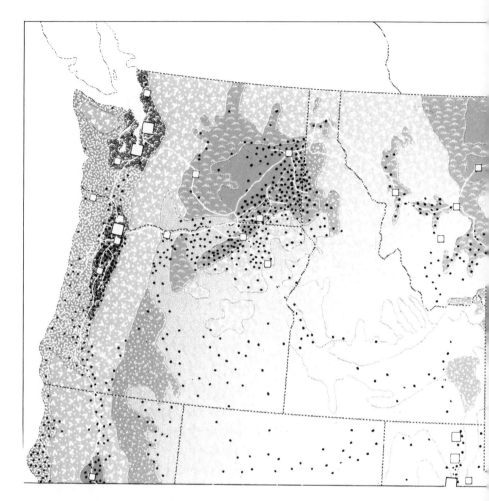

Map 3. Railroads and cities in the northwestern states in 1890. Square symbols proportional to population show the location of urban centers (places with at least 2500 inhabitants). Each dot represents 10,000 acres of improved farm land.

nesota, and Nebraska. Between Grand Forks and Great Falls on the Great Northern and between Fargo and Livingston on the Northern Pacific there were only smaller communities. Apart from the in-filling that had taken place in the eastern Columbia Basin, there was no conspicuous pattern of urbanization in the entire area bounded by the Willamette Valley, the Wasatch Front in Utah, and the Missouri and

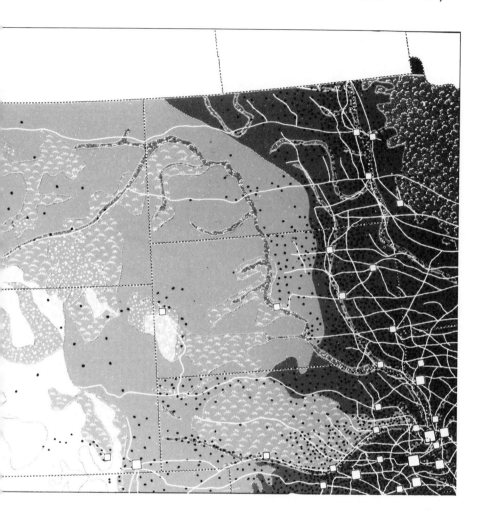

Platte valleys in Nebraska, the lone exception being the newly emerging copper mining, smelting, and refining district of Montana. Only a handful of places created by the railroads had attained urban status. Cities had not followed automatically the building of transcontinental railroads, at least not this soon after construction.

The Northern Tier in 1940

The next half-century saw many modifications in these patterns. A tide of agricultural settlers swept into the trans-Missouri dry farming districts between 1900 and 1910. Another rush took place into even

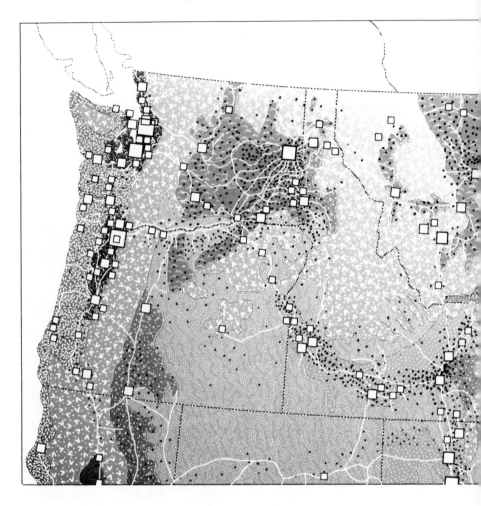

Map 4. Railroads and cities in the northwestern states in 1940. Square symbols proportional to population show the location of urban centers (places with at least 2500 inhabitants). Each dot represents 10,000 acres of cropland.

drier lands in Montana between 1910 and 1920, but many retreated by 1940 following two decades of agricultural depression. Railroad companies extended new branch lines into these grain farming districts and into the Wheat Triangle district of Montana and the rest of the Palouse country as well. Irrigation and dry farming almost totally changed the landscape of the Snake River plain in Idaho, so that by

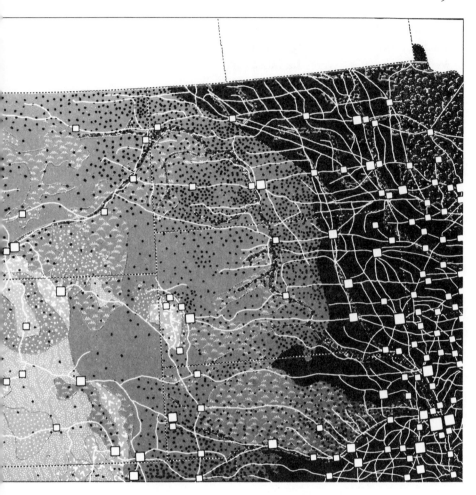

1940 there was a coherent pattern of urban centers as well as millions of acres of cropland blanketing that section.

Some areas, such as northwestern South Dakota and central Montana, continued to hope for railroad connections, but in vain. Dry, hilly grasslands would not produce good grain crops, and railroad companies avoided such areas. But new, short lines of track were extended into logging areas in the Cascade Mountains and coastal ranges. Logging and lumber manufacturing, although extensive in the area, nonetheless were town- or city-based activities. Resource extraction and processing stimulated scattered urban concentrations in the Pacific Northwest, and by 1940 the Puget Sound Lowland and the Willamette Valley were the most urbanized regions west of Minneapolis.

What is most evident on the 1940 map, however, is not the existence of cities in the Northern Tier states but rather their comparative absence. North Dakota contained only eleven communities of more than 2,500 population in 1940, although less agriculturally focused Idaho had more than twice as many. It is plain that croplands and railroads were closely associated, but cities were not part of that package except in areas of irrigation development. The population threshold of 2,500 inhabitants, used by the United States census as the minimum size for an urban place, might well be challenged for a sparsely settled territory where agriculture was the overwhelmingly most important activity and where the primary purpose of towns was to serve as trade centers. But to argue this lower limit downward and to claim that places of, say, a thousand inhabitants were the real "cities" of the Northern Plains is to effectively make the same point about the lack of urban growth in the region.

Railroads simply did not bring about urbanization. All of those miles of railroad branch lines that were constructed away from the transcontinental trunks were designed for a single purpose: to haul grain out of the region. Railroad companies and their townsite affiliates platted hundreds of tiny communities along those branch lines for the purpose of creating convenient collection points for the region's grain surplus.[20] This was the true role of railroad companies in shaping the settlement pattern: creating chains of small trade centers, not chains of great cities. It took more than a trade-center role, usually even more than a county-seat role, for one of these places to grow into urban status in the system that existed until the 1940s.

Platting small trade centers during the early twentieth century earned even less money for railroad companies than their earlier efforts, such as Cheyenne or Livingston or Yakima on the transcontinental routes. The settlement in-filling that took place between 1890 and 1940 came very late in the evolution of American retailing, at the very end of the period when small towns were necessary in order to serve a predominantly rural population that was bound to a locality through the circumstance of poor roads. Railroads were a maker of small towns, especially grain-elevator towns, and a good share of the places they created along the branch lines extended into the various farming districts and never achieved stability even as local trade centers.

The railroad brought three kinds of logistics to the Northern Tier states. It created a system for moving goods and people *through*, from the Pacific to the Middle West or vice versa, and for hauling *out* the products of farms, forests, mills, smelters, and refineries. A third role was to bring *in* nearly everything else, especially manufactured goods, from the cities of the East and Middle West. This third role certainly was known fifty or one hundred years ago, but its full impact probably was unanticipated. The lack of cities in the Northern Tier states during the first half-century of development is a logical result of the fact that trains can run both directions on a track. One need not resort to more sinister explanations, such as "anti-urban bias" or "colonial dependency" to explain the lack of urbanization. Transportation systems achieve regional complementarity; they make regional specialization possible. The urban pattern that had evolved by 1940 was a product of this specialization: grain-producing areas had few cities because only a few were needed. Mining and forest products specialty areas were more urbanized because of the labor requirements of those industries, but they, too, were specialized, local economies linked through the transportation network with other regions producing other kinds of products.

Conclusion

Urban growth in the Northern Tier states has been more rapid in the last half-century than it was until 1940. Interstate highways and jet air travel increased the accessibility of the region to outsiders, many of whom came not only to visit but to make permanent residences as well.[21] Energy booms stimulated urban growth (sometimes short-lived) in sections of Montana and Wyoming, skiers took to the mountain slopes, and refugees from the metropolis invaded just about every place that had a nice view. With these changes came new urban growth of a sort that was unanticipated at the time when railroads were perceived to be the prime agency of development.

The creation of cities at the hands of railroad companies thus amounted to much less than was hoped in the mid-nineteenth century and much less than has been credited in retrospect. From the first town—Cheyenne on the Union Pacific in 1867—to the end of branch-line construction and townsite creation around 1920, railroad companies were overwhelmingly the most important factor in creating new towns, although they had little to do with population growth once a town was platted. The railroad's purpose, after all, was transportation and not real estate. Companies engaged in extensive promotion in many instances, yet the towns they founded tended to remain small—partly because there were too many towns and partly because "small" was all the local economy could sustain. The railroad's own network of lines, efficiently lacing together various regional economies of the nation, practically guaranteed that sparse population and limited urbanization would characterize the agricultural and resource-based Northern Tier states for as long as the railroad was the dominant form of transportation.

Notes

1. James E. Vance Jr., *Capturing the Horizon: The Historical Geography of Transportation* (New York: Harper & Row, 1986), Chapter 4.

2. G. K. Warren, "Map of Routes for a Pacific Railroad . . . 1855," in *Railroad Maps of North America: The First Hundred Years*, by Andrew Modelski (Washington, D.C.: Library of Congress, 1984), plate 17.

3. James E. Vance Jr., "The Oregon Trail and Union Pacific Railroad: A Contrast in Purpose," *Annals*, Association of American Geographers, 51 (1961): 357–79.

4. R. E. Talpey to G. M. Dodge, October 29, 1867, in Grenville M. Dodge Papers, Box 152, Iowa State Historical Society, Des Moines [Dodge Papers].

5. J. A. Evans to G. M. Dodge, February 13, 1867, Box 153, Dodge Papers.

6. G. M. Dodge, "Plan for the Organization of the Union Pacific Town Lot Department," May 23, 1867, Box 170, Dodge Papers.

7. Ibid.

8. Ibid.

9. John W. Reps, *Cities of the American West: A History of Frontier Urban Planning* (Princeton, N.J.: Princeton University Press, 1979), 572.

10. Asa Whitney, untitled map of 1849, reproduced in Modelski, *Railroad Maps*, plate 19.

11. As shown on the map by Warren, "Map of Routes."

12. Vance, *Capturing the Horizon*, 323.

13. Reps, *Cities of the American West*, 565–8.

14. John C. Hudson, "Main Streets of the Yellowstone Valley: Town-Building along the Northern Pacific in Montana," *Montana, the Magazine of Western History* 35 (Autumn 1985): 59.

15. John C. Hudson, *Plains Country Towns* (Minneapolis: University of Minnesota Press, 1985), 55.

16. John C. Hudson, "Two Dakota Homestead Frontiers," *Annals*, Association of American Geographers, 63 (1973): 453.

17. Reps, *Cities of the American West*, 572.

18. Paula M. Nelson, *After the West Was Won: Homesteaders and Town Builders in Western South Dakota, 1900–1917* (Iowa City: University of Iowa Press, 1986), 21.

19. Donald W. Meinig, *The Great Columbia Plain: A Historical Geography, 1805–1910* (Seattle: University of Washington Press, 1968), Chapter 8.

20. Hudson, *Plains Country Towns*, Chapter 5.

21. Robert G. Athearn, *The Mythic West* (Lawrence: University Press of Kansas, 1986), Chapter 7.

9

Protest Movements
on the Northern Tier

The Pullman Boycott of 1894 and the
1922 Shopmen's Strike

W. THOMAS WHITE

THE PULLMAN BOYCOTT IN 1894 AND, NEARLY THREE DECADES later, the Shopmen's Strike in 1922 paralyzed most of the nation's rail network. They aroused powerful and, from some quarters, almost hysterical opposition by those who feared the specter of communism in America—the Paris communards in the first instance and the Russian bolsheviks in the second. Calmer opponents were only slightly less anxious when they contemplated the economic and social effects of the stoppage of rail traffic, upon which industrial America was absolutely dependent. Equally vehement were the strikes' supporters, which included a wide variety of elected officials, small businessmen, some large businessmen, workers, reformers, revolutionaries, and other unlikely bedfellows.

In the young states of Montana, Idaho, and Washington, the two conflicts proved to be particularly important. The Pullman Boycott, as fought in the far Northwest, was essentially a Gilded Age conflict occurring at the very close of the region's frontier phase; the Shopmen's Strike erupted at the onset of the Jazz Age, when the region was firmly settled and Victorian America was in sharp decline. In an important sense, the Pullman and Shopmen's disputes serve as benchmarks, marking the transition from a frontier to a settled society in the region. Consequently, they shed light on the developing socioeconomic milieu and the reactions of northwesterners—railroaders and non-railroaders alike—to the emerging modern order of the twentieth century. Significantly, then, the grassroots unrest manifest in both conflicts meshed well with broader protest movements, such as the Populist Revolt of the 1890s and the Robert M. LaFollette-Burton K. Wheeler independent presidential campaign of 1924. In the strikes and the broader political movements, the citizens of Montana, Idaho, and Washington played an important and not accidental role as they sought the political and economic autonomy promised, but not conferred, by statehood in 1889–1890.

The Pullman Boycott and Strike of 1894

The Pullman Boycott and Strike of 1894 erupted less than two months after the labor conflict on the Great Northern Railway and was the capstone to labor turbulence on the railroads during the depression of the 1890s. Although the Pullman conflict was conducted on a grander scale than either the Great Northern strike or the Coxeyite movement—the Pullman Strike paralyzed the railroad system in twenty-seven states and territories—the action was fought along lines closely resembling the patterns of local sympathy for insurgent railway workers and the behavior of American Railway Union strikers that had been manifest the previous spring. The economic hardships, which included draconian layoffs and wage reductions that grew directly out of the Panic of 1893, combined with the cultural patterns of labor militancy and general populist resentments to form a crucible of discontent in which embittered native white and northwest European workers retaliated against the railroads' policies. Only the Great Northern Railway, which had so recently fought with the American Railway Union, was exempt from the general transportation strike that halted traffic on all other major roads from Chicago to the Pacific Coast.

Triggered by a sympathetic boycott of Pullman Palace Cars by the American Railroad Union, the larger Pullman Strike represented the high point of the loosely knit, community-based industrial unionism practiced by the year-old union. At the same time, the strike demonstrated the impotence of that approach in the face of the modernizing roads, which had constructed a tightly centralized, disciplined organization to contend with general labor disturbances. As James J. Hill had found earlier, the railroads discovered willing allies among the leaders of the established, skilled operating brotherhoods. More important for their final victory, the roads successfully enlisted the aid of President Grover Cleveland's administration, which established a precedent by ordering out the army's entire western garrison to enforce federal court orders and open the roads. In doing so, Cleveland showed scant regard for states' rights, calling on the federal judiciary and military establishment despite explicit and loud protests by the governors of Oregon, Colorado, Texas, Kansas, Missouri, and Illinois.[1]

In the Pacific Northwest, the strikers' conduct revealed the Gilded Age pattern of geographically disparate, community-based militancy at its height. Encouraged by local support, the strikers exhibited remarkable strength, particularly in the more isolated towns immediately east and west of the Rocky Mountains. That local support helped moderate ARU behavior during the contest, and the Northwest escaped the large-scale violence that erupted at the strike's center in Chicago and other areas. At the same time, however, the ARU's defeat demonstrated the inability of disparate, community-supported locals to effectively combat nationally centralized railroads. The railroads were able to coordinate strategy through the General Managers Association, a trade association of all railroads with terminals in Chicago, while they secured the aid of the federal government to shatter the ARU's effort to establish industrial unionism in the industry.[2]

ARU President Eugene V. Debs considered the West a bastion of support. Within the region, Montana's mountain communities registered the strongest endorsement of the boycott and strike as they had two months before in the Great Northern strike and the Coxeyite movement. The state's ARU locals enjoyed substantial support from the general populace and much of the business community, and sentiments of both groups dovetailed easily with the growing populist revolt in the state. A fundamental factor in those sentiments was the attempt by the Northern Pacific to claim a large portion of Montana's mineral lands as part of its land grant. In response, an otherwise unlikely populist alliance of mine owners, laborers, farmers, and middle-class reformers had emerged by 1894.[3]

As soon as they learned that the Northern Pacific had discharged several men in St. Paul for honoring the Pullman car boycott, ARU leaders in Livingston, Montana, took the initiative. When the road's managers rebuffed their demands that the St. Paul men be reinstated and increased its use of Pullman cars, the ARU in Montana reacted swiftly. Ignoring calls for moderation from Debs and other national leaders, Montana workers immediately called a strike on Northern Pacific and Union Pacific lines and added their own demands for a restoration of wages and other issues. Local responses were rapid and decisive, and the conflict spread east and west across the Northern Tier of states.[4] The region's entire rail network, except for those areas serviced by the Great Northern, was suddenly paralyzed.

During the initial stages of the strike, Livingston's conductors defied the Order of Railway Conductor's national leaders and openly endorsed the action. Although the town's chapter of the Brotherhood of Locomotive Engineers initially denied that it was a party to the conflict, its members refused to work with inexperienced "scab" labor, thereby reinforcing the ARU's position. Meanwhile, unskilled and semi-skilled workers flocked to the unions' banner. As an anonymous spokesman in Washington state observed: "The power of the American Railway Union rests in the fact that it has taken in the wipers, trackmen, bridgemen, freight clerks, and others who have not heretofore been organized."[5]

The opposing railroads, allied with the General Managers Association, also mobilized, as J. W. Kendrick of the Northern Pacific put it, to "clean house thoroughly now that we have opportunity." The GMA set aside earlier rivalries and vowed "to do anything it could for his company [the Northern Pacific]."[6] Subsequent events, including legal maneuvers, calls for federal troops, and the importation of non-union workers, suggest that the Northern Pacific, like the Union Pacific, received considerable advice and aid from the General Managers Association.

The American Railway Union discovered its own grassroots allies in Montana. Perhaps most galling to the railroads was the position taken by the state's mine owners through the newspapers they controlled. The state's largest paper, *The Anaconda Standard*, did not openly endorse the ARU cause, but it clearly reflected the anti-Northern Pacific views of its owner, Marcus Daly of the Anaconda Company. The paper defended the strikers' conduct and character and insisted that they "are showing constantly that they have the interests of the community at heart." Outraged, the Northern Pacific's Kendrick charged that "the Marshal owes his appointment to Marcus Daly, and I am reliably informed that Daly is fomenting disturbance for the purpose of estranging the men from the road and securing their votes for his miserable capital removal scheme." (At the time, Daly was attempting to have Anaconda named capital of the new state.) The *Butte Miner*, controlled by rival copper baron William Andrews Clark, took a different stand, demanding that Pullman car workers consent to arbitration so that a settlement could be reached quickly.[7]

Feelings about the strike ran high throughout the Northwest, particularly in towns near the Rocky Mountains. In the less isolated states of the Pacific Northwest, comparatively more diversified economies and more varied notions of self-interest encouraged a more pronounced opposition to the strike in the business community. For instance, chambers of commerce in Seattle, Tacoma, and Portland roundly denounced the Pullman boycott.[8] In Northern Tier states outside Montana, where there was less dependence on a single industry, the land grant roads did not seem to threaten all elements of society.

Despite such qualifications, pro-strike passions were intense throughout the region. As early as June 28, reports from Wallace in Idaho's mining panhandle indicated that "all" of the Northern Pacific was on strike there, where employees were demanding a return to the pre-January 1 wage schedule.[9] Attorney General Richard Olney was alarmed and instructed the United States attorney at Moscow to "procure warrants or any other available process from United States Courts" against anyone obstructing U.S. mail trains and to "direct marshall [*sic*] to execute the same by such numbers of deputies or such posse as may be necessary." [10]

U.S. District Judge James H. Beatty obliged the Department of Justice on June 30 and ordered federal Marshal Joseph Pinkham to northern Idaho to protect the Northern Pacific's property. He also instructed Pinkham to arrest "any persons whose accustomed duty it is to operate said trains, who claim to still be in the service of said [Northern Pacific] receivers, but who refuse to perform such duty." [11]

Although it proved fairly simple to obtain federal warrants from a sympathetic judiciary, officials found it difficult to enforce such instruments in Idaho. On July 5, Judge Beatty wired Olney that, although a federal marshal and deputies were in place on the Northern Pacific in the north and the Union Pacific in southern Idaho, the railroads could get crews "when known troops will protect them, but [they] will not trust to marshals, as strikers do not fear latter." Beatty was particularly eager to obtain federal troops for northern Idaho: "To attempt to run trains by marshals alone is a long and uncertain struggle, with a bloody ending . . . marshals alone can not control the situation and operate trains."[12]

On July 7, events took an ominous turn. At Wardner, Idaho, someone dynamited the powerhouse and ore bins of the Bunker Hill and Sullivan Company. Two days earlier, Ed Boyce, president of the Wardner Miners' Union, had informed Spokane's ARU Local 94 that the "Coeur d'Alenes miners promise you their united support in whatever shape it comes."[13] Observing the alliance between miners and railway workers, the *Spokesman-Review* warned of "Anarchy in the Coeur d'Alenes." Although the Spokane paper preferred that local forces handle the situation, it rejoiced that "the American spirit is beginning to assert itself, and its influence will spread like wildfire. The strike may continue for weeks but rioting will have to cease." Meanwhile, Governor McConnell asked that one or two companies of regulars be dispatched to Shoshone County.[14]

In southern Idaho, railworkers manifested their resentments most clearly in Pocatello. On July 6, local opinion makers, including a Colonel Ferguson, *Populist Educator* editor Frank Walton, and Baptist and Congregationalist ministers who made an appeal to non-Mormons, registered their support of the Pullman Strike. The conflict escalated when the strikers took possession of the Pocatello yards immediately after Marshal Pinkham left to escort a Union Pacific mail train. Both Pinkham and Judge Beatty immediately requested that Olney dispatch troops to the area.[15] S. H. H. Clark of the Union Pacific warned Major General John M. Schofield, commander of the army, "that the feeling there has been so intensified by the news received from Chicago that it would be absolutely dangerous to attempt to run trains through there under existing conditions."[16] By July 7, General John R. Brooke had ordered two companies to Pocatello, where fed-

eral authorities arrested a number of ARU men allegedly involved
in the occupation of the Union Pacific yards and Frank Walton was
incarcerated for "inflammatory talk."[17]

In Idaho's panhandle, six men were arrested for dynamiting an
engine at Hope, and there were other disturbances as well, usually
involving miners. On July 20, sixty-two individuals and businesses
from Spokane, including the Old National Bank, Washington Water
Power Company, Edison Electric Illuminating Company, Snake River
Fruit Company, and Traders National Bank, petitioned Senator Watson Squire and congressmen John L. Wilson and W. H. Doolittle to
pressure the Cleveland administration for more troops for Shoshone
County.[18] Five days later, Governor McConnell added his voice to the
clamor, calling on senators George Shoup and Fred DuBois to urge the
retention of troops in northern Idaho. Having recently talked "with
the representatives of the different property interests in Shoshone
County," McConnell believed that at least two companies should remain to curb the "Miners Union which is controlled by a lot of Molly
McGuires . . . [with] re-enforcements of hard characters sent from
Butte to the Coeur d'Alenes. Our State Militia is as you know in such
a condition as to be unserviceable," the Idaho governor complained.
"The last Legislature controlled by the Populist contingency refused
to appropriate any thing for the National Guard. However, it would
not matter in my opinion if they had. The regular troops are much
better in cases of this kind than is the State Militia."[19]

On July 28, 133 men arrived at Wardner under the command of a
Captain Thompson, who took a more moderate view of conditions in
the troubled mining region. After two days, Thompson observed that
"ninety per cent of the people are law abiding citizens" and informed
his superiors that the Northern Pacific would have little trouble operating its trains. He sharply criticized "the false reports that are commonly being sent to the press from these mining towns evidently the
work of alarmists or willful liars."[20]

The response to the Pullman Strike in Washington state was similar
to that in Idaho and Montana. Nonetheless, when the strike reached
the state, not all Washington workers were willing to transfer their
allegiance to the American Railway Union. Northern Pacific Grievance
Chairman J. B. W. Johnson of the Conductors denounced the strike

in Tacoma when he first heard news of ARU actions in Montana, but his was a minority view.[21] The pro-labor *Tacoma Morning Union* estimated that most railway workers in the town were members of the ARU, who like their counterparts in Seattle, Ellensburg, Sprague, and Spokane, voted to boycott the Northern Pacific's Pullman cars. "The thoughtless will blame the men who quit work," the *Morning Union* observed, "the just and reasoning will blame the one company that seeks to decrease the already insufficient earnings of the employees, thus causing them to strike for their rights as free white men." [22]

On June 29, the strike spread to the Union Pacific and the Seattle, Lake Shore and Eastern railroads when workers, particularly switchmen and firemen, refused to handle any Pullmans.[23] As alarmed as many of his peers by the escalating conflict, United States District Judge Cornelius H. Hanford ordered United States marshals to take appropriate measures to open the railroads.[24] But the ARU cause was gaining popular, grassroots support throughout the state. Crowds gathered at railroad depots to jeer the marshals and non-ARU workers recruited to run the trains.[25] Farmers in the Big Bend area demonstrated their resentments by donating flour and bacon to the striking railroaders. In Pasco, the citizenry refused the marshals food and lodging, and they were compelled to hire their own cook and live off the contents of the boxcars they were guarding.[26]

The ARU enjoyed other support as well. In Seattle, individual unions held a series of fund-raisers for the strikers, and the Western Central Labor Union endorsed the ARU's actions. Alarmed by the escalating violence, the WCLU also criticized "the unlawful acts of so-called sympathizers, who in their fanaticism, are dealing a serious blow to the glorious cause we represent." The Tacoma Trades Council also "heartily" endorsed the strike, as did Tacoma's Longshoremen's Union No. 2, Knights of Labor.[27]

Strike sentiment was particularly strong in the Spokane/Sprague area. There, Great Northern workers refused to handle Union Pacific freight, and the Freeman's Silver Protective Association applauded the ARU's "valiant and patriotic battle in the cause of human liberty." Meanwhile, local ARU chapters joined with Spokane's trade unions to form a common front in the Citizens' Protective League.[28]

The most spectacular indication of popular sentiment in Washington was the swirl of events surrounding the mutiny of national guard units from far eastern Washington. The Washington National Guard was on maneuvers in the Puget Sound area when the Pullman Strike erupted. The Northern Pacific supplied a train for their return home on July 7, but Company G of Spokane refused to board, reportedly because it was manned by a non-ARU crew. The unit later agreed to ride the train, claiming that bomb threats and the presence of an inexperienced engineer were the real causes of its earlier reluctance. Nonetheless, on September 18, 1894, a military court of inquiry found Company G guilty of mutinous conduct and recommended the unit be disbanded.[29]

The actions of other eastern Washington units—or, rather, exaggerated reports of their actions—alarmed many residents. Despite rumors of mutinies by Troop A (Sprague) and Troop D (Spokane), a military court could unearth no instance of insubordination by members of those cavalry units. Some guardsmen did honor Debs' general plea for a show of support, however, and "flew the white ribbon" as they returned to their homes.[30]

The guardsmen's return trip on July 8 highlighted the rising level of violence that was becoming almost commonplace in the state. The troop train was delayed by a bomb planted in the roadbed, a number of sniping attempts, and repeated jeers and threats by crowds that gathered at various points along the line. Upon its arrival at Sprague, the train was greeted by burning trestles and boxcars, and an angry crowd pelted the train with rocks and other missiles. Meanwhile, firings, derailments, and scattered snipings were reported near Tacoma, Puyallup, Ellensburg, and Pasco.[31]

Coming on the heels of the widely reported refusal of two militia units to break up ARU demonstrations at Sacramento, those incidents and the rumored mutiny of the Washington National Guard contributed to alarmists' fears. Of additional concern was an incident on July 6 in Spokane, where a crowd derailed three engines and two boxcars. The rioting ended only when three policemen and three ARU representatives—H. S. Luddington, D. H. McGinley, and Michael Whaley—replaced deputies as guards in the Northern Pacific yards.[32]

United States Marshal James E. Drake clearly was alarmed when he informed Olney that he would have serious trouble enforcing Judge

Hanford's June 29 order. With similar fears, Hanford, Seattle Mayor Byron Phelps, and U.S. Attorney William H. Brinker wired the attorney general on July 7:

> We are assured strikers and industrial army are conspiring to commit mischief at Seattle, Tacoma, Spokane, and along railroad lines. . . . His [Drake's] force for lack of arms and discipline, not adequate to quell mobs in case of actual riots in cities. The revenue cutter *Grant*, with officer, men, and guns, under Captain Tozier, would quickly and thoroughly clear the streets. If force necessary, it should be a superior force.[33]

That same day, James McNaught, counsel for the Northern Pacific receivers, wired Major General Schofield: "Mob at Spokane Falls tearing up Northern Pacific tracks and destroying other railroad property. Marshal powerless. Cannot operate trains without assistance."[34]

The Cleveland administration responded promptly to the real problems in Washington, as it did in states where there was little or no violence or property destruction. When General Elwell S. Otis received his instruction to open the Northern Pacific as a military and post road, he ordered "all available troops" at Vancouver Barracks, Fort Walla Walla, Fort Sherman, and Fort Spokane to move to strategic points in Washington and Idaho.[35]

The arrival of federal troops, the roads' enlistment of non-union workers, and the erosion of popular support for the ARU following the incidents in Spokane and elsewhere broke the strike in Washington. "Striking employees are daily and rapidly sending in their applications for employment," McNaught informed Schofield by mid-July, "and we expect to run through trains regularly hereafter." The Northern Pacific had "found it necessary to send a large number of men principally engineers and firemen from St. Paul . . . to operate in Montana," and the road anticipated "some trouble in Dickinson [North Dakota], Glendive, Livingston, and North Idaho." But McNaught assured federal authorities that "we are declining to reinstate agitators and strikers' leaders." He believed there would be few serious obstacles to the railroad's operations.[36]

The Northern Pacific counsel's lingering reservations over Montana, particularly Livingston—Kendrick called it "the worst place of all" on the entire Northern Pacific line—had a solid foundation. Throughout Montana, which had so far escaped violence, ARU spokesmen and their numerous supporters vehemently denounced the introduction of the U.S. Army into what they considered a private dispute.[37] On July 9, for example, the ARU called a mass meeting in Helena to protest the Cleveland administration's intervention. James H. Calderhead, leader of the powerful Butte ARU local and a major figure in the state's Populist party, was the principal speaker. Reportedly, he received a thunderous response to his address condemning the railroads and the Cleveland administration on moral and economic grounds. The following day, occupying troops aboard a Northern Pacific train confronted the civilian populace at Livingston. Although that confrontation further inflamed anti-railroad, populist sentiment in the state, it had little effect on the outcome of the Pullman Strike.[38]

Federal troops rapidly completed their occupation of the affected roads. During the final phase, troop trains faced no major obstructions by the civilian populace, although demonstrations and hostility surfaced in many localities. Despite isolated incidents of property destruction and sabotage, the Pullman Strike in the Northwest was over. Under the combined weight of federal and state injunctions, imported non-union workers, and the presence of federal troops and marshals, most strikers simply gave up the fight. For their part, the victorious railroads quickly retaliated, fulfilling what Kendrick described as their "duty to annihilate the American Railway Union." In Chicago, the General Managers Association and its allies blacklisted thousands of former employees, while federal grand juries issued indictments charging ARU leaders, including Eugene Debs, with conspiracy and contempt of court.[39] Arrests also followed in Washington, Oregon, Idaho, and Montana, although sentences tended to be light. When James Calderhead was convicted of contempt of court, for example, he was fined one hundred dollars and sentenced to thirty days in jail.[40]

The general policies of the Northern Pacific, Union Pacific, and Southern Pacific railroads affected far more of the former strikers. Northern Pacific Superintendent Brimson warned that it would not rehire "agitators," a category that included employees who refused to renounce their ARU affiliation, and "dynamiters," as determined by company dossiers compiled by the Thiel and Pinkerton agencies. The Northern Pacific denied over eight hundred workers their former positions; the Union Pacific discharged two thousand men for similar reasons.[41] The Southern Pacific took perhaps the most extreme position, not only refusing to rehire strikers but also determined to pursue them throughout the United States and Canada to prevent them from finding new jobs.[42]

The ARU's defeat ended any serious attempt at pure industrial unionism in the railroad industry, but it did have immediate consequences. In the short term, those strikers who remained in the region probably joined in the populist revolt that raged throughout the 1890s.[43] Robert Burns Smith, Montana's Populist governor, appointed Calderhead commissioner of Agriculture, Labor and Industry in 1896; four years later, the former ARU chieftain successfully campaigned for the office of state auditor. Washington Governor John R. Rogers appointed Seattle ARU leader W. P. C. Adams as the first head of the state's labor bureau. Adams was succeeded by fellow Seattle ARU leader William Blackman, who was also president of the Washington State Labor Congress and its successor, the Washington State Federation of Labor.[44]

Fought in an immediate post-frontier setting, the Pullman Strike was a watershed for labor relations on the Northwest's railroads. During that insurgent moment, the American Railway Union enjoyed enormous popular support, most notably in the region's smaller, more isolated communities. In that sense, the dispute epitomized common patterns of community-based and supported labor disputes in the Gilded Age. But that era was fading, and the roads' successful strategy demonstrated the superiority of new forms of centralized organization and disciplined action, executed in concert with a sympathetic national government. Those trends were tested again in the modern, post-World War I environment of the Jazz Age.

The 1922 Shopmen's Strike

The 1922 Shopmen's dispute—the first national work stoppage since 1894—was "the greatest strike of the decade," according to historian Irving Bernstein. Like the Pullman Strike, it had a profound impact on labor relations. In one sense, the effect was a negative one for railway workers. The strike failed, and that failure ushered in the era of company unionism that prevailed in the industry until the advent of the New Deal. But the strike had positive effects as well. Its militant, often radical conduct proved to be an important factor in political matters, influencing the election of many pro-labor senators and congressmen in 1922, the Robert M. LaFollette-Burton K. Wheeler protest ticket of 1924, and the passage of the 1926 Railway Labor Act, which abolished the hated Railroad Labor Board and established the basic legal framework for labor relations that still operates today.[45]

The shopmen's demands included a return to the benefits they had briefly enjoyed during World War I—better wages, restoration of overtime pay for Sunday and holiday work, and the abolition of the hated practice of contracting out shop work. The shopmen also expressed their resentment of the Railroad Labor Board's apparent inability or unwillingness to enforce decisions unfavorable to the roads' management. With their demands unanswered, on July 1, 1922, over four hundred thousand shopcraft and other non-operating employees went on strike. Within two weeks *Labor* claimed that six hundred thousand workers were out.[46]

The national walkout came on the heels of the widely reported violent clash between striking miners and strikebreakers in Williamson County, Illinois, heightening the sense of crisis that permeated the nation in 1922. President Warren G. Harding quickly took a hard-line stand on the strike, declaring his intention to force both parties to accept the decisions of the Railroad Labor Board. Both he and the Republican party, however, were uncertain about the proper response to the labor crisis. Attorney General Harry M. Daugherty insisted that the strikers were outlaws and urged drastic action. Secretary of Labor James J. Davis and Secretary of Commerce Herbert Hoover disagreed, contending that there was some justice in the strikers' demands while urging appeals to moderates, such as Baltimore and Ohio President Daniel Willard, to effect some compromise.[47] Harding wavered between the two poles of opinion. Outside the administration, individual Republicans expressed different views. Idaho Senator William E. Borah sounded a strong pro-labor note in a guest editorial in the June 17 issue of *Labor*. Damning the board's wage reduction for maintenance-of-way workers, the peripatetic senator thundered that the decision was "IN ITS NATURE PEONAGE."[48]

While the Harding administration vacillated, the workers' bitterness grew as the roads issued ultimatums demanding that the striking shopmen return to work or be fired. To combat the strikes and mobilize public opinion, the Hill Lines attempted to coordinate strike policy with other transcontinentals, such as the Milwaukee Road, and with the National Association of Railway Executives. By the end of July, however, NP President Ralph Budd was disgusted with such efforts and ready to go it alone. "I think it most unfortunate that further aid is given the strike leaders in holding their men in line by having more conferences," he informed Howard Elliott, now chairman of the Northern Pacific, "and also by calling together all the roads, the labor leaders are going to have their contention that the railroad Presidents are dictated to by a small group apparently sustained by our action, which speaks louder than words." Budd believed that "it would be to the very best interest of the railroads to immediately disband the Association of Railway Executives. Otherwise . . . by these conferences we are enmeshing ourselves deeper and deeper into the tangle of national recognition of labor matters."[49]

Increasingly, any settlement of the strike turned on the issue of seniority—for example, whether all striking shopmen would be reinstated with full seniority if they returned to work.[50] On that issue, the Hill Lines remained firm, pursuing their own policy. Union Pacific managers took a different tack, and on September 7 they announced that employees who returned to work by September 15 would "be given any pension rights which he had as of date June 30, 1922."[51]

The seniority issue was related to the retention of experienced workers, most of whom had gone on strike. On the Northern Pacific, for example, 7,950 shopmen out of a normal work force of 8,421 had walked out. Although the road had recruited 4,724 replacements by September 23, it was still short 3,226 shopmen. Many returned to work over the ensuing months, but by March 27, 1923, only a little over 36 per cent of the railroad's pre-strike work force was employed.[52]

Not all were welcomed back. The Northern Pacific began compiling its "black list" in August 1922. "This is the time to carefully analyze the situation," General Mechanical Superintendent H. M. Curry insisted, "and if opportunity offers when final settlement is made to rid the service of chronic agitators, fault finders, time servers, etc."

To that end, Curry's office compiled a detailed list of over eighteen hundred "undesirables" and over twenty-three foremen, including six at Tacoma, two at Glendive, one at Livingston, one at Butte, five at Missoula, and one at Auburn.[53]

The Great Northern experienced a high percentage of walkouts and probably pursued similar policies of weeding out "undesirables." Of its authorized 9,252-man work force in June 1922, only 596 stood by the road. By January 1923, roughly two thousand had returned to work, and a total of only 27.7 percent of the Great Northern's original shopcraft workers remained on the job after the strike ended.[54]

Other roads faced varying degrees of strike activity. "U.P. reports from Omaha indicate 71% normal force," C. R. Lonergan wired from Spokane, an important center of strike activity. The hard-pressed Milwaukee Road, where a pattern emerged reminiscent of the disputes of the 1890s, was hit harder. "They lost 100%, including all electricians" at Spokane with heavy defections at other points, Lonergan reported.

> Their situation [is] more difficult than N.P., because division headquarters in small towns where employees control local situation and hold public offices, making it difficult to protect strikebreakers, also experiencing more trouble than we are having on account [of] sympathetic attitude of train and engine men towards strikers.[55]

As the full magnitude of the strike became apparent, powerful forces mobilized to defeat the insurgents. The roads effectively enlisted—far more successfully than they had in 1894—the support of individual shippers, banks, newspapers, and small businessmen represented by commercial clubs and chambers of commerce.[56] A number of elected officials also supported management, including Montana Republican Senator Henry L. Myers. "If the Government will not try to compromise this issue [seniority] and will afford adequate protection to those who are working the roads," Myers confided to Donnelly, "in my opinion, the roads will win this strike and the issue will be settled once and for all and settled right." Insisting that there was a basic "principle" involved in holding fast against employee demands, Myers was confident that if the roads won an unconditional victory, "railroad employees would think a long time before again plunging the country into the throes of a nationwide strike."[57]

Unable to secure a national compromise and anxious over the political effects of the coal strike and the threat of a complete breakdown of the transportation network, Harding threw off his ambivalent stance and moved to compel the unions to settle. On August 18, the president addressed a joint session of Congress on the industrial crisis, and less than two weeks later he overrode moderates in his cabinet and his party by authorizing Daugherty to seek an injunction against the strikers from Judge James Wilkerson of Chicago, who issued the order on September 23.[58]

The Daugherty-Wilkerson injunction bore a striking resemblance to the "omnibus injunctions" levied against the American Railway Union in the Pullman Strike. The 1922 measure rested primarily on the grounds of preventing interference with interstate commerce and the mails, while it also stipulated that there was sufficient evidence of conspiracies to violate the Sherman Anti-Trust Act and the Transportation Act of 1920. "Among the most far-reaching labor dicta to which the federal government had ever resorted," Robert Zieger argued, the injunction went to the extreme of prohibiting union officials from "picketing or in any manner, word of mouth, or interviews encouraging any person to leave the employ of the railroad."[59]

Despite the harshness of that measure and similar orders issued by lower courts, the injunctions had little impact on the strike's outcome. Most strikers had either already left the industry or were in the process of reaching agreements with individual roads along the lines of the September 13 Baltimore and Ohio formula, which allowed for seniority rights. The Northwest proved an exception to that general rule. There, only the Milwaukee Road signed the B&D agreement. All had ample opportunity to reach a compromise settlement, since both regional RED officials and those of the operating brotherhoods made a number of attempts to effect a reasonable solution. The other carriers in the Pacific Northwest, however, had decided to make a clean sweep of the matter as most of their counterparts in other regions did later, despite the B&D agreement. The Hill and Harriman lines simply recruited their own company unions.[60]

In the face of the intransigence of the Great Northern, the Northern Pacific, the Union Pacific, and the Southern Pacific, a variety of opponents to the roads' policies emerged. An analysis of the character of strike supporters suggests both the change and continuity of regional attitudes toward railway workers. Viewed from the standpoint of community loyalties, pro-strike sentiment was basically threefold. Respectable moderates, especially influential in the area's small towns, supported the AFL organizations and persisted in their hope for an equitable settlement of the dispute. Outside the boundaries of polite society, the Industrial Workers of the World experienced a resurgence of strength among those inclined toward the older forms of radical protest in the more isolated towns of the interior. Finally, adherents of the new radicalism surfaced, most clearly in Tacoma with the arrival of William Z. Foster, leader of the Communist-affiliated Trade Union Educational League, to preach the gospel of "amalgamation."

A remarkably strong current of moderate, pro-strike sentiment existed in the Pacific Northwest, despite the hysteria connected with the Red Scare of 1919–1920 and the general industrial crisis of 1922. The persistence of such restraint seems all the more notable in view of local violent clashes and the militant stance adopted by insurgents at Tacoma, Seattle, Everett, and Spokane in Washington; Pocatello, Glenns Ferry, Nampa, and Montpelier in Idaho; and Great Falls, Havre, Wolf Point, Cutbank, Whitefish, Laurel, Missoula, and Miles City in Montana.[61]

Senator Borah, with an uncommon sense of his constituency's mood in 1922, became a leading critic of the Daughtery injunction, which, he charged, was a flagrant violation of the Bill of Rights and common justice and likely would "break down the courts of the country." [62] In *Labor's* August 5 issue, he lashed out at employers who, since the end of the war, had been cutting wages "irrespective of whether they were reduced below the poverty line or not." Further, Borah contended, the real cause of the coal and railroad strikes was the employers' unabashed intention to destroy the unions.[63] Outside Idaho, political figures such as Burton K. Wheeler found restive railway workers' support an important asset in his successful run for Myers' Senate seat, as did Clarence C. Dill who defeated Miles Poindexter that same year. Dill, formerly a congressman and an active Plumb Plan supporter, proclaimed on the front page of *Labor* that it was the railway men, farmers, and common people who had made his campaign successful.[64]

Another measure of respectable opinion was manifested in sentiments expressed in the region's smaller communities, where remnants of older patterns and loyalties persisted. Of course, there was nothing approaching unanimity on this score, and the solidarity so clearly apparent in the populistic 1890s had been much eroded by 1922. Yet, despite the general trend of modernization, the Red Scare, local clashes between strikers and authorities, and an upsurge of IWW and Communist party activity on the roads, a substantial body of community support for striking shopmen did exist, particularly in the region's small towns. Main Street in the Pacific Northwest was sufficiently aroused in places like Havre and Wolf Point to compel Great Northern officials to concede that it was "useless" to dispatch strikebreakers there. A "mob of about four hundred" had greeted the last train, and the "sheriff is up for office and [we] cannot expect much assistance," the railroad managers complained.[65]

Another hotbed of strike activity was the Billings-Laurel area, which registered strong pro-strike sympathies cutting across class lines. The strike had run smoothly through October, prompting Northern Pacific District Claim Agent F. D. Tilton to rejoice that Laurel, which had "always been more or less of an eye-sore, . . . has . . . showed a wonderful improvement." Tilton reported it "an inspiring, soul-warming privilege to come in contact with those fighting sons-of-guns" who were winning the strike at that point.[66]

When an estimated two hundred of those "fighting sons-of-guns" rampaged through the town's business section, however, it was the Northern Pacific that became the promoter of violence and discord in the eyes of the local populace. On December 2, fifty businessmen and citizens telegraphed their disaffection to Attorney General Daugherty. They clearly did not share the perception of U.S. Marshal Joseph L. Asbridge and United States attorneys John L. Slatery and Ronald Higgins that "especially at Livingston and Laurel, mobs of howling men, women, and children composed of strikers and their sympathizers, would follow [scab] shopmen from and to work, using all kinds of threats and insulting remarks."[67] To them, it was the Northern Pacific's management that was "employing and harboring lawless characters they can not or will not control and who have become a menace to our community." Further, the Laurelites demanded that United States deputy marshals "be investigated for their part in aiding and abetting" the armed raid "on the business part of town . . . shooting up and completely wrecking a billiard hall frequented by striking shop-men and shooting one man in the arm although no resistance was offered."[68]

Other communities in the Northwest protested the railroads' conduct. Consequently, Burton K. Wheeler, as one of his first official acts, joined with fellow Montana Senator Thomas J. Walsh in a protest to the Interstate Commerce Commission. The complaints emanating from Billings are particularly instructive, since the Northern Pacific assigned one of its own detectives to investigate the signatories. As the prejudiced and not always accurate J. E. Spurling reported to his superiors in St. Paul:

> . . . M. M. Moss is a livestock buyer and does considerable business. He is inclined to be aggrieved because on two occasions the past fall he was not supplied with stock cars promptly on the date ordered.
>
> Geo. White is President of the White Transfer Company, who do quite a little business, but is in no way prominent, although apparently a good citizen.
>
> Mr. R. A. Haste has been for a number of years publisher of a farm paper here. He is really the brains of the Socialist labor combination, is a very bright man, using his talents in the wrong direction. He has been chosen as Secretary to United States Senator Elect Wheeler and will have a big part in shaping Wheeler's policy in Washington. Because of his great ability, he is a dangerous man.
>
> Mr. A. G. Van Segle is a Socialist barber, a defeated candidate for sheriff and an agitator of the extreme type.
>
> Mr. Richard Kirk runs a little suburban grocery and enjoyed a good deal of trade from our former employees.
>
> Mr. Fred F. Holliday is a dealer in second hand goods, a fairly good fellow, who is undoubtedly influenced by the fact that he is getting more stock on hand than he can well dispose of.
>
> Sam Chicas a Greek, who conducts some suburban groceries and who undoubtedly feels the loss of some former customers.
>
> Mr. Hyme Lypsker a Jew Clothier dealing in the cheaper grades of clothing who also is affected by the loss of former customers.
>
> Mr. A. G. Hammond is the only signer who is at all prominent in the civic or business life of Billings. He is a first class citizen, a splendid fellow, a clever business man and during the entire period of the strike has expressed his feelings as friendly to the Northern Pacific. He is a

good patron of ours and one of my very best personal friends. I cannot understand why he has signed such a petition.

Barry O'Leary is a Contractor, building up a fair business. Do not know him very well, but apparently he is the right kind of man, but judging from residence shown he lives among the former employees of the Northern Pacific and they have probably enlisted his sympathy.

The balance are largely rabble, the majority unknown to me, but residences shown class them as laborers, who undoubtedly are members of Unions or Union sympathizers. A Good many are Wops, Greeks and Slavs, two at least are bootleggers (this is court record not personal knowledge).

I have overlooked F. E. Fisher of the Searchlight, a labor union paper published here of the extreme Socialist type. Fisher is a very bright well educated man, therefore, dangerous. He was formerly connected with the State University at Missoula. Has an unsavory record there. . . .

I am accepting the signatures as bona-fide and presume that the majority are residents of Billings and vicinity and probably the majority are, through our lax emigration laws, citizens of the United States and entitled to voice their sentiments and also to a fair hearing, but as representatives of our business interests they simply "Ain't."[69]

In addition to his obvious class and ethnic prejudices, Spurling was far too hasty in dismissing such individuals and their position in the community. Certainly, they were not the Northern Pacific's allies, but many, including White, Haste, Lypsker, and O'Leary, were important men in the town.

B. R. Albin of the Hart-Albin company, who was critical of the railroad, was singled out for special attention. A Democrat who "was very instrumental in his [Wheeler's] election," Albin was co-partner in the largest department store in eastern Montana. Northern Pacific Vice-President Rapelje took special pains to have his general superintendent, J. E. Craver, personally discuss the railroad's position with Albin. Craver did so, although long after the strike had ended, and found Albin "a first class merchandiser, which of course is characteristic of his race," and infected with "political ambitions [that] were something of a joke." Although Craver doubted the interview had "any effect on Mr. Albin," who was only "catering to labor" and concerned over high freight rates, the bigoted railroad official believed he had accomplished as much as could be expected.[70]

The pro-strike sentiments expressed by such community leaders were characteristic of the mood of an earlier time. By 1922, their influence was strongest in the more isolated towns of the Northwest. This is not to suggest that moderate opinion was nonexistent in the region's cities, but that it carried more weight in smaller, more isolated locales. A key factor in the persistence of those patterns was the tendency of citizens in those smaller towns to band together, their comparative insulation from the shocks of modernity and its changes, and their continued dependence on the railroads.

The second form of protest in the Shopmen's Strike came from the IWW. Never particularly strong within the railroad industry, the Wobblies made a concerted effort to expand their influence on the roads after the devastating attacks on the organization during the war and the Red Scare. In late 1920, Charles Donnelly relayed "a Secret Service Agent's report" to Northern Pacific Vice-President W. T. Tyler. After conversations with IWW General Secretary-Treasurer George Hardy and Railway Organization Committee Chairman Robert Russell in Chicago, the agent warned: "they are making preparations for the biggest campaign in the history of the I.W.W. to get members from the different Brotherhoods . . . [and] to get good live speakers into the center of all of the A.F. of L. organizations and blow them up from the inside." Harry Trotter was named to head up the western organizing effort based in Seattle; and although it was "a little early for this movement to have spread to our territory," Donnelly still believed it was "desirable to keep [a] pretty close watch of the situation."[71]

During the Shopmen's Strike, IWW activity increased notably, particularly in the more isolated towns along the Great Northern line. Commenting on a December 26, 1922, article in the *Boston Transcript*, L. C. Gilman of Seattle offered Ralph Budd his view of the extent of radical activity on the road: "in Washington and Montana there is enough radicalism to furnish a foundation for such an article . . . but so far as there being any danger of the I.W.W. and other radicals undertaking to overthrow the Government I do not think such danger exists." The Great Northern work force did include "a pretty large I.W.W. element . . . particularly on that section between Spokane and Williston, and there is no doubt . . . that our trainmen and enginemen sympathized with the strikers." The strike's failure, however, and the roads' agreement to take back some strikers "rather curbed the activity of the radicals elements in our employ." By February 1923, Gilman saw "more danger from radicalism among the farmers than among the workingmen."[72]

Gilman's assessment was essentially accurate, although he was too sanguine about the Wobblies' tenacity. Substantial IWW activity at remote points on the Great Northern, Northern Pacific, Milwaukee, and Soo lines continued through 1924, despite the best efforts of the railroads and sympathetic elected officials such as North Dakota Governor R. A. Nestor.[73] In 1922, the Great Northern's lines in Montana were the center of IWW activity in the Northwest. The most dangerous points from management's viewpoint were the repair shops at Great Falls, Havre, Wolf Point, Cut Bank, and Whitefish.[74]

In the remote town of Whitefish, Montana, the Great Northern's W. R. Smith relayed the news to his superiors that the Wobblies had threatened local officials who were uncooperative. "This town very strong on radical I.W.W.," his agent reported, "and if any riotous action takes place do not feel it would be striking employees but the radical I.W.W. element and very likely coupled with moonshine." The railroad's managers were sufficiently apprehensive to request that a special agent, "who carried a red card," be sent to Whitefish "so that we may be in a position to know what is going on and who the radicals are after this is over."[75] Later, the road reported that, although the county sheriff was cooperative, "the mayor and officers at the city . . . were themselves strikers, and the chief of police . . . had advised that he would arrest new employees that appeared on the streets of Whitefish. Trouble was avoided only by the railway company and its new employees exercising discretion."[76]

In general, the railroads were so alarmed by the specter of the IWW threat that they went to unusual and, in at least one instance, bizarre lengths to combat the Wobblies. After several attempts, W. A. "Three Fingered Jack" Godwin persuaded the Great Northern to hire him so that he could preach an anti-IWW gospel to the strikers and persuade them to return to work. In early 1922, before the strike, Godwin wrote Louis Hill about an alleged meeting between himself and James J. Hill at Spokane in 1908. Having "turned my back upon a criminal or careless career," Godwin claimed to possess "the gift of speech" and felt equipped to carry the gospel to the railroad towns and abolish "the rabid radical anarchism from the minds of the most violent men." Then working in Pendleton, Oregon, Godwin hoped to add to the forty thousand IWW cards he falsely claimed to have collected by offering his services to the region's railroads.[77]

When the Shopmen's Strike erupted, the Great Northern inexplicably took the huckster's claims seriously and hired Godwin to spread the word from Seattle to the Dakotas. Great Northern Special Agent H. H. Hanson ran a hurried background check. Clearly, Godwin had wildly exaggerated his claimed conversions, but "there are several of my informants who seem to think that this man has done a lot of good in keeping down agitation among the I.W.W. in lumber and logging camps throughout Washington." Hanson was never able to determine whether the man was "a reformed gambler or 'card shark' " or a convicted felon who "had done 'his bit.' "[78] The Hill Lines blinked away that ambiguity in early September, and commissioned Godwin to roam the Northwest and North Dakota preaching the gospel of company unionism and collecting IWW membership cards until the company dispensed with his services in December.[79]

While the upsurge in IWW sentiment in comparatively isolated small towns represented the old radicalism, a new variety surfaced with its principal center in Tacoma. There, William Z. Foster arrived to preach the gospel of "amalgamation" under the auspices of the community-affiliated Trade Union Educational League. Foster had worked briefly on the Oregon Railway & Navigation line in Oregon and, as a reporter for Seattle's Workingman's Paper, had covered the Wobblies' free speech fight in Spokane.[80] Accordingly, he had some reason to expect a favorable reception among the Northern Pacific's shopmen at Tacoma.

Foster had outlined his plan for the railroads in a 1921 pamphlet, *The Railroaders' Next Step*. He saw railway labor's historical experience as a progression from individual craft unions to cooperative endeavors, such as those of the operating brotherhoods in the Progressive Era and those of the non-operating unions in their creation and refinement of the Railway Employees Department within the AFL. Shared experiences in the Railroad Administration, the Plumb Plan campaign, the launching of *Labor*, and the wage movements of the immediate postwar era were important events in the creation of permanent alliances between the operating and non-operating unions.

The next logical step was "amalgamation," or the formation of one industrial union by existing organizations. "It will be the logical and inevitable climax to all the get-together movements, radical and conservative, among railroad men for a generation. Amalgamation of the sixteen railroad craft unions into one industrial union," Foster declared, "that's the railroaders' next step." Once that was achieved, "we will go on and on, building up still greater combinations of Labor, until finally we have the whole working class solidly united in one militant union. . . . That hour will sound the death knell of capitalism."[81]

Not surprisingly, the roads kept a close watch on the proponents of such doctrines. The National Civic Federation kept its members well informed of the activities of the Trade Union Educational League and the dangerous "Lenin-Foster plan to destroy the American Federation of Labor and the railway brotherhoods preliminary to the establishment of a 'Soviet Republic' in this country."[82] The roads also received detailed reports on TUEL activities from the Thiel Detective Agency, the Corporations Auxiliary Company, and the Pinkerton's National Detective Agency.[83]

When the strike began, the Great Northern took special pains to discover the extent of TUEL influence in the region. Foster had only "a skeleton organization in the Northwest." Although some train service and shopcraft employees were sympathetic, J. A. Cochrane opined that "such movements go in cycles . . . [and] in the end, the trend of thought will revert back to the conservative methods adopted by labor organizations in years past and which built them up to their present financial and business success."[84]

Cochrane's analysis was fair enough, but Foster discerned a different spirit in the Northern Pacific's Tacoma shops. On the eve of the strike, he prepared to embark upon his western tour. Earlier, Foster had arranged with the Tacoma Central Labor Council for his appearance in the city as part of the council's campaign to organize a local TUEL.[85] The July 18 meeting "was in our opinion a success," the Tacoma groups informed Earl Browder, another future leader of the American Communist party. With an audience of over seven hundred, "we sold enough tickets to cover expenses and a little surplus for the Strike Committee," while distributing a larger number of Foster's pamphlets.[86]

But neither the TUEL's efforts in the more urbanized areas nor those of the IWW in the interior towns significantly affected the strike's resolution. Although the roads worried over the potential effect of radicalism spreading among their employees, the Left remained divided, isolated, and nearly powerless to mount a sustained, effective challenge to management. The more moderate, established shopcraft unions fared little better. They enjoyed the public sympathy of some merchants, farmers, the operating brotherhoods, and a substantial segment of the general populace, yet they lost the strike. Only the Milwaukee railroad agreed to the Baltimore & Ohio compromise. The Hill and Harriman lines rehired a few repentants but immediately replaced all others and implanted their version of the company unionism so characteristic of the "lean years," a system that obtained in the Northwest and the nation until the Great Depression and the New Deal.

Despite those subsequent developments, what remains clear is that by the early 1920s, the frontier legacy so apparent during the first decade of statehood was on the wane. In the 1894 conflict, residents of the Northern Tier states presented a relatively solid front that cut along community lines—which tended to override class and other divisions—to combat railroad management. That Gilded Age pattern was reinforced in the Northwest by the prevalence of dashed expectations, geographical isolation, the lack of alternative jobs, and the populist revolt to forge a crucible of discontent that united railroaders and much of the general populace against the hated carriers.

Elements of that pattern persisted into the post-World War I era and was evident during the 1922 Shopmen's Strike. But the conflict also highlighted new trends that worked to erode the community-based support accorded the American Railway Union nearly three decades before. Among railroaders, the desire for unaffiliated, independent industrial unionism had diminished, while others participated in a short-lived resurgence of the IWW or joined in the new radicalism of William Z. Foster and the Communist Left. Among non-railroaders, pro-labor support paralleled the 1894 pattern in some ways but was also much diminished, owing largely to the broader socioeconomic trends sweeping the nation. In short, the 1922 railroad labor conflict signaled the marked decline in the force of Main Street-based protest movements that were so evident on the northern frontier at the outset of statehood. After World War I, the Northwest—and the nation—entered upon a new, if no less uncertain, era in American life.

Notes

1. Arnold M. Paul, *Conservative Crisis and the Rule of Law: Attitudes of Bar and Bench, 1887–1895* (Ithaca, N.Y.: Cornell University Press, 1960), 139; John L. Blackman, *Presidential Seizure in Labor Disputes* (Cambridge, Mass.: Harvard University Press, 1967), 9, 237.

2. *Railway Times* (Chicago), June 1, June 15, 1894. For accounts concerned largely with the Pullman Strike in Chicago, see United States Strike Commission, "Report on the Chicago Strike of June-July, 1894," S. Ex. Doc. 7, 53d Cong., 3d sess. (Serial 3276); "Annual Report of the Secretary of War, 1894," H. Ex. Doc. 1, 53d Cong., 3d sess. (Serial 3294); *Proceedings of the General Managers' Association of Chicago, 1893 and 1894* (Chicago: Knight, Leonard & Company); Almont Lindsey, *The Pullman Strike: The Story of a Unique Experiment and of a Great Labor Upheaval* (Chicago: University of Chicago Press, 1942); Ray Ginger, *The Bending Cross: A Biography of Eugene Victor Debs* (New Brunswick: Rutgers University Press, 1949); Stanley Buder, *Pullman: An Experiment in Industrial Order and Community Planning, 1880–1930* (New York: Oxford University Press, 1967). For treatments of the strike that deal more fully with developments outside Chicago, see Shelton Stromquist, *A Generation of Boomers: The Pattern of Railroad Labor Conflict in Nineteenth-Century America* (Urbana: University of Illinois Press, 1987); James H. Ducker, *Workers on the Atchison, Topeka & Santa Fe Railroad, 1869–1900* (Lincoln: University of Nebraska Press, 1983); Nick Salvatore, *Eugene V. Debs: Citizen and Socialist* (Urbana: University of Illinois Press, 1982); Jerry M. Cooper, *The Army and Civil Disorder: Federal Military Intervention in Labor Disputes, 1877–1900* (Westport, Conn.: Greenwood Press, 1980).

3. Thomas A. Clinch, "The Northern Pacific Railroad and Montana's Mineral Lands," *Pacific Historical Review* 34 (August 1965): 323–35; Robert W. Larson, *Populism in the Mountain West* (Albuquerque: University of New Mexico Press, 1986), 74–102; Michael P. Malone, *The Battle for Butte: Mining and Politics on the Northern Frontier, 1864–1906* (Seattle: University of Washington Press, 1981), 92–110.

4. See W. Thomas White, "Boycott: The Pullman Strike in Montana," *Montana, the Magazine of Western History* 29 (Autumn 1979): 2–13.

5. *Anaconda Standard* (Montana), January 3, June 26–28, 1894; Stromquist, *Generation of Boomers*, 86–95, 103; Salvatore, *Eugene V. Debs*, 118–19; General Manager's Miscellaneous Subject Files, Labor File, Northern Pacific Rail-

way Company Records, Minnesota Historical Society, St. Paul [NP Records]; *Helena Independent* (Montana), June 29, July 2, 1894; *Weekly Missoulian* (Missoula, Montana), July 4, July 11, 1894; *Seattle Post-Intelligencer*, July 2, 1894 (quotation).

6. *Anaconda Standard*, June 28–29, July 1, 1894; *Helena Independent*, June 28, 1894; Thomas A. Clinch, *Urban Populism and Free Silver in Montana: A Narrative of Ideology in Political Action* (Missoula: University of Montana Press, 1970), 114; Lindsey, *Pullman Strike*, 219; *Butte Miner* (Montana), July 1, 1894; J. W. Kendrick to G. W. Dickinson, July 4, 1894, General Manager's Miscellaneous Subject Files, NP Records; *Proceedings of the General Managers' Association*, June 29, 1894.

7. *Glendive Independent* (Montana), June 30, 1894; *Billings Gazette* (Montana), July 7, 1894; *Daily Times* (Billings), July 5–7, 1894; *Butte Miner*, July 1, 1894; *Anaconda Standard*, July 1–11, 1894; Kendrick to NP Receivers, July 5, 1894, General Manager's Miscellaneous Subject Files, NP Records. The "Copper Kings" controlled nearly all the state's principal newspapers by 1894. By 1888, William Andrews Clark owned the *Butte Miner*; shortly thereafter, Marcus Daly established the *Anaconda Standard*, the largest and most influential paper in Montana. John M. Schiltz, "Montana's Captive Press," *Montana Opinion* 1 (June 1956): 3–4; Malone, *Battle for Butte*, 88–89.

8. *Weekly Missoulian*, July 4, July 11, 1894; Lindsey, *Pullman Strike*, 245; *Anaconda Standard*, July 7, 1894; *Butte Miner*, July 2, July 8, 1894; *Tacoma Daily Ledger*, July 8, 1894.

9. *Spokesman-Review* (Spokane), June 29, 1894.

10. Richard Olney to James H. Forney, June 29, 1894, "Annual Report of the Attorney General of the United States, 1896," Appendix H. Doc. 9, 54th Cong., 2d sess. (Serial 3499), 50 [AG Report, Appendix].

11. Jas. H. Beatty to Joseph Pinkham, June 30, 1894, AG Report, Appendix, 50–51.

12. Beatty to Attorney General, July 5, 1894, AG Report, Appendix, 51; *Spokesman-Review*, July 6, 1894.

13. *Spokesman-Review*, July 7, 1894.

14. *Spokesman-Review*, July 8, 1894. That same day, Marshal Pinkham wired the U.S. attorney general requesting that one company be sent to Hope to protect Northern Pacific property. See AG Report, Appendix 52.

15. AG Report, Appendix, 52. See also Richard J. Bonney, "The Pullman Strike of 1894: Pocatello Perspective," *Idaho Yesterdays* 24 (Fall 1980): 23–28, which takes a different view than is argued here.

16. S. H. H. Clark to John M. Schofield, July 7, 1894, Records of the Adjutant General's Office Pertaining to the Chicago Pullman Strike of 1894, RG 94, U.S. Navy and Old Army Branch, Military Archives Division, National Archives, Washington, D.C. [AG Strike Records].

17. Brooke to Schofield, July 7, 1894, AG Strike Records; *Spokesman-Review*, July 11, 1894; *Idaho Falls Times*, July 12, 1894.

18. Petition of Spokane citizens to Senator Watson Squire, Congressman John L. Wilson, and Congressman W. H. Doolittle, July 20, 1894, AG Strike Records.

19. McConnell to Senator George Shoup and Senator Fred Dubois, July 25, 1894, AG Strike Records.

20. Captain Thompson to Assistant Adjutant General (Vancouver Barracks), July 30, July 31, 1894, AG Strike Records.

21. *Post-Intelligencer*, June 28, 1894.

22. *Tacoma Morning Union*, June 29–30, 1894; *Post-Intelligencer*, June 29, 1894; *Spokesman-Review*, June 28–29, 1894. For an important example of opposition to the strike in Tacoma, see *Tacoma Daily Ledger*, July 8, 1894.

23. *Spokesman-Review*, June 30, 1894. The strike on the Seattle, Lake Shore and Eastern, which handled the terminal facilities for the Northern Pacific, was a spasmodic affair. T. S. Blondo, the ARU leader on that line, announced a return to work on July 1. On July 3, however, Blondo again called a strike when non-union crews began arriving with the westbound trains, an action that resulted in the firing and replacement of ARU strikers. See *Post-Intelligencer*, July 4–5, 1894.

24. *Spokesman-Review*, June 29, 1894.

25. U.S. Marshal James E. Drake enlisted a number of "conductors, engineers, etc." as deputies during the strike. Drake to Attorney General, July 30, 1894, AG Report, Appendix, 204. Such practices caused consternation in the Tacoma Trades Council. On July 12, the locomotive Firemen protested the conductors' actions during the strike, whereupon the council requested the ARU furnish it with "the name of every scab working on the N.P. during the trouble." On August 16, however, the Firemen informed the Tacoma body that the complainants had left the country; because the conductors' names could no longer be ascertained, the matter was dropped. Minutes of the Tacoma Trades Council, July 12-August 16, 1894, Central Labor Council Records—Pierce County, Archives and Manuscripts Division, University of Washington Library [CLC Papers].

26. *Spokesman-Review*, July 1, 1894; *Walla Walla Statesman*, July 7, 1894.

27. *Tacoma Morning Union*, July 10, 1894. After the strike was broken, the WCLU endorsed a petition asking Congress to impeach Attorney General Olney for his role in the strike. Minutes of the Western Central Labor Union, July 11, July 25, 1894, CLC Papers. For a more skeptical view of the WCLU's support of the ARU and the strike, see Jonathan Dembo, *Unions and Politics in Washington State, 1885–1935* (New York: Garland, 1983), 18–19; Meryl E. Rogers, "The Labor Movement in Seattle, 1885–1905" (M.A. thesis, Pacific Lutheran University, Tacoma, 1970), 103–5; Minutes of the Tacoma Trades Council, July 25, 1894; *Tacoma Morning Union*, July 12, 1894.

28. *Spokesman-Review*, July 3, July 10, 1894. Great Northern Vice-President W. P. Clough informed General Merritt that "practically every one of these

men [enginemen and trainmen] are members of the American Railway Union. We have been reliably informed that the governing bodies of that organization have either decided to issue or have actually issued instructions to its men to decline to handle trains carrying troops. . . ." Clough later reported that Great Falls Local 89 had ordered its members between Havre and Butte to "quit work the moment an attempt is made by the company to move troops." Clough to Merritt, July 10, July 12, 1894; "Report of the Secretary of War, 1894," 127–8.

29. Patrick Henry McLatchy, "The Development of the National Guard of Washington as an Instrument of Social Control, 1854–1916" (Ph.D. diss., University of Washington, Seattle, 1973), 290–1.

30. Ibid., 284–6.

31. Ibid., 287–8; *Tacoma Morning Union*, July 5–11, 1894. See also James McNaught to Schofield, July 11–12, 1894, AG Strike Records.

32. *Spokesman-Review*, July 6, 1894.

33. Drake to Olney, July 6, 1894, Byron Phelps, William H. Brinker, and Cornelius H. Hanford to Olney, July 7, 1894, AG Report, Appendix, 201.

34. McNaught to Schofield, July 7, 1894, AG Strike Records.

35. "The Boise garrison, which was reserved for service on the Union Pacific road, where conditions appeared threatening, was not summoned for detached duty, as the employees of that road remained quiet." "Report of the Secretary of War," 1894, 155–6.

36. McNaught to Schofield, July 12, 17, 1894, AG Strike Records.

37. Kendrick to Jas. McNaught, July 13, 1894, General Manager's Miscellaneous Subject Files, NP Records. Despite the passions engendered by the military's arrival, white Montanans manifested relatively little racial prejudice against the black soldiers of the 10th Cavalry, which constituted a substantial element of the troops employed against the strikers. The *Helena Independent* reported that a large number of Missoulians felt that, although the use of troops was unnecessary, they "would much prefer if any are used to guard property, that they be white troops." Such concerns seem to have been neither universal nor particularly intense. In fact, the ARU chapter in Livingston had formerly denounced the Chicago convention's decision to bar blacks from membership in the ARU. The lack of reported anger over the use of black troops— the *Independent* was virtually alone in its report of racial concerns—coupled with positions such as that taken by the Livingston local suggests that anti-black prejudice in Montana was comparatively restrained. *Helena Independent*, July 9, 1894. In a similar vein, Tacoma Local 103 voted on July 5 to support an amendment to the ARU's constitution to admit blacks. *Tacoma Morning Union*, July 10, 1894.

38. For the confrontation in Livingston, see White, "Boycott"; "Investigation in the Case of Captain Lockwood, Accused of Striking I. F. Toland with a Sword at Livingston, Montana, July 10, 1894," AG Strike Records; Letters Sent

by the Headquarters of the Army (Main Series), v. 32 (Microcopy 857, Roll 13), RG 108, U.S. Navy and Old Army Branch, Military Archives Division, National Archives, Washington, D.C.

39. Lindsey, *Pullman Strike*, 279–81, 236–7; *Railway Times*, August 1, September 1, 1894; Kendrick to Thomas F. Oakes and H. C. Payne, July 11, 1894, General Manager's Miscellaneous Subject Files, NP Records.

40. *Anaconda Standard*, September 25, 1894.

41. *Anaconda Standard*, July 22, 1894; C. M. Weber to J. H. Mitchell, July 17, W. W. Cooley to Kendrick, August 21, 1894, "Classified Statement, by Divisions, of Men Not Re-employed at Close of Strike, July, 1894" [the NP's "blacklist"], General Manager's Miscellaneous Subject Files, NP Records.

42. Lindsey, *Pullman Strike*, 337.

43. *Railway Times*, August 15, 1894; August 1, 1896; Carlos A. Schwantes, *Radical Heritage: Labor, Socialism, and Reform in Washington and British Columbia, 1885–1917* (Seattle: University of Washington Press, 1979), 59; David Burke Griffiths, "Populism in the Far West, 1890–1900" (Ph.D. diss., University of Washington, Seattle, 1967), 417–19.

44. Schwantes, *Radical Heritage*, 66. At the 1894 Populist convention in North Yakima, Adams was a contender for the Populist congressional nomination. *Walla Walla Statesman*, June 29, 1894.

45. Irving Bernstein, *The Lean Years: A History of the American Worker, 1920–1933* (Boston: Houghton Mifflin, 1960), 211; David Montgomery, *The Fall of the House of Labor: The Workplace, the State, and American Labor Activism, 1865–1925* (Cambridge, England: Cambridge University Press, 1987), 422–3; Robert Zieger, *Republicans and Labor, 1919–1929* (Lexington: University of Kentucky Press, 1969), 141; Phillip I. Earl and Guy Louis Rocha, "The National Railroad Strike of 1922 and the Decline of Organized Labor in Nevada," *Journal of the West* 25 (April 1986): 44–51.

46. *Labor* (Washington, D.C.), July 1, July 15, 1922. See also the June 30, 1923, issue for *Labor*'s summary of the conflict in conjunction with Edward Keating, *The Story of "Labor": Thirty-Three Years on the Rail Workers' Fighting Front* (Washington, D.C.: Rufus H. Darby, 1953), 110–14. For the strike in the Northwest, see *Seattle Union Record*, July 1, 1922; *Great Falls Tribune*, July 2, 1922; *Tacoma Labor Advocate*, July 7, 1922; *Oregon Labor Press* (Portland), July 7, 1922.

47. Zieger, *Republicans and Labor*, 119–20.

48. *Labor*, June 17, 1922.

49. Ralph Budd to Elliott, July 28, 1922, President Subject File 10538, Great Northern Railway Company Records, Minnesota Historical Society, St. Paul [GN Records].

50. S. M. Felton to Budd, July 6, Budd to L. C. Gilman and W. F. Turner, July 20, H. E. Bryan to Budd, July 22, 1922, GN Records. See also Zieger, *Republicans and Labor*, 121, 130–1.

51. Union Pacific System announcement, September 7, 1922, President Subject File 10598, GN Records.

52. See September 23, 1922, "General Strike Situation Report," September 23, 1922, and report of the General Mechanical Superintendent, March 27, 1923, President Subject File 591-G-38, NP Records.

53. See "Personal" memoranda from H. M. Curry to his subordinates, November 27, December 22, 1922, with attached lists, Mechanical Engineer Subject File 15-E-8, NP Records.

54. "Statement Showing Old Employees in Mechanical Crafts Now Employed," January 25, 1923, President Subject File 10598, GN Records. For a detailed analysis of the number of replacements recruited by the GN and the positions it filled, see the periodic "Report[s] of Men Received" and C. O. Jenks to Ralph Budd, with enclosures, October 5, 1922, GN Records.

55. C. R. Lonergan to J. G. Woodworth, July 27, 1922, President Subject File 591-G-38, W. F. Turner to Budd, September 5, 1922, President Subject File 1389-A-16, NP Records. See also the 1922 "scab" lists kept by the Pocatello Local Federated Shop Crafts, O.S.L.R.R., Union Pacific System in the August Rosqviest Papers, Idaho Historical Society, Boise.

56. A large number of letters from such individuals and organizations supporting management's position may be found in President Subject File 591-G-38, NP Records, and in President Subject File 10538, GN Records.

57. H. L. Myers to Charles Donnelly, July 27, 1922, President Subject File 591-G-38, NP Records.

58. Zieger, *Republicans and Labor* 135–9. For Harding's August 18 address, see "Address of President of the United States on Strike Crisis," S. Doc. 240, 67th Cong., 2d sess. (Serial 7988).

59. Zieger, *Republicans and Labor*, 139; Edward Berman, *Labor Disputes and the President of the United States* (New York: Columbia University Press, 1924), 235–9. See also John D. Hicks, *Republican Ascendancy, 1921–1933* (New York: Harper and Row, 1960), 72–73; Philip Taft, *The A.F. of L. in the Time of Gompers* (New York: Harper and Brothers, 1957), 404–6; Robert K. Murray, *The Politics of Normalcy: Governmental Theory and Practice in the Harding-Coolidge Era* (New York: W. W. Norton, 1973), 80–81.

60. Harry D. Wolf, *The Railroad Labor Board* (Chicago: University of Chicago Press, 1927), 258; Walker D. Hines, *War History of the American Railroads* (New Haven, Conn.: Yale University Press, 1928), 226–9.

61. For strike correspondence with the attorney general's office, see "Annual Report of the Attorney General, 1922," Appendix, H. Doc. 409, 67th Cong., 3d sess. (Serial 8117). See also President Subject File 591-G-38, *passim*, NP Records; President Subject File 10538, *passim*, Great Northern Records; *Machinists Monthly Journal* (Washington, D.C.), 34 (November 1922); 745–52.

62. Quoted in Zieger, *Republicans and Labor*, 140.

63. *Labor*, August 5, 1922. For more on *Labor*'s enthusiastic support, see the

Edward Keating-B.M. Jewell correspondence, June-July 1922, American Federation of Labor-Congress of Industrial Organizations, Railway Employee's Department of Records, Labor-Management Documentation Center, M. P. Catherwood Library, Cornell University, Ithaca, New York [Keating-Jewell Correspondence].

64. September 30, October 28, November 4, November 18, 1922, Keating-Jewell Correspondence.

65. Miller to M. J. Lins, July 19, 1922, President Subject File 10538, GN Records.

66. J. E. Craver to C. L. Nichols, July 27, F. D. Tilton to Curry, October 12, 1922, President Subject File 591-G-38, NP Records.

67. John L. Slattery, Ronald Higgins, and Joseph L. Asbridge to Attorney General, November 24, 1922, AG Report, Appendix, 391–393.

68. Ibid., 402–3. The protesting telegram was also carried by *Labor*, December 9, 1922.

69. J. E. Spurling to R. W. Clark, January 18, 1923, President Subject File 591-G-38, NP Records.

70. B. R. Albin to J. G. Woodworth, January 6, J. E. Craver to Rapelje, January 27, May 13, 1923, NP Records.

71. Donnelly to Tyler, November 12, 1920, President Subject File 591-G-7, NP Records. For more on IWW activities at this time, consult the Globe Inspection Company's April 13, 1921, report, President Subject File 6860, GN Records; Randolph Boehm, ed., *U.S. Military Intelligence Reports: Surveillance of Radicals in the United States, 1917–1941* (Frederick, Md.: University Publications of America, 1984), reels 2, 6, 18, 20.

72. L. C. Gilman to Budd, President Subject File 6860, GN Records.

73. August 14, 1924, memorandum, President Subject File 3191 and File 6860, GN Records.

74. For a summary of striker militancy at these points, see AG Report, Appendix, 384–403.

75. W. R. Smith to C. O. Jenks and William Kelly, July 15, 1922, President Subject File 10538, GN Records. See also J. H. O'Neill-Jenks correspondence of April 1923, President Subject File 3191, GN Records.

76. AG Report, Appendix, 397.

77. W. A. Godwin to Louis W. Hill, January 17, 1922, President Subject File 6860, GN Records.

78. H. H. Hanson to H. G. Keith, August 13, 1922, Vice President-Operating Subject File 7-10, GN Records.

79. A copy of Godwin's speech and his reports to the GN management are in Vice President-Operating Subject File 7-10, GN Papers.

80. Schwantes, *Radical Heritage*, 97, 177. See also William Z. Foster, *From Bryan to Stalin* (New York: International Publishers, 1937), 26–39. For more on Foster and the TUEL, see Theodore Draper, *American Communism and Soviet*

Russia: The Formative Period (New York: Viking Press, 1960), 61–74; William Z. Foster, *Pages from a Worker's Life* (New York: International Publishers, 1939), 44–51; Max Nomad, *Rebels and Renegades* (New York: Macmillan, 1932), 338–91.

81. William Z. Foster, *The Railroaders' Next Step* (Chicago: The Trade Union Educational League, c. 1921), 26–28.

82. Ralph M. Easley to Donnelly, with enclosures, March 25, 1922, President Subject File 2084, NP Records.

83. President Subject File 10538, Vice President-Operating, General Manager Subject File 17-2, GN Records.

84. J. A. Cochrane to C. O. Jenks, July 7, 1923, President Subject File 10538, GN Records.

85. William Z. Foster to W. T. Morris, June 14, Earl Browder to Comrade McIlvaigh, June 16, F. B. Clifford and Friends of Soviet Russia to W. T. Morris, June 17, Tacoma Central Labor Council to Foster, June 26, 1922, CLC Papers.

86. Tacoma Central Labor Council to Earl Browder, July 20, 1922, CLC Papers. See also *Tacoma Labor Advocate*, July 21, 1922.

10

New Deal Economic Programs in the Northern Tier States, 1933–1939

LEONARD J. ARRINGTON and DON C. READING

WE ARE ALL AWARE OF THE DEPRESSED STATE OF THE AMERICAN economy during the 1930s. From 1929 to 1933, the gross national product declined by one-third, personal income dropped 50 per cent, more than one-fourth of the working force was unemployed, and ten thousand banks failed. Building construction was almost at a standstill, and businesses were being liquidated at the rate of several thousand per year. Agriculture was particularly distressed. Wheat prices fell from $1.04 per bushel to 38 cents, and farm income as a whole declined from $5.8 billion in 1929 to $1.4 billion in 1932.[1] Added to the depressed economy was the nation's worst natural disaster: giant black blizzards, or dusters, that punished much of the western United States in 1934 and 1935. "Never before in the weather history of the United States," the chief of the U.S. Weather Bureau declared, "has so little rain fallen over so wide a territory throughout the growing season."[2]

The usual response to recessions, depressions, and natural disasters in the United States had been to depend primarily on "private" philanthropy from individuals, churches, and civic groups. Families and businesses were expected to adjust as best they could until better days arrived. But in 1932, a new factor was introduced with the election of Franklin D. Roosevelt and a supporting Congress that was willing to launch a federal recovery program in what came to be known as the New Deal. The New Deal included a mild attempt to counteract disinflation by a modest increase in currency and credit; a mild attempt to create jobs by various public works programs; a mild attempt to help cities and states with welfare problems by relief assistance; and an attempt to save the distressed farm population by agricultural programs. The total expenditure for all programs from 1933 to 1939 amounted to less than $45 billion, an average of less then $7.5 billion per year, or $57 per capita. Even considering that the general level of prices has risen considerably since the Depression, the expenditure is not impressive today, when the expenditures for defense, space, welfare, and international aid are nothing less than massive.

Among the states hardest hit by the Depression and drought—and those, therefore, in need of federal assistance—were the six Northern Tier states. Their experience suggests that the federal government, in a rare assumption of responsibility, initiated programs that helped these states, however inadequately, to recover from the effects of drastic deflation, grievous want, and ruinous drought.

What is the story of the six Northern Tier states? How were they affected by the Depression and how did they fare under federal programs?

There is a litany of disastrous declines along the Northern Tier. In Washington, manufacturing employment dropped from 114,635 in 1929 to 67,752 in 1933. In Idaho, average farm income slumped from $686 to $250, and in Wyoming per capita farm income declined from $798 in 1929 to $330 in 1932. In the 1937 census of total and partial employment, Montana had the highest unemployment rate of any state in the Union—22 per cent of its work force. There was a catastrophic decline in income in North Dakota and South Dakota, which had the highest percentage of their citizenry on farms of any states but Mississippi and Arkansas. Farm income declined 64 per cent in North Dakota and 68 per cent in South Dakota, the highest of any states in the nation (see Table 1).

How did Roosevelt's New Deal respond to conditions in these states? The national programs can be summarized under six headings: expenditures for relief, expenditures for agriculture, youth programs, social welfare programs, works programs, and lending programs. Tables 2 and 3 give the total and per capita spending on these programs during the six years from 1933 to 1939. The amount of expenditures and loans in each state are partly due to the special needs of the state and partly to the generalized effort to promote recovery nationally.[3]

TABLE 1

Conditions in Northern Tier States, 1930–1939

	Washington	Idaho	Montana	Wyoming	North Dakota	South Dakota
Population in 1930	1,563,396	445,032	537,606	225,565	680,845	692,849
Per capita personal income, 1929	1,019	758	859	993	565	608
Per capita personal income, 1933	685	466	539	696	362	329
Percentage decline, 1929–1933	33	39	37	30	36	46
Percentage of work force unemployed, 1937	17	14	22	11	19	21
Percentage drop in average farm income, 1929–1933	57	64	61	59	64	68
Per capita federal expenditures, 1933–1939	373	399	710	626	431	446
Per capita federal loans, 1933–1939	118	251	264	234	272	249

Sources: Abner Horwitz and Caryle P. Stallings, "Interregional Differentials in Per Capita Real Income Changes," *Studies in Income and Wealth*, vol. 21, National Bureau of Economic Research (Princeton, N.J.: Princeton University Press, 1946), 195–265; Don C. Reading, "A Statistical Analysis of New Deal Economic Programs in the Forty-eight States, 1933–1939" (Ph.D. diss., Utah State University, Logan, 1972), 370; Leonard J. Arrington, "Western Agriculture and the New Deal," *Agricultural History* 44 (October 1970): 342–43; Arrington, "The New Deal in the West: A Preliminary Statistical Inquiry," *Pacific Historical Review* 38 (August 1969): 313–14; and Office of Government Reports, Statistical Section, Report no. 10, vol. 2, Washington, D.C., 1940. There is a separate report for each state. These figures do not include expenditures of state and local agencies when they participated financially in the programs listed.

Washington

Washington state was the beneficiary of an enormous expenditure to construct the Grand Coulee Dam on the Columbia River. The largest building project ever undertaken in the nation at that time, Grand Coulee cost about $400 million, most of it administered by the Public Works Administration and the Bureau of Reclamation. The Bureau of Reclamation allotted $9 million to Washington, $3 million more than that given any other state. Washington ranked fifth among the forty-eight states in PWA expenditures, with money going to finance projects in flood control, water power, educational construction, and streets and highways. Washington also ranked ninth nationally in Works Progress Administration expenditures, and the result was 181 miles of new highway, 2,000 miles of improved roads, and 246 new public buildings. Washington also received large allocations from the Forest Service and the Civilian Conservation Corps to aid in the maintenance and development of the state's vast forests.

Idaho

The $76 million in loans from the Farm Credit Administration was the largest single New Deal program in dollar amount in Idaho from 1933 through 1939. On a per capita basis, Idaho ranked fourth among states, with a per capita allocation of $170. Idaho also ranked high in other agricultural loan programs. The state was fifth in per capita loans from the Farm Security Administration, which included aid to low-income families to make it possible for them to become self-supporting. Idaho ranked first in per capita loans from the Rural Electrification Administration, which helped Idahoans establish six electrical cooperatives and construct eighteen hundred miles of power lines into rural areas. As a result, the number of Idaho farms receiving central station service rose from 30 per cent in 1934 to 54 per cent in 1939.

Idaho also ranked first among the forty-eight states in Forest Service expenditures, primarily because the Forest Service controlled a large amount of Idaho land and because there had been an epidemic of forest fires set by arsonists who wanted employment as firefighters. For similar reasons, Idaho received large expenditures from

TABLE 2

Federal Expenditures and Loans in Northern Tier States, Fiscal Years 1933–1939

	Washington	Idaho	Montana	Wyoming	North Dakota	South Dakota
Expenditures for relief						
Federal Emergency Relief Administration	37,765,959	15,984,218	25,322,858	10,268,744	39,648,734	43,446,478
Other Relief	15,620,306	6,806,882	5,767,618	1,908,581	4,318,983	3,695,345
Expenditures in agriculture						
Agricultural Adjustment Administration	32,492,656	27,713,892	49,368,092	11,741,173	104,624,071	85,986,334
Soil Conservation Service	2,526,179	1,738,217	12,229,824	1,732,827	23,132,309	22,631,348
Farm Security Administration	2,668,818	466,848	1,318,292	1,282,094	1,416,402	2,356,569
Research Extension and Education	2,383,511	1,949,449	2,069,672	1,685,861	2,406,276	2,475,322
Forest Service funds	4,167,079	5,627,890	3,629,635	1,867,785	15,637	528,282
Youth programs						
Civilian Conservation Corps	60,073,985	57,178,559	32,731,095	25,376,237	15,156,929	27,290,641
National Youth Administration (included in WPA, 1935–1938)	930,553	473,772	561,000	157,849	786,158	843,427

TABLE 2

Federal Expenditures and Loans in Northern Tier States, Fiscal Years 1933–1939 (continued)

	Washington	Idaho	Montana	Wyoming	North Dakota	South Dakota
Social welfare programs						
Social Security Act	19,521,588	5,738,614	5,334,963	2,026,326	3,388,312	5,151,878
U.S. Employment Service	1,164,175	386,154	590,083	293,664	487,356	408,941
Veterans Administration	65,906,314	15,907,267	23,251,190	13,883,305	15,563,098	21,850,153
Works programs						
Bureau of Public Roads	27,100,972	19,398,120	31,251,183	19,469,927	24,345,145	24,185,546
Public Works Administration	97,135,613	11,623,238	126,294,611	10,665,032	7,048,062	8,921,035
Bureau of Reclamation	88,521,147	6,105,258	4,405,942	19,624,388	0	353
Civil Works Administration	13,468,000	5,425,000	6,265,000	2,463,000	5,040,000	6,733,583
Works Progress Administration	102,411,974	22,873,480	46,934,995	10,953,540	39,946,133	45,971,854
Other expenditures	8,820,427	3,660,740	4,056,642	5,785,098	6,000,089	6,490,131
Total nonrepayable federal expenditures	582,679,256	209,057,598	381,382,693	141,185,431	293,323,694	308,967,220

Lending programs

Reconstruction Finance Corporation	52,819,719	12,726,688	13,981,049	5,584,792	12,616,330	14,840,305
Farm Credit Administration	63,896,883	76,269,709	94,309,943	31,397,119	144,583,537	122,521,044
Commodity Credit Corporation	7,935,733	3,233,316	7,127,969	500,277	5,913,244	7,271,183
Farm Security Administration	5,926,340	5,715,477	9,143,189	6,781,079	9,397,107	12,564,689
Rural Electrification Administration	1,225,876	2,107,163	1,104,373	833,721	752,450	438,234
Public Works Administration	1,717,300	997,200	7,852,952	983,900	1,150,566	2,932,351
Home Owners' Loan Corporation	49,712,377	10,694,878	7,755,837	6,554,085	10,410,366	11,599,819
Other Loans	1,557,390	60,500	560,640.	244,000	232,110	38,625
Total repayable expenditures	184,791,618	111,804,931	141,835,952	52,878,973	185,055,710	172,206,250
Total nonrepayable and repayable expenditures	787,470,874	320,862,529	523,218,645	194,064,404	478,379,404	481,173,470
Private loans insured by FHA	57,441,306	10,287,395	7,415,036	8,639,232	3,662,512	5,047,320
Total expenditures, loans and insured loans	824,912,180	331,149,924	530,633,681	202,703,636	482,041,916	486,220,790

Source: Office of Government Reports, Statistical Section, Report no. 10, vol. 2, Washington, D.C., 1940. There is a separate report for each state. These figures do not include expenditures of state and local agencies when they participated financially in the programs listed.

TABLE 3

Per Capita Federal Expenditures and Loans in
Northern Tier States, Fiscal Years 1933–1939

	Washington	Idaho	Montana	Wyoming	North Dakota	South Dakota
Expenditures for relief						
Federal Emergency Relief Administration	24	36	47	45	58	63
Other Relief	10	15	11	8	6	5
Expenditures for agriculture						
Agricultural Adjustment Administration	21	62	92	52	154	124
Soil Conservation Service	2	1	2	6	2	3
Farm Security Administration	2	4	23	8	34	33
Research, Extension and Education	2	4	4	7	4	4
Forest Service funds	3	13	7	8	0	1
Youth programs						
Civilian Conservation Corps	38	128	61	112	22	39
National Youth Administration (included in WPA, 1935–1938)	1	1	1	1	1	1
Social welfare programs						
Social Security Act	12	13	10	9	5	7
U.S. Employment Service	1	1	1	1	1	1
Veterans Administration	42	36	43	61	23	32
Works programs						
Bureau of Public Roads	17	44	58	86	36	35
Public Works Administration	62	26	235	47	10	13
Bureau of Reclamation	57	14	8	87	0	0
Civil Works Administration	9	12	12	11	7	10
Works Progress Administration	66	51	87	48	59	66
Other expenditures	6	8	8	26	9	9

TABLE 3

Per Capita Federal Expenditures and Loans in
Northern Tier States, Fiscal Years 1933–1939 (*continued*)

	Washington	Idaho	Montana	Wyoming	North Dakota	South Dakota
tal nonrepayable federal expenditures	373	470	709	625	431	446
nding Programs						
construction Finance Corporation	34	29	26	25	19	21
rm Credit Administration	41	171	175	139	212	177
mmodity Credit Corporation	5	7	13	2	9	10
rm Security Administration	4	13	17	30	14	18
ral Electrification Administration	1	5	2	4	1	1
blic Works Administration	1	2	24	4	2	4
me Owners' Loan Corporation	32	24	14	29	15	17
her loans	1	0	1	1	0	0
tal repayable expenditures	118	251	264	234	272	248
tal nonrepayable and repayable expenditures	491	721	973	859	702	694
ivate loans insured by FHA	37	23	14	38	5	7
tal expenditures, loans and insured loans	528	744	986	897	708	702

rce: Office of Government Reports, Statistical Report no. 10, vol. 2, Washington, D.C., 1940. There is a arate report for each state. These figures do not include expenditures of state and local agencies when y participated financially in the programs listed.

the Civilian Conservation Corps, ranking second among all states. In addition to the conventional CCC camps, Idaho and other Northern Tier states benefited from twenty-nine Indian Conservation Camps, where 4,875 Indians worked on conservation and forest development projects. CCC workers put up telephone lines, constructed firebreaks, built truck trails and vehicle bridges, constructed reservoirs, and built range fences.[4] On an overall per capita basis, Idaho ranked sixth in the nation in federal expenditures and fourth in loans.

Montana

Because of its high unemployment, Montana ranked first in the nation in two New Deal works programs and second (behind Nevada) in per capita federal expenditures and loans. The Public Works Administration allocated $126 million in Montana at $233 per capita, Montana received $144 more than Delaware, the state that ranked number two. This large disparity is explained by the $50 million in funds awarded for the construction of the $100 million Fort Peck Dam in northeastern Montana. This single expenditure exceeded the estimated cost of all non-federal projects in Montana, and the town that sprang up near the project bore the name "New Deal." PWA also participated in a wide range of other projects in the state, including the construction of streets and highways, waterworks, and other dams.

Montana also ranked first in per capita expenditures by the Works Progress Administration, an agency that provided work relief. From 1933 through 1939, Montana received $87 per person, leading second-place New York by more than $5 and taking in $16 more per person than Colorado, the second-ranked Rocky Mountain state. WPA projects included not only the construction of public buildings, storm and sanitary sewer systems, water mains, and highways, but also such non-construction projects as distribution of foodstuffs to needy families and hot lunches for school children.

Wyoming

A sparsely populated state with a large land area, Wyoming received fewer federal expenditures and loans on an absolute basis than other states, but on a per capita basis it ranked third among all states—just behind Nevada and Montana. Wyoming ranked highest per capita in loans from the Farm Security Administration, with a per person allocation of thirty dollars—twelve dollars greater than for any other state. Nearly all of this money was administered by the Rehabilitation Loan Program and consisted of loans for feed, seed, fertilizer, and farming equipment. Wyoming was also high in Bureau of Public Roads expenditures for highways and Bureau of Reclamation allocations for irrigation works.

North Dakota and South Dakota

Because North Dakota and South Dakota had about the same size population, land area, and percentage of farm population during the Depression, it makes sense to consider them together in this analysis. In addition, both states received essentially the same amount of aid from most New Deal agencies on an absolute and a per capita basis and were ranked together in nearly all categories.

The largest single expenditure from a federal agency to North Dakota and South Dakota was from the Agricultural Adjustment Administration. North Dakota ranked first and South Dakota ranked second on a per capita basis in allocation from the AAA; they were the only two states to receive an allocation of more than $100 per person. The Dakotas also ranked first and second on a per capita basis in disbursements from the Farm Security Administration, which was created to help low-income farm families become self-supporting. FSA helped nearly 120,000 families in the two states from 1935 through 1939.

The largest lending program in North Dakota and South Dakota dealt with the states' agricultural sector. The Farm Credit Administration loaned $144 million to North Dakota and $122 million to South Dakota from 1933 through 1939, with the two states ranking first and second in the nation on a per capita basis. In addition to loans to individual farmers, FCA extended credit to farmers' cooperatives and privately organized agricultural financing institutions. The two states also ranked relatively high on a per capita basis in loans from the Farm Security Administration.

For the three years that the Federal Emergency Relief Administration was active, from 1934 through 1936, North Dakota and South Dakota placed high on a per capita basis in relief payments. But the states ranked low (forty-eighth and forty-sixth) in per capita allocations from the Public Works Administration. The Dakotas were last (forty-seventh and forty-eighth) on both absolute and per capita bases in loans from the Home Owners' Loan Corporation and on insured loans from the Federal Housing Administration—no doubt due to the loss in population by the two states. The Dakotas were two of only five states that lost population during the 1930s.

It is clear that the six states on the Northern Tier obtained their share of federal help from 1933 through 1939. On a per capita basis, Montana received more federal assistance than any state except Nevada, with Wyoming ranking third, Idaho fifth, North Dakota sixth, South Dakota seventh, and Washington thirteenth among the forty-eight states. One study concluded that the primary object of federal programs during the 1930s was to restore incomes to the levels obtained before the Depression started.[5] The Northern Tier states, heavily dependent on mining, agriculture, and lumbering, had suffered tragic declines in prices and employment. States that had not experienced declines of the same magnitude did not receive as much help from federal agencies. Connecticut, for example, which received only $237 in benefits per capita—less than one-fourth as much as Montana— had a more balanced economy and presumably had better withstood the Depression. Other states that ranked well below the Northern Tier states were those in the Southeast, which received benefits averaging $306 per capita compared with $761 per capita for the Northern Tier states. North Carolina, South Carolina, Georgia, Alabama, Mississippi, and Arkansas had traditionally ranked low on the economic scale; their average per capita personal income, even in 1929, was only $403, compared with $800 for the six Northern Tier states and $1,336 for the top six states. The government's goal seemed to be to restore each state's depressed income to its 1929 level, not to attempt an equalization among states.

Unquestionably, the funds expended by federal agencies in the Northern Tier states during the 1930s helped solve many of their problems, and by the time war broke out in Europe in 1939, residents of the Northern Tier were grateful for what had been accomplished. What would they have done without the Grand Coulee and Fort Peck dams; the control of blister rust and the construction of roads through the forests; the construction of highways, country roads, school buildings, and public buildings; the electrification of farms; the establishment of Social Security; the conservation of productive soil; and the support of low-income youth to attend high school and college?

The list of accomplishments over the six-year period from 1933 through 1939 is impressive.[6] In Washington, bank deposits rose from $265 million to $482 million; the Federal Land Bank made 9,400 long-term loans; the Rural Rehabilitation Division aided 9,400 needy farm families; the Home Owners Loan Corporation made 21,492 loans to distressed homeowners; and the Public Works Administration completed 427 projects, including 92 schools, 28 waterworks systems, 205 bridges, 10 sewers, and other projects covering university buildings, hospitals, disposal plants, libraries, auditoriums, recreational centers, and school gymnasiums.

In Idaho, silver production rose from $2 million in 1933 to $15 million in 1939; over the same period, farm marketings rose from $52 million to $80 million. The Civilian Conservation Corps provided healthful and productive outdoor labor for almost twenty thousand sons of poor families. The National Youth Administration provided part-time employment for some five thousand needy high school and college students. The Reconstruction Finance Corporation, Federal Emergency Relief Administration, and other agencies provided relief for some twenty thousand destitute Idaho families. Some four thousand laborers were employed on an expanded highway program, involving thousands of miles of new and improved roads. Other Idaho workers constructed the Owyhee Reclamation Project, several storage reservoirs, 78 educational buildings, 25 airports, 125 public buildings, and hundreds of athletic fields, fairgrounds, and parks throughout the state.

In Montana, the Farm Credit Administration made 7,187 long-term farm real estate loans and 41,493 crop-producing loans. The Farm Security Administration aided 20,186 needy families. Federal land utilization established six projects, consisting of almost two million acres in central and eastern Montana, to convert marginal and abandoned cropland from wheat cultivation to profitable range. The Public Works Administration completed 113 projects, including 52 school buildings, 22 waterworks systems, 6 dormitories, 7 courthouses, 3 city halls, and other projects. The WPA built 114 public buildings, 27 athletic fields, 10 playgrounds, 27 swimming and wading pools, 4 golf courses, 58 tennis courts, and 19 parks. The Civilian Conservation Corps operated 27 camps to restore and increase the state's natural resources. New residential building construction rose from $252,985 in 1933 to $1,376,539 in 1938.

In Wyoming, farm marketings rose from $25 million in 1933 to $41 million in 1938, to which government payments of $3 million were added, for a total of $44 million. The Farm Credit Administration made 4,376 long-term loans to farmers on farm real estate and 5,547 crop-producing loans. The Farm Security Administration aided 6,463 needy families. The Public Works Administration completed 43 projects, including 16 school buildings, 4 waterworks systems, 1 airplane hangar, 2 jails and courthouses, and one fire station. The Works Progress Administration completed 103 miles of highway and made improvements on 2,235 miles of other roads, 106 new public buildings, 4 new athletic fields, 2 playgrounds, 9 new swimming pools, 3 golf courses, 6 tennis courts, and 4 parks. Sewing-room projects produced 130,000 garments, and more than 235,000 lunches were served to school children. The Civilian Conservation Corps operated 27 camps in Wyoming and furnished employment to 7,104 Wyoming enrollees and 1,922 non-enrollees. These young men completed 480 miles of truck trails, controlled pests on 220,000 acres, controlled rodents on 594,000 acres, and developed 2,233 acres of public campgrounds. The Bureau of Public Roads completed 2,254 miles of highway.

In North Dakota, the Farm Credit Administration made 38,814 long-term amortized loans to farmers on farm real estate; 125,763 crop-producing loans and 16,651 crop and livestock loans were granted through Production Credit Associations. The FCA also made 44,404 drought relief loans. The Farm Security Administration aided 55,601 needy families. The Land Utilization Division of the Department of Agriculture (formerly the Resettlement Administration) established five projects in western and southeastern North Dakota to convert more than one million acres in submarginal lands from cultivation to grazing. The Public Works Administration completed 146 projects, including 50 schools, 16 waterworks systems, 18 bridges and street improvement projects, and 7 disposal plants. The Works Progress Administration constructed 148 public buildings, including 28 schools, 49 recreational buildings, and 5 firehouses.

In South Dakota, farm marketings rose from $68 million in 1933 to $94 million in 1938, plus government payments of $18 million, for total farm receipts of $112 million. The Farm Credit Administration made 26,524 long-term amortized loans to farmers on farm real estate; 65,338 crop-producing loans were made through the Emergency Seed and Feed Loan Section and 17,748 crop and livestock loans through the Production Credit Associations. The Farm Credit Administration also made 43,989 drought relief loans. The Farm Security Administration aided 59,153 needy families. The Land Utilization Division of the Department of Agriculture established three projects totaling 666,500 acres in South Dakota to convert submarginal land to range and wildlife use. The Public Works Administration completed 146 projects, including 42 schools, 28 waterworks systems, 4 disposal plants, 8 sewers, and 2 swimming pools. The Works Progress Administration completed 2,066 miles of new highways and roads, improved 4,310 miles of other roads, and erected 131 new public buildings, including 24 schools and 62 recreational buildings. The Civilian Conservation Corps operated 18 camps, furnishing employment to 20,658 South Dakota enrollees and non-enrollees.

But even with all these federal dollars and programs, by 1939 employment and payrolls in the six states of the Northern Tier had not reached 1929 levels. There was still widespread unemployment, rural poverty, and thousands of families on relief. New Deal spending had achieved no more than half a recovery. If the political atmosphere had permitted it, a more effective program could have been placed in operation. It is likely that the recovery would have been more rapid if the deficit had been greater. This is not to suggest that New Deal programs were always wisely administered or that they were always consistent and carefully planned. There were examples of misuse and corruption in each state, although an observer of the current scene would surely declare that the corruption was insignificant, if not excusable. The New Deal was experimental; it was important not only for its physical attainments and morale-boosting effect but also because it established a precedent for government's acceptance of responsibility to maintain the health of the national economy. Above all, the Depression established the principle that the federal government should take herculean efforts, if necessary, to maintain a strong and compassionate economy, whether threatened by natural disaster, financial panic, or runaway inflation.

That the expenditures should have been greater is evidenced by what happened after 1939. With the German attack on Poland in September 1939 and the beginning of war in Europe, America had to beef up her defense. Total federal expenditures, which were less than $5 billion in 1933 and just under $9 billion in 1939, rose to $14 billion by 1941. When America became an active participant in the war in December 1941, the federal budget adjusted accordingly, shooting up to $32 billion in 1942. By 1945, total federal spending was at the rate of $93 billion per year. Unemployment plunged, the economy moved ahead, and farmers prospered. We found that what we were unwilling to do for recovery we were quite willing to do for defense.

Notes

1. See Dixon Wecter, *The Age of the Great Depression, 1929–1941* (New York: Macmillan, 1948); Broadus Mitchell, *Depression Decade: From New Era Through New Deal, 1929–1941* (New York: Rinehart & Company, 1947); David A. Shannon, *The Great Depression* (Englewood Cliffs, N.J.: Prentice-Hall, 1960); Lester V. Chandler, *America's Greatest Depression, 1929–1941* (New York: Harper & Row, 1970); Michael A. Bernstein, *The Great Depression: Delayed Recovery and Economic Change in America, 1929–1939* (New York: Cambridge University Press, 1987). The impact of the Depression on the West is described in Gerald D. Nash, *The American West in the Twentieth Century: A Short History of an Urban Oasis* (Englewood Cliffs, N.J.: Prentice-Hall, 1973), 139–91.

2. J. B. Kincer, "Data on Drought," *Science* 80 (August 24, 1934): 179. Recent studies include A. Paul Bonnifield, *The Dust Bowl: Men, Dirt, and Depression* (Albuquerque: University of New Mexico Press, 1979); Donald Worster, *Dust Bowl: The Southern Plains in the 1930s* (New York: Oxford University Press, 1979). See also John T. Schlebecker, *Cattle Raising on the Plains, 1900–1960* (Lincoln: University of Nebraska Press, 1963).

3. See Leonard J. Arrington "The New Deal in the West: A Preliminary Sta-

tistical Inquiry," *Pacific Historical Review* 38 (August 1969): 311–16; "Idaho and the Great Depression," *Idaho Yesterdays* 13 (Summer 1969): 2–8; "Arizona in the Great Depression Years," *Arizona Review* 17 (December 1968): 11–19; "Western Agriculture and the New Deal," *Agricultural History* 44 (October 1970): 337–353; "Utah, the New Deal, and the Depression of the 1930s" (Dello G. Dayton Memorial Lecture, Weber State College, Ogden, Utah, 1982), 7–31; "The Sagebrush Resurrection: New Deal Expenditures in the Western States, 1933–1939," *Pacific Historical Review* 52 (February 1983): 1–16; "New Deal Programs and Southwestern Agriculture," in *Southwestern Agriculture: Pre-Columbian to Modern*, ed. Henry C. Dethloff and Irvin M. May Jr. (College Station: Texas A&M University Press, 1982), 275–92.

4. Dean D. Lundblad, "The Indian Division of the Civilian Conservation Corps" (MA thesis, Utah State University, Logan, 1968).

5. Don C. Reading, "New Deal Activity and the States, 1933 to 1939," *Journal of Economic History* 33 (December 1973): 792–807. See also Gavin Wright, "The Political Economy of New Deal Spending: An Econometric Analysis," *Review of Economics and Statistics* 56 (February 1974): 30–38.

6. There are summaries of accomplishments in the mimeographed reports, one for each state, in Office of Government Reports, Statistical Section, Report no. 10, vol. 2, Washington, D.C., 1940. Copy is in the library of the Superintendent of Documents, Washington, D.C., and photocopies are in the Utah State University Library, Logan.

11

Traveling the Hope Highway
An Intellectual History of the West River Country of South Dakota

PAULA M. NELSON

HOW DO PEOPLE DECIDE WHO OR WHAT THEY ARE? WHY DO PEOPLE
do what they do? How do individuals justify the choices they have
made? When those kinds of questions are asked of a region, the answers compose an ethos; they provide a portrait of the attitudes that
shape a people. I have asked these questions of identity and purpose
of one particular region, the west river plains of South Dakota. The
west river country includes the portion of the state west of the Missouri River, which geographically and culturally divides South Dakota
neatly in half. For my purposes, I have excluded the Black Hills region because its history, beginning a generation earlier and driven by
mining rather than agriculture, is very different from that of the plains
portion of the state.

The history of the settlement of the west river plains has been
marked with uncertainty and struggle. It first reached public con-
sciousness as the Great Sioux Reservation, the home of the most noble
and most feared of the Plains tribes. By 1889, it had become the focus
of expansionist dreams. It was in that year that Dakota promoters and
boosters saw their dreams realized. The Great Sioux Reservation was
greatly reduced, a system of individual allotments was developed for
future implementation, and the "excess" land was opened to non-
Indian settlement. But boosters' hopes were dashed, initially, by the
national depression of the 1890s and the lack of rail transport to the
region. After 1900, with the economy again strong, two railroads announced plans to build roads west from the Missouri River to Rapid
City. The federal government contributed to the excitement when it

announced plans to distribute more "surplus" reservation lands to the public by lottery. The rush for west river lands had begun.[1]

The people who participated in the settlement boom came from all walks of life. The chance for a free farm lured secretaries, teachers, clerks, big-city policemen, and store owners as well as farmers to what promoters billed as "the last, great frontier." The immigrants built their farms and towns with high hopes, but they were struck a fearful blow by the drought of 1910–1911. Water sources dried up and the grass refused to grow. Seeds planted in the spring sprouted in August when the first rains of the growing season fell. Suffering and hardship marked those years, and one-third to one-half of the population packed up and moved to more appealing climes. The drought lingered in milder form until 1915. After that good year, some settlers returned to enjoy the happier circumstances and the higher prices of the war years. But west river settlement had been indelibly marked. The lesson was hard. This country was not like the humid Midwest, and it never could be. Settlers who stayed would always face a higher risk of economic failure, isolation born of a low population, and social disorganization. The drought of 1910–1911 and the difficult years that followed brought the first test of west river mettle and warned of trials to come.[2]

The pioneers who built the towns and farms of the west river country arrived at a time of tremendous social change in the United States. The growing urban and industrial order required a commitment to life in groups, a life in which individual desires had to bend to the good of the community. West river settlers fled those changes and chose to migrate to a place where the old virtues of individualism, independence, freedom, self-reliance, and healthy self-interest might be better realized. Of course, they believed they would be successful economically as well; failure was not a word in their lexicon. They planned to succeed in the context of the old ways, not the new. West river pioneers could and frequently did cooperate with their neighbors, but they did so in a context that allowed them maximum freedom of opportunity for themselves. In its most strident expression, west river people wanted to "live each day so that you can look every damn man in the eye and tell him to go to hell," as a wall plaque hanging in a Mellette County claim shack proclaimed.[3]

The west river country was built on faith rather than reality—faith in the future and faith in the abilities of the settlers to conquer the frontier and build a prosperous society. This faith was built on enduring Christian truths: that God had created the world for man to conquer and improve; that God had not made a land that could not be farmed; that there was a promise to man that God would grant success and prosperity to those who lived right and worked hard. In its secular form, that truth was stated as "the man who works is the man who wins," the slogan enshrined on a *Dakota Farmer* premium and posted on a kitchen wall in Meade County.[4]

The slogan said nothing about people who worked and struggled, who lived right and did the good work God commanded, and failed anyway. But that was the west river experience. The drought of 1910–1911 dried the hopes and withered the faith of many west river pioneers. Those who stayed had to reassess their priorities and redefine their faith to fit their straitened circumstances. The idea that life is more than economic success developed early in the west river experience, becoming an article of faith among people whose primary motivation in immigrating there had been quick success but who then chose, in the most extreme adversity, to make a virtue of necessity. The joy of the struggle, not its successful conclusion, became central to west river ideology. E. L. Keith, a Philip lumberman, wrote a "Sermon for the Discouraged" that articulated the developing ideal. In his lengthy analysis of condition and prospects, Keith replied to "the knocker . . . abroad in the land." While his piece was a spirited defense of the country and a holy injunction to stay and do the farmer's hard duty, it also admitted that conditions were different in western South Dakota and always would be. Keith called for the use of scientific farming methods and adaptation to the land. "Our problems here are very different from what most of us have encountered before coming here," he wrote, but "we will learn to know our land and its problems in time and when nature once comes to have a familiar look to us, we will go forward to grapple with the problems of agriculture joyously and with confidence in our strength. We will not only learn much about conservation of moisture, but we will learn much about the crops and their adaptation to conditions that we find here." He rated "knockers" with the "adverse conditions that characterize this new country" and consigned them to "the beaten track . . . some little eastern town," because "they are not the stuff of which nation builders are made." Keith concluded his exhortation with an appeal to pride and duty:

> The real empire builder will stay right here. They will grapple with the difficulties of pioneer life joyously, like "the strong man who goes forth to run a race." Undaunted by obstacles in their path and never for one moment discouraged at seeming defeats, they will go on with the work yet hardly commenced.[5]

The complex juxtapositions of advantages and disadvantages and the trials and joys of west river life were captured in a newspaper piece written by the Reverend Carl Weirauch, a local homesteader, teacher, and minister. Weirauch created a fictional couple, Eb and Kate, who discussed the west river crises in the post-drought years and always arrived at reasons to hope. "I have always told you there would be no shadow were there no sun," Kate began.

> I have been thinkin' a great deal about what the future of this country is goin' to be myself. I have decided that what folks stayed here are the best, they are the salt of the earth. They are to be depended upon and I think, worth tying to. . . . We are in Western South Dakota now, the land of sunshine and clear skies, the land that flows with milk and alkali water, the land of the cactus and the mosquito, the land of opportunity and hard work where the promise still holds good for those to come who have a good strong back and are willing and wanting to build for their future happiness, welfare and prosperity. And seems to me Eb, that of all times this is the time for them to come.[6]

The faith that God would reward those who stayed and did his bidding remained strong, but the expected reward became indefinitely postponed and spiritualized. Yet, it was still assured, in much the same way that early Christians had dealt with the unseemly delay in the Second Coming. Because work did not always bring rewards, an important corollary was added to the faith: while this year was always hard, next year would be better. Each bad year, each year of hard work without result, became the planting of yet another acorn from which a mighty new country would grow. In the meantime, as one woman wrote, "We have learned to follow the custom of the country, and get along as best we can with what we have."[7]

The boom in American agriculture brought about by the devastation and starvation in Europe during World War I reached into the west river country and brought a temporary reprieve. For a brief period after the war, those who had stuck with the country despite the drought congratulated themselves on their good judgment and prepared for another boom. It never materialized. The agricultural depression that struck in 1920–1921 devastated the agricultural economy, rural banks, and small-town businesses quite as thoroughly as the drought had. The shock of the 1920–1921 crash was nationwide, but it struck especially hard in the west river country, where settlement was relatively new, the economy was precarious, and there were few reserves to help people through the crisis. The agricultural depression permanently damaged prospects for future growth and development and hastened the region's slide to the margins of American society. It was the second great time of testing for the west river country, and it lasted for several years.

The big shake-out of farmers in the west river country came with the crash of the early 1920s. Farmers and ranchers who had borrowed money for livestock to feed the starving masses of Europe now faced foreclosure on debts as high as $40,000 at a time when most farm loans rarely topped $3,000. With cattle prices at rock bottom, the ranchers now joined ranks with the masses of Europe. In Perkins County, 799 farms—38 per cent of all farms in the county—were foreclosed between 1921 and 1925. In Haakon County, the number was 389 farms, or 47.5 per cent; in Jackson County, 212, or 53 per cent of farms were foreclosed before mid-decade. Sixteen of the eighteen counties of the west river plains experienced their highest foreclosure rates between 1920 and 1925.[8]

Even the foreclosures could not save the banks. A number of west river banks failed in the 1920s, leaving some towns with no bank at all. Investors lost heavily, and those with savings or checking accounts—those who had invested in their neighbors—lost most of what they had. The town of Kadoka had two banks in 1920; in January 1924, the two banks merged, hoping to create a stronger institution, but the merged bank failed in May 1924. In the fall of 1924, one of the two

Belvidere banks (the only banks that survived in Jackson County of the six in operation in 1920) moved to Kadoka. The bank failed in 1927 and Kadoka was without a bank until 1948. It took two and one-half years for the first bank to pay dividends to depositors who had lost money when the bank closed. Depositors received back 10 per cent of their investment; the other 90 per cent went toward two years of crop failure and the expensive maintenance of bank property, including foreclosed farms.[9]

Because struggling or failed farmers could not pay their taxes, the government also felt the pinch of the crisis. Governments paid their bills in warrants at 7 per cent interest, and a few counties issued bonds to raise cash to pay the skeptics. The only alternative was strict enforcement of tax collection, which would drive county residents from their homes when they could not pay and would not have appreciably increased revenues in any event. But the west river country needed more people, not fewer, and county officials did not want their citizens driven out because they were in debt. The downward spiral continued, as fewer paid taxes and government debts mounted. There seemed to be no solution other than prosperity, and prosperity, it was said, was as scarce as hen's teeth.[10]

The rationale for "sticking," as it was called, was again widely discussed during the early 1920s. Again, the operative ideals were faith and the hope that next year would be better, combined with the belief that an individual could control his or her destiny. The newspapers tried to sound encouraging; boosterism, not reporting, was their primary mission. On 1922, the *Dakota Farmer* tried to capture the spirit of the west river country:

> This story is about a land where young men still have dreams and hopes that reach into the days of tomorrow. It is the land where they work and toil today. The dwellers of this land, unlike the fly-by-night settlers who appear upon the first page of the abstract of the title, are tied to the country by stronger bonds than a mortgage. They have spent so much of their time here that they have become attached to the country and the ideals that guide her destiny.

West river residents had come to love the prairie, the author continued, and no longer missed more wooded and better watered land.

They had also "learned to love the golden sunset and the boundless youth" of the west river country.

> These uncomplaining frontiersmen would not trade their debts and hardships for the false ease of the eastern renter who pays $10.00 per acre cash rent and never knows from one year to the next whether or not he is going to live under the same roof.[11]

"Mrs. A. F. A." from Meade County expressed a similar spirit. She and her family lived fifty to one hundred miles from medical care, wore old clothes or hand-me-downs sent by relatives, traded clothes and patches with neighbors, and was in need of all the "common decencies of life" that her neighborhood lacked. Yet, she observed, "we are absolutely independent in our ways of living and of thinking . . . we like it and stay if we do starve for many things, for we have room for our minds and our bodies." Although the community needed railroads, schools and other services, she concluded, "We are always on the Hope Highway . . . and can always find many stretches where we can hit it on high even though much of the trip is a daily grind in low."[12]

The editors of the *Kadoka Press* maintained their belief in the individual's ability to make the west river country bloom. At the beginning of 1922, in their annual New Year's message, the *Press'* editors repeated their governing faith: "Whether the coming year will be for us one of happiness and prosperity or otherwise is largely written within our own making, and if we but determine to make it the best year of all so it will be, for with that determination will come forth the effort to make it so." In 1926, after many farm foreclosures, bank failures, and other hardships, the *Press* emphasized the need for faith:

> "We need a good crop this year and every year to come if possible, but more than that we need faith in the country. We need faith of the kind that will compel a man's better judgment to come to the front—the kind that will make our people stay on the job through the lean years as well as the fat ones. When we have developed that faith that enables us to carry on and have learned to love a booster and to be one ourselves, THEN THE PEOPLE WILL COME AND PROSPERITY WILL NO LONGER BE JUST AROUND THE CORNER. It will have arrived."[13]

The nationwide depression and the Dust Bowl that accompanied it on the Plains provided the third great test of west river life. The challenges to life and spirit were unremitting for over a decade; the solution—government aid and control—was precedent shattering and disquieting to many. The depth of the crisis cannot be overstated. Prices fell to rock bottom and cash virtually disappeared. The drought, hot winds, dust storms, and insect plagues began in 1930 and continued with few interruptions until World War II. The trials of nature prevented west river residents from engaging even in subsistence agriculture, which might have eased their suffering. There was little to eat, clothes were tattered and patched, bedding was worn out, and families huddled together to stay warm. Neighbors with food helped those without. Farmers cut Russian thistles to provide feed for their stock, but many animals starved to death.

The Red Cross undertook early relief efforts and Herbert Hoover's Reconstruction Finance Corporation provided some money for work relief, but neither effort appreciably eased the crisis. In 1933, the first New Deal money and aid arrived, creating a new world of regulations, social workers, and relief. While some west river residents resisted aid on ideological grounds, most were too desperate to care about the issue of dependency. In county histories written during the last thirty years, relief programs receive more gratitude than complaint.[14]

World War II and the return of the rains in the 1940s ended the crisis. By that time, the population had dropped by 21,249, or 14 per cent from that in 1930, and those remaining had changed their connections to the land. Many towns had grown considerably, rural areas had diminished, and some areas had become virtually depopulated. The depression and Dust Bowl years, especially the year 1936, replaced 1910–1911 in west river country lore as the time of greatest troubles.[15]

The bitter combination of depression, drought, insect plagues, and temperature extremes had created incredible hardships in the west river country. When the Carmichael family in Perkins County lost the lease on their rented farm, they built themselves a dugout. Son Vern helped build the shelter: "We dug a hole in the side of a hill near 'Raggy Simmons' Butte. We went to the reservation and cut ash poles and hauled them home to make a roof for a den." To heat their "hole in a hill," as they called it, the children gathered cow chips. A Fall River

County family took over two old homestead shacks, located twelve yards apart. For two years they lived with their bedroom in one shack and the living area in the other. The family lived on fruit they had picked and canned during an abortive relocation to Oregon, trading some for coal when needed. The Moelter family in Meade County rented some unimproved land in 1932 and put up a one-room sod house with no ceiling; the exposed rafters were boards covered with tar paper.[16]

Food was often in short supply. Many people in the Adrian family's neighborhood in Mellette County roasted wheat and used it as a coffee substitute. Lorraine Herrig in Tripp County remembered using vinegar to remove mold from bacon to make it edible. Her brother developed rickets because of the family's poor diet. A Meade County family survived on a meager ration of pancakes, macaroni, and potatoes. Agnes Whiting remembered "how utterly futile our efforts were to save the garden and our crops. The resulting hard winter and food shortage is one I'd rather not talk about."[17] Livestock also suffered. Agnes Whiting of Tripp County was later haunted by the memory of

> the bellowing of the hungry cattle that we could not feed; no hay except mounds of thistles which were the only vegetation the grasshoppers and drought had left us. The milk cows staggering and falling over barn door sills, following us, bawling for forage which we couldn't give them; cattle eating manure piles.[18]

Along with the drought came furious winds and wild dust storms, which darkened the sky at midday and filled houses, furniture, and food with dirt. The storms blasted the paint from buildings, and cattle sometimes died from ingesting the dirt the wind blew into their feed. In Tripp County, weeds sprouted from the backs of cattle that had been left out in the winds. In 1934, the River Park correspondent to the *Bison Courier* reported a common problem: "How to be cheerful in the continual dust storms, that is our task." A year later, after another bad bout with wind, she simply asked, "Don't you still taste the dust in your mouth?"[19]

The heat of summer and the cold of winter added to the misery. In 1931, a young boy had suffered a sunstroke one morning when the temperature reached 109 degrees in the shade before eleven o'clock.

In 1934, local news columns listed people on the sick list because of the heat. But the summer of 1936 was the worst. Temperatures that summer reached 117 degrees, and west river residents spent the days in their cellars and slept outdoors at night. To avoid rattlesnakes, families made their beds on hay wagons or truck beds.[20]

The winter of 1936 brought the most dramatic cold and the worst storms. In Bison, the temperature did not rise above zero for thirty-five days in January and February of 1936. A Pennington County family with a "good" house—not a shack—recorded a temperature of eighteen degrees below zero in the upstairs and downstairs bedrooms. A train crew was stuck in a massive drift near Eagle Butte in a February storm that dropped the temperature to fifty-three degrees below zero and brought winds of sixty to seventy miles per hour. After three days without food, two members of the crew walked two and one-half miles to a farm, where they found a family, "gaunt, hungry and poorly clothed" clinging to their stove and burning the boards from their corral to keep warm. The crew traded coal for a loaf of bread, some coffee, and a chunk of pork, and the farmer spent the night hauling coal from the train to his house. In George Reeves' neighborhood, people alerted by the telephone helped hand-shovel twenty-eight miles of snow-clogged roads to get a dying man to the doctor.[21]

As if trials by fire and ice and drought were not enough, the 1930s also brought insect plagues to the west river country. The grasshoppers remained year after year but other pests, including Mormon crickets and blister beetles, might attack one year and be gone the next. William Schoulte lived in Lyman County during the depression years and of all the crises the dust and the hoppers made the biggest impression on him. "The hoppers would move in and in just a few short hours after a whole year's work would be ruined," he remembered. "They would start in a field of corn and when they finished, a hole in the ground would mark the spot where a stalk of corn had stood." But the lack of a crop did not stop the hoppers' assault. "When the farm was devoid of vegetation, they started eating the bark off the fence posts and then the paint on the house; when all else was gone they started to eat each other." On the Schoulte farm, "hoppers died by the millions and piled up around the house, giving off a sweet, sickening smell." Grasshoppers ate coats left in the fields and nylon underwear hanging on the clothesline. Towns were not immune to property damage either. In Kadoka, grasshoppers ate gardens and flowers. A large swarm arrived in Dallas on a busy Saturday night. A clerk in the Farmer's Store remembered the invasion:

> The insects moved into the store en masse and began devouring everything that seemed edible to them. They had soon consumed the fruits and vegetables, the crepe paper and other related items and were eating the labels from the canned and dry goods. We battled them all night.[22]

Some farmers tried to take advantage of the situation. They loaded the grasshoppers in sacks and kept the bags tied tightly shut until all the insects had died. Then they spread the dead hoppers out to dry in the sun and rebagged them for poultry feed. The combination of grasshoppers and drought created a grim landscape; nothing green grew anywhere during the worst years. The stripping of paint from the dust-scoured buildings and the desolation of the countryside created a monochromatic picture of misery and despair.[23]

As the struggle to make a living grew ever more difficult, as people began to leave for Oregon and Washington, and as the government became more involved in daily life, west river people who stayed with the country justified their decision and articulated their philosophies in small-town newspapers and farm papers like the *Dakota Farmer*. The *Farmer*, in fact, became a forum for arguing the advantages and disadvantages of the country and of government's intervention in west river life.

White Americans had always confronted the frontier (or the wilderness) in religious terms as well as natural ones. The Bible is filled with imagery of the wilderness as a dark and threatening abode that imposes terrible tests on the faithful, who are challenged to convert the wilderness into the Garden and in the process be purified and reborn. God's command in Genesis to "be fruitful and multiply, and replenish the earth and subdue it" had a literal meaning for all American generations except the most recent. The mission had not been dulled by the passage of time; twentieth century pioneers recalled it frequently and cloaked their endeavors in the age-old language of conquest. When they struggled and failed, the pioneers turned to the Bible for solace. God's warning to Adam, "In the sweat of thy face shalt man eat bread," reminded them that they had to work for their comfort and success. As the dust blew and as crops died year after year, God's promise that "while the earth remaineth, seedtime and harvest . . . shall not cease" comforted them. God had not forsaken them, they believed, although the test was severe.[24]

Throughout the depression, T. E. Hayes sought to reinvigorate this faith in *Dakota Farmer* readers, writing letters that are like a chorus enjoining the faithful. A Perkins County farmer for twenty-five years, Hayes served in the state legislature, was active in his community club and taxpayers' league, and wrote letters, columns, and doggerel for the *Farmer*. He had his critics, but they were few.

Hayes argued from the beginning that all would turn out well for those who had patience and faith, and he recorded every reason why that would be so. In 1931, he used the theme "things at their worst will mend or end" in a column about the depression. The taxing drought in the summer of 1930 had ended, he reported, "and although too late for the grain, alfalfa and sweet clover soon responded to these refreshing rains, late flax fields began to bloom and inside of two weeks we appeared to be living in a new world." He added a word about his faith that all would be well. "The old book has promised," he reminded his readers, "that seedtime and harvest shall not fail; it might also add, the law of supply and demand shall not fail." Hayes remained convinced that old promises and the laws of the marketplace would eventually correct the economy, no matter how badly humankind erred.[25]

As the New Deal developed its programs for relief and production control for agriculture, Hayes began to worry about the inevitable loss of independence that government presence entailed. He and his neighbors were concerned about the deliberate destruction of excess crops and stock; they worried that God would exact retribution in the drought and in the dust. And yet, even as Hayes recounted his neighbors' oft-asked question, "What are we going to do?" he echoed his oft-stated faith. "Personally," he wrote, "I am not afraid of the future. I for one cannot believe God has forgotten us . . . I believe His promise that seedtime and harvest, summer and winter, shall not fail while the earth remains." The prairie would come back, Hayes believed, and the crops would grow and rains would fall. "What are we going to do?" he asked. "That to a great extent depends on the individual who is willing to join with his hopeful neighbors whose great hope is in God and freedom." [26]

Two of the most discussed features of the New Deal conservation and agricultural policies were the shelterbelt program, which was based on the premise that thick lines of trees planted on the plains would slow the damaging winds, and the submarginal lands program, which entailed the large-scale purchase of inferior farmland in so-called submarginal areas and the relocation of affected residents to homes in more manageable environments. The west river country lay on the west (that is, the windy) side of the proposed shelterbelt, and much of it was designated as submarginal land. Hayes, along with his friends and neighbors, did not respond positively to the bureaucrats' conclusion that they had hitched their wagons to a submarginal star. He argued that west river "people have and are still going through a process of adjusting themselves to conditions as they find them, and if left alone will find the way out without advice of eastern profs." Hayes was defiant in defense of his region: "Even if they build a shelterbelt and leave us on the outside, we will still plant a few trees of our own; still plow and sow and reap if we get a little moisture." He concluded: "We have reclaimed this country, and in spite of all the ballyhoo, we shall stay here and keep the home fires burning . . . and anyone or combination that tries to move us out will be up against the old pioneer spirit that knows no defeat." Butte County's William Greenberg argued in the *Dakota Farmer*: "Western South Dakota is still a poor man's country—the land of promise to him who has the pioneering spirit." While times were hard, he went on, the problems could be surmounted: "The end can never be doubted, we are engaged in our old set task of subduing the earth, and the men on the ground can be trusted to do it successfully, if the federal government does not step in to remove the opportunity." [27]

As the 1930s drew to a close, a Jones County man, J. B. Hartz, wrote to the *Dakota Farmer* to encourage his friends and neighbors to hold on. "All too many of us have found that 1939 was just another year of failure," Hartz observed. "The figures in red have become so common and familiar to us during the past 18 years that they do not appall us any more . . . we have taken so many lickings that another defeat or failure means little to us." Although some among them might feel defeated, he found larger meanings of success that went beyond wealth. "We can all go down in history," he reminded his readers,

> as having led successful lives if we wish it that way and are willing to do the best we know how to make it that way. To be successful we need neither riches, position, power, eloquence or great learning. All we need is a right heart, a sensible mind and two willing hands. Success depends on what is within us and on the efforts we put forth, not on the results of those efforts.

He concluded by invoking the reward that would surely come: "Let us do the very best we know how and leave results to Him who knows our hearts and sees our every effort and will reward us accordingly in due season."[28]

But not everyone had faith, and they moved out when the trials became unendurable. Harry Putnam, born on Plum Creek near Wendte in Stanley County, was one who left the country. In 1982, he contributed a poem to the Bad River regional history:

> Depression, drought assailed us, summer's heat and winter's cold
> Wreaked their worst upon us, yet we were always told
> That next year would be better, and when my youth was past
> I learned the promised next year was no better than the last.

Putnam left the west river country in the 1930s, returning only rarely to visit.[29]

Critics of the prevailing ideology assailed the country and the idea that freedom in poverty was better than having some comforts that came with a modicum of controls. Philip Beck of Dewey County complained:

> Who can call a country like this a farm country, where you can not raise more than one crop in three? . . . And that crop is not a big crop. . . . In the first place we have no soil to farm; on the other hand we have not the climate. . . . I never did see anything grow on a hot stove, even if it had moisture. . . . And yet, some will holler and say we have just as good a country as anywhere else.

Harry Hibner wrote an even more scathing report on the country. In response to William Greenfield's hopeful letter to the *Dakota Farmer*, Hibner claimed:

> This west river country is not a newly settled country; it is no frontier. It is a bankrupt, desolated, poverty-stricken, over-populated, over-grazed semi-desert. . . . The picture Greenberg draws of subduing the earth, of green fields, and bursting granaries and schools and a house on every section of land is very fine indeed; but how does he propose to supply sufficient rainfall, or if he could, then how to prevent this thin, poor soil from leaching? What about the poor, broken poverty-stricken ones who have tried to live on a couple of quarters of this land?

Hibner insisted that the prevailing faith and efforts were wrong. He condemned Greenberg and other optimists like him: "It is people like you who are trying to make of this country something that it was never intended for. It can't be done. If it could it would have been done many years ago. It has been tried for 25 years and it can't be done."[30]

A few people argued that the freedom claimed by west river partisans was not true freedom and was, in fact, detrimental to west river life. R. Jones was the most articulate defender of New Deal efforts to take chances and try new solutions to stubborn problems. The person he targeted for criticism was T. E. Hayes, the standard bearer of the west river faith. Jones argued:

> Those who sit in the scorner's seats advocate our return to the old policy of blind drifting and inaction . . . they talk of losses of freedom, of independence. What do they mean? Freedom to go wherever you please when your farm is foreclosed? . . . That we are not dependent on Minneapolis, Pittsburgh, Birmingham, and Tulsa for fuel, textiles, and markets?

Jones maintained that some liberties had to be given up so that people could prosper. He chose as one example "the right of individual farmers to use, for costly grain production, land better suited for grazing, forest, or golf courses." In a second letter in the same issue of the *Dakota Farmer*, Jones expanded upon his theme. "There is no such thing as absolute 'freedom.' Even the sturdy individualist in the gone but not forgotten (unfortunately) pioneer days, did not have complete liberty." It was necessary for some "liberties" to disappear so that planning might take place that would promote the general welfare. It was a new world, Jones argued, and people would have to recognize the need to experiment and accept change.[31] The critics of the prevailing ideology were few, however. Most editors, rural newspaper correspondents, and letter writers held onto their faith and hope in better times next year, although they sometimes qualified their position with humor or cynicism. Their defenses of the country and its people were spirited and they were occasionally discouraged, but they showed little public anger.

But there was another approach to life in the west river country, one filled with belligerence and rage. In this view, the struggle was between man and a harsh and uncaring Nature, a battle with no reassuring promises. In *A Man from South Dakota*, George Reeves focused on his years on a South Dakota ranch during the 1920s and 1930s. Reeves began ranching on his own in 1926. As an educated, rational college man, he initially believed he could bend the force of Nature to his will. But when he watched his wheat and flax die and saw a tantalizing cloud slip away without giving rain, he reacted with rage:

> I cursed the enemy wind, I cursed the cloud, I cursed the goddam country that I had chosen for a place to live. When my rage had worn itself out, I was disturbed. My voice hadn't been that of a reasoning educated man. It had been the hoarse, irrational bellowing of a wounded cave man. . . . It was irrational but I couldn't escape the feeling that somehow I could bend this force to do my will. The cave man was slow to learn that he could only duck.[32]

The battle became very personal during the 1930s: Reeves versus "Dakota," tricky, vicious, unpredictable. Reeves worked to develop techniques and strategies to outwit Dakota, but he needed money to finance his ideas. Money was extremely scarce, and the federal government had become the only source of cash for farm operators. But Reeves viewed the government with contempt. Government officials, he said, "lined up facts in perpendicular columns and life didn't come that way." The requirements they forced him to meet and the time it took for them to fill his requests got in the way of his very personal struggle with Dakota. Even before the New Deal, Reeves proclaimed: "I hate government." After Roosevelt took office, the farmer's anger and scorn grew. Reeves believed he could beat Dakota—that was his faith—but he "was afraid of governments, for they had eyes, and with them they could make themselves brutal tyrants." He angrily refused a neighbor's request to participate in the corn/hog allotment program: "This is my land, and I'll put a hole through the first guy that tries to tell me what to do." He had seen famine and surplus in Dakota, and he doubted if any government policy maker had personally confronted those conditions. Until they did, they had no right to solve the Dakotans' problems.[33]

As the drought deepened, Reeves' cattle began to suffer and he was forced to participate in the government's cattle buy-up program. It was a shotgun wedding, and Reeves adopted a cynical strategy of bilking the government as a kind of revenge for his dependency. He was confident that he knew more than any government official and that he could manipulate the government to aid in his fight with Dakota. "There was nothing in my rule book that prevented me from taking this sucker's money," he said. Dakota was his adversary, and an admirable foe, "an opponent who would never tire, who always offered something new to imperil—and improve—the flavor of next year." Government officials, planners, and anyone else who had never "looked up from his work with his eyes full of grit and dust to see the Devil standing there spraddle legged above the black clouds of a duststorm" and yet had refused to give up, were not worthy of Reeves' respect. Reeves' brand of west river ideology is tough and hard, self-righteous and stubborn, and guided by uncompromising self-interest. He shared none of the faith in the promise that helped many west river people stay afloat during hard times. The force he fought is blind and unfeeling; God may have been a source of consolation for Reeves, but the Devil was running the show.[34]

Since the World War II era, the west river people have endured other tests of commitment and courage but none to match the earlier three. The economy has become dependent more on ranching than farming, and the culture has been modernized; west river residents, in keeping with the new and more private styles of journalism, no longer pour their hearts out in the local papers. Life continues to be more difficult than it is in more populated areas, but better roads and access to electricity, telephones, and television have eased the daily lives of those in the west river country. Distance remains a problem, and the population has continued to decline. A recent study by Frank Popper and Deborah Popper of Rutgers University forecast the abandonment of the Great Plains within the next decades due to the hardships, isolation, and economic precariousness of life there. Yet, those who stayed believe that it is worth the struggle. As the editor of *South Dakota Magazine* wrote in a recent issue: "Any spreadsheet study of why people live in South Dakota . . . has to include wide columns for sunsets, independence, neighborliness, clean air, proximity to wild life and opportunity." [35]

A new generation has now taken up the challenge of west river life, yet many of the themes of their lives remain the same. Linda Hasselstrom, a rancher and writer who lives near Hermosa, has described her way of life in terms similar to those used in 1912—the struggle with Nature is dominant and immediate in a way that is no longer even a memory for most Americans. Unlike Reeves, however, the relationship for Hasselstrom is one of coexistence rather than war. "It's not really a battle," she said of her ranch work, "it's a war of nerves, of tactics. If we considered it a fight we could only lose; instead we try to outmaneuver her, to survive." She suggested that west river ranchers have a "covenant with Nature," one that is "less like a battle than a marriage." The challenges they confront "enhance our feeling of accomplishment when we succeed." Some ranchers even speak of the land in the first person, Hasselstrom noted, as in "I'm so dry I had to sell" or "There ain't enough grass on me to feed a bird." [36]

Faith and hope in next year continue to govern the lives of many west river people. They believe that the promise still holds good for those who will work, and they continue to see adversity as a sign and portent rather than as a defeat. In 1984, Lucille Mann wrote about the hardships that she had endured during the 1930s, and found the signs of the faith that had sustained her still around today in the form of volunteer trees. "The drought years of the 'thirties' sent dust storms to our country," she explained,

causing erosion and much discouragement, both materially and spiri-
tually. But, riding in the winds of fury were untold number of tree
seeds. . . . Landing on barren soil, these tiny seeds awaited the snows of
winter and the spring showers that followed, resulting in the thousands
of volunteer trees growing in Tripp County today. These trees, born in
adversity standing alone or in groves, are a testimony of abiding faith
and hope.

And in 1985, a middle-aged Meade County woman wrote about her
faith: "This country has been good to us. We love it here . . . no one
can tell what tomorrow will bring, so we'll just hold on as long as we
can. Though drought, heat, storms and 'hoppers, we will hope and
pray for a better next year."[37]

Notes

1. Paula M. Nelson, *After the West Was Won: Homesteaders and Townbuilders in Western South Dakota, 1900–1917* (Iowa City: University of Iowa Press,
1986). All material from *After the West Was Won* is used by permission of the
University of Iowa Press.

2. Ibid., 14–23, 42–50, 120–41.

3. Ibid., 14–16; Winifred Reulter, ed., *Mellette County Memories: Golden Anni-
versary Edition, 1911–61* (Stickney, S.D.: Argus Printers, 1961), 38.

4. Nelson, *After the West Was Won*, 144–54; Esther Marousek Letellier, *The
Man Who Works* (Pierre, S.D.: State Publishing Company, 1984), iii.

5. Nelson, *After the West Was Won*, 125–6.

6. Ibid., 145–6.

7. Ibid., 157.

8. *The Kadoka Press* (South Dakota), September 19, 1922, carried notice of
foreclosure on three debts totaling $55,877 contracted by William Rooks on
cattle and horses. The case of Lee and Viola Croft recorded in the August 11,
1922, *Press* is more typical. They owed $1,267.75 in principal, interest, and
fees on 240 acres of land; the debt was contracted in November 1921 and was
foreclosed in August 1922. Almost every issue of the *Press* carried notices of
mortgage foreclosures, and in the early 1920s there were several per issue. See
Harry A. Steele, *Farm Mortgage Foreclosures in South Dakota, 1921–1932*, Agricultural Economics Department, Circular no. 17 (Brookings: South Dakota Agricultural Experiment Station, May 1934), Table 1; Gabriel Lundy, *Farm Mortgage
Foreclosures in South Dakota, 1933-1934-1935-1936-1937*, Agricultural Economics
Department, supplement to Circular no. 17 (Brookings: South Dakota Agricultural Experiment Station, August 1938), Table 1, 2, 4–7. The compilers of the

farm mortgage figures did not include the reservation counties of Shannon, Todd, Washabaugh, or Washington.

9. *Kadoka Press*, January 25, May 23, November 21, 1924, April 28, 1927, November 18, 1926. The *Press* frequently mentioned failed banks in other communities. See, for example, February 1, 1924, where bank failures are attributed to malicious gossip, and May 2, 1924, which reports an unwarranted run that caused a bank to close.

10. *Bison Courier* (South Dakota), March 9, March 16, 1922; *Kadoka Press*, December 9, 1921, January 13, February 24, 1922.

11. *Dakota Farmer* (Aberdeen, South Dakota), June 1, 1922.

12. *Dakota Farmer*, March 15, 1922.

13. *Kadoka Press*, December 29, 1922, July 8, 1926.

14. *Kadoka Press*, January 21, March 3, October 13, 1932, January 5, March 2, 1933; Winner Chamber of Commerce, *Tripp County, South Dakota, 1909–1984* (Freeman, S.D.: Pine Hill Press, 1984), f-51; American Legion Auxiliary, *Eastern Pennington County Memories* (Marcelline, Mo.: Walsworth, 1965), 355; Lavonne R. Butler, ed., *Faith Country Heritage* (Pierre, S.D.: State Publishing Company, 1985), 621, 630–1; 646; 731; Elsie Hey Baye, *Haakon Horizons* (Pierre, S.D.: State Publishing Company, 1982), 87.

15. U.S. Bureau of Census, *Sixteenth Census of the United States: Population*, South Dakota tables, 1940; *Dakota Farmer*, July 17, August 14, 1937.

16. Butler, *Faith Country Heritage*, 365–6, 591; Northwest Fall River County Historical Society, *Sunshine and Sagebrush* (Pierre, S.D.: State Publishing Company, 1976), 200.

17. Reutter, *Mellette County Memories*, 10; Colome Book Jubilee Committee, *Colome, South Dakota, Diamond Jubilee, 1908–1983* (Winner, S.D.: Sodak Printers, 1983), 75; Butler, *Faith Country Heritage*, 593; Dallas Historical Society, *Dallas, South Dakota: The End of the Line* (n.p., 1971), 137.

18. Dallas Historical Society, *Dallas, South Dakota*, 137.

19. Colome Book Committee, *Colome Diamond Jubilee*, 74; Dallas Historical Society, *Dallas, South Dakota*, 80; *Kadoka Press*, August 9, 1934; *Bison Courier*, November 9, 1936; *Kadoka Press*, March 22, 1934; *Bison Courier*, April 19, 1934, April 11, 1935.

20. *Kadoka Press*, July 16, 1931, July 26, 1934, *Bison Courier*, August 9, 1934; U.S. Department of Agriculture, Weather Bureau, *Climatological Data*, South Dakota section, vol. 41, no. 13, 1936, 50; *Bison Courier*, September 3, 1936; Butler, *Faith County Heritage*, 810.

21. *Bison Courier*, February 27, 1936; American Legion Auxiliary, *Eastern Pennington County*, 361; Butler, *Faith Country Heritage*, 822–4; George S. Reeves. *A Man from South Dakota* (New York: E. P. Dutton, 1950), 165–7.

22. Mrs. Delmer King, *Early Settlers in Lyman County* (Pierre, S.D.: State Publishing Company, 1974), 136; Northwest Fall River, *Sunshine and Sagebrush*, 234; Dallas Historical Society, *Dallas, South Dakota*, 139.

23. *Kadoka Press*, August 6, 1931.

24. Roderick Nash, *Wilderness and the American Mind*, rev. ed. (New Haven, Conn.: Yale University Press, 1973), 8–43; Genesis 1:28, 4:19, 8:22.

25. *Dakota Farmer*, January 1, 1931.

26. *Dakota Farmer*, July 7, 1934.

27. *Dakota Farmer*, February 16, May 11, 1935.

28. *Dakota Farmer*, February 10, 1940.

29. Irene Caldwell, ed., *Bad River (Wakpa Sica), Ripples, Rages and Residents* (Fort Pierre, S.D.: Bad River Women's Club, 1983), 182.

30. *Dakota Farmer*, August 3, July 6, 1935.

31. *Dakota Farmer*, September 1, 1934.

32. Reeves, *A Man from South Dakota*, 117. His point of view, though harsh, has struck a responsive chord. South Dakotans have told me that it is the best and most realistic depiction of west river ideology available.

33. Ibid., 143, 146, 149.

34. Ibid., 156, 221, 244.

35. Frank Popper and Deborah Popper, "The Great Plains: From Dust to Dust: A Daring Proposal for Dealing with an Inevitable Disaster," *Planning* 53 (December 1987); Bernie Hunhoff, "Publisher's Letter," *South Dakota Magazine* (January-February 1989): 4–5.

36. Linda Hasselstrom, *Windbreak: A Woman Rancher on the Northern Plains* (Berkeley, California: Barn Owl Books, 1987), 54, 72–73, 168.

37. Winner Chamber of Commerce, *Tripp County*, 39; Butler, *Faith Country Heritage*, 753.

12

Summing Up
Grounds for Identity

DONALD WORSTER

THE RAW MATERIAL FOR THE PAPERS IN THIS VOLUME HAS COME
from what now amounts to a rather long, tangled history. Support
for exploring the history of the Northern Tier comes from the eight
million people who live there, more than half of them dwelling in
the single state of Washington, mainly west of the Cascades, the rest
dispersed over five states that rank among the least densely populated in the nation—thinly spread but still able and willing to support
historical studies and creative minds.

What, besides an increase in scholarship and population, do these
states have to celebrate? Has a common identity emerged over this
century of statehood? Have the people who have come to live in the
six states of the Northern Tier joined with the people living there before 1889 to find a character of their own, setting them apart from
Americans elsewhere? Is there anything unique or distinctive in that
heritage?

In 1889, a large part of the identity of the Northern Tier could have
been summed up in a single image: "Great Northern Railway." It was
the railroad and its maker, James J. Hill, living far off in Minneapolis, who summoned the Northern Tier into being and made statehood
come when and as it did. Part of that early identity was the shipment
of western commodities—wheat, cattle, copper—via the railroad lines
to points east. In the beginning, the Northern Tier was whatever it
could sell to markets elsewhere. Today, we can suggest, that is still
largely the case. The Northern Tier has emerged as a more or less
permanent hinterland.

The concept of a hinterland comes from a Canadian tradition of
scholarship. Simply put, it refers to an area remote from cities and

industry, from the core or heartland of economic and political power, which in turn is conventionally referred to as the "Metropolis."[1] Hinterlands are areas that have grown less rapidly than others; consequently, they are left in a dependent or subordinate position, ruled over, or at least heavily influenced, by the Metropolis. With a few qualifications, that seems to characterize the six states of the Northern Tier. They began largely as an extension of Hill's imagination westward, and they exist now, despite many ambitions to the contrary, as a physically large but politically weak producer of staples for metropolitan consumers.

"Metropolis" refers to an entity that is more than any one city; it includes all the centers of the nation-state and of the industrial economy and of cultural innovation. Traditionally, those centers lay somewhere due east of the Northern Tier—in Minneapolis, Chicago, New York, Washington, London. Over the past hundred years, however, the Metropolis has moved west, and finding it on a map has become more difficult. It has come to include many points south of the Northern Tier—Denver, Dallas, Salt Lake City, Los Angeles, San Francisco—and some farther west, some even within the Tier itself—Boise, Seattle, Vancouver, Tokyo. Commodities move back and forth in those directions, too—and so does capital, and so do workers and ideas.

We can also characterize the Northern Tier as a borderland, an area located on or near an international border, a frontier in the European sense of the word, in this case a border marked "United States-Canada," running more than a thousand miles from the Red River Valley to the Strait of Juan de Fuca, traversing plains, mountains, and salt water, separating (but only just, we are proud to say) two friendly neighbors, really kinfolk. In comparison to the southern borderland shared by the United States and Mexico, this northern one has gotten little attention from historians, though both have had a similar past of imperial struggles between European powers, of declarations of independence and nationality, of confrontations over sovereignty, of migration back and forth. We have no real school of northern borderlands history, no Herbert Bolton or John Francis Bannon for these parts, though a few tentative moves toward a comparative and transnational perspective have been made.

Understanding the six Northern Tier states as they progress into their next century will require focusing on both their hinterland and borderland status, on determining how those two characteristics may have interacted or are interacting now. To do that means learning to think about the geography of these states in new ways as an area standing not only on one end of an east-west axis but also as standing in the middle of a north-south axis. Put another way, the Northern Tier has become more integrated over the past century into the larger region of the American West as it has, to a lesser extent, become more tied to its international neighbors, the western provinces of Canada, and through them to a world of affairs very different from that of, say, Louisiana or Pennsylvania.[2]

It is the first of those points, the Northern Tier's integration with its general region, that I want to examine in more detail. Specifically, I want to suggest that the critical issue left unresolved in this volume is what constitutes the underlying cultural identity of the Northern Tier. I will argue that its identity can only be found by finding the identity of the American West as a whole—that is, by looking southward and asking what it is that holds *all* these states together. What, despite the many hinterland and borderland complications, do they have in the way of common bonds? What does it mean to live in any of them—to be a westerner?

For a long while Americans who came to live in the West—the lands reaching from the plains to the Pacific Coast—were not much troubled by questions of identity. There was little sense of need to find a special character for themselves, to be distinguished from Americans back East. They were simply, unreflectively confident that they were the best the nation had to offer, the advance guard of a rising national giant, the fist thrust boldly into a wilderness. Everywhere they attached names to the landscape that spoke of an uncomplicated assurance that they were preparing the way to the nation's future: the American River, Independence Rock, Virginia City, the state of Washington, the future state of Lincoln, the county of Jefferson, of Lewis, of Clark, of Madison, of Fremont, of Custer, and of Sheridan. The spirit behind that naming was at once intensely nationalistic, devoted to extending the grand entity called America, and egregiously superior, certain that the nation would be reborn in a bigger and better form as it went west.

One could get no better picture of that early devotion to Americanism than by examining the Fourth of July celebrations once held religiously in the western territory. From the days of the first wagon trains down to the twentieth century, it was on that day that westerners affirmed their unequivocal loyalty to the United States of America. In the fervor of their nationalism, they tried hard to put their eastern fellows to shame. William Swain, on his way to the California gold camps, told of one such celebration: July 4, 1849, eight miles below Fort Laramie on the North Platte River. He and his companions on the trail lined up at noon and marched to the tune of "The Star Spangled Banner" toward an improvised reviewing stand, where they stood and listened to a reading of the Declaration of Independence, a patriotic address, and a rendition of "Hail Columbia." Then, in a grand banqueting hall formed by two rows of wagons and a roof of wagon covers, they sat down to gorge on their country's wealth—ham, beans, biscuits, johnnycake, apple pie, sweet cake, rice pudding, pickles, vinegar, pepper sauce and mustard, coffee, sugar, and milk. After that affirmation of American abundance, the toasting commenced, round after round after round. "The boys had raked and scraped together all the brandy they could," wrote Swain, "and they toasted, hurrayed, and drank till reason was out and brandy was in." In all directions from that boisterous scene the high plains stretched silently away, utterly oblivious to their claims; but Swain and company made them anyway, in a strident if inebriated voice: "We are Americans and we will make this place America—and everything we pass on our way to wherever we're going will become America."[3] That was a full forty years before Wyoming became a state, but it may stand for the long hold of a nationalistic sense of identity, one that was still present in 1890 and is still strong at times along the North Platte River today. With William Swain, the westerner as distinctive creature did not yet exist and would not for a long time.

The first dissent from that uncritical nationalism among residents of the western states and the first doubts about who they were began to appear in the last decade of the nineteenth century. Particularly up and down the Great Plains and through the mountain valleys people began to fear that they might not, after all, be the young future-dominating America as they had once hoped—that they might not be wresting power and wealth away from older areas, but might become impoverished waifs, exploited, disinherited, forgotten. We call this moment of doubt the Populist uprising, but it did not end with the defeat of the Populists in 1896. Decade by decade the doubts grew, until by the 1920s and 1930s historians and other intellectuals began to take up the question of where westerners really stood in the national order. The most noted of them was Walter Prescott Webb (b. 1888), a young man from Stephens County, Texas, located in the middle of a triangle formed by Fort Worth, Abilene, and Wichita Falls. The future historian grew up with a strong sense of being far removed from the centers of American influence. "None of the books he read as a child," wrote G. M. Tobin, "told him anything that would suggest that the placid routine he saw around him had any place in the wider experience of the nation as a whole; their frame of reference invariably assumed Eastern or European norms."[4] So Webb set out to write his own books and, in effect, to use history to find out who he was by finding out what his West was and how it was different from the rest of America. Similar motives animated Bernard De Voto of Utah, Joseph Kinsey Howard of Montana, and others in the years between the first and second world wars.

The answer to that quest for identity was the notion of the West as a colony, or "plundered province." Except for California, the one golden child in the regional family, all the western states were seen to be joined together as victims of eastern capital, and the victimizers, men like James J. Hill, took a roasting. This dependent condition was one that, paradoxically, only the eastern-based federal government could set right. And it tried to do so. Stirred by a rising self-consciousness in the West, pressured for recognition and aid, the federal government sent a great flood of dollars to western states during the New Deal; as a consequence, in the postwar period the West began to take off into sustained economic and demographic growth, until it was able to shift the national balance of power considerably its way.[5]

Of course, the growth in status and redistribution of power has been uneven. Most new residents coming into the West during the last half century have moved to the warmer states toward the south. Vast sections of the region have remained rural, sparsely settled, and disadvantaged and are likely to remain so in the foreseeable future.

Idaho is simply never going to become a competitor of southern California, for there are not enough people in the nation to populate it; nor are there enough water resources or accessible lands in Idaho to allow it. A lot of this sparsely settled West, as William Robbins has insisted, is still being plundered.[6] So, to be sure, are Maine, West Virginia, and Indiana; so are rural citizens in every state, along with urban workers, women and children of all races, various people of color, the old, the handicapped, the uneducated—anyone and everyone who is not sitting at the top of the global market economy. What is most remarkable is not the continuing fact of exploitation in many areas, though some westerners have still to accept that fact and deal with it; rather, the most astonishing thing is that all these postwar economic patterns have not stopped the search for identity. On the contrary, it has become more determined and urgent. Westerners may have gone from being the avant-garde of American nationalism to a province plundered by eastern corporations to an integral, sometimes dominating, sometimes subordinate part of global capitalism. But playing a kind of counterpoint to all those shifting relations with the outside world, there has been a steadily increasing tendency for westerners to look within themselves and ask just what sets them apart from others.

If Webb was the first western historian to be self-consciously regional, his progeny are numerous today. There are several hundred members of the Western History Association, founded in 1961; and many more are active in state and local history societies. They are joined by a growing number of novelists and painters, along with advocates of historic preservation and the decorative arts, to form a thinking community in the region that is essential to any quest for distinctiveness. Whatever the West is, its identity is rooted in the past. It will be revealed by historians and artists examining the past and writing about it, in a spirit of sympathy but also of critical detachment. The process of forging an identity is already going on. I think it is safe to say that the imaginations of those historians and artists are no longer out there with William Swain, singing "Hail Columbia" loudly over the Wyoming plains. But what *are* they singing? What *should* they be singing?

A few years ago, I recommended that the search for western identity come down from the wispy, mythic clouds of frontierism, where the talk has been about savages and civilization, virgin land and manifest destiny, and get its feet firmly planted on the ground—that it wedge down to the hard material reality of the region.[7] Specifically, I urged that primacy be given to agriculture and human ecology or to the distinctive ways in which westerners have tried to get their livelihood from the earth. Two such distinctive ways have been widespread over the western states, setting them off from their eastern counterparts: first, an older pastoral mode of sheep and cattle ranching, and second, a later hydraulic mode of controlling water on a large scale for the purposes of irrigated farming, which has brought a more intensive use of land, close rural settlements, and densely packed urban oases. To be sure, those two ways are not wholly self-contained; both are expressions of the larger capitalist order of human and environmental relations, though they respond to regional conditions of climate, water supplies, and vegetation. Nor are the pastoral and hydraulic modes always mutually exclusive, commonly overlapping as they do through much of the country. Nonetheless, they have had different historical associations, different patterns of development, and, for the sake of analysis, can be usefully isolated. Historians who want to contribute fundamentally to our understanding of western identity must, it seems to me, pursue the history of those modes of using the land. In other words, they must become informed about the ecological processes of adaptation that have gone on in this particular part of the world.

I do not mean to argue that a regional identity is determined *only* by that material base. It also is the outcome of the way people *think* about each other and about the place where they live. There is, in other words, an inner cultural history as well as an outer ecological one that must be written about the West, and it is still largely unwritten. We have hardly begun to understand that inner history of the Northern Tier.

One of the reasons I am so enthusiastic about the work of Patricia Nelson Limerick is because she is the first scholar in a long while to pay serious attention to that inner history. Her recent book, *The Legacy of Conquest*, challenges us to transcend all the details of our research to ask more broadly how people in the West have thought and felt in distinctive ways. Specifically, Limerick has asked us to consider what people have thought and felt about each other—what they have thought or felt, or failed to think and feel, when they looked across the racial lines. What she found is a mental life that has gone on apart from, or even in opposition to, the external reality.

> To analyze how white Americans thought about the West, it helps to think anthropologically. One lesson of anthropology is the extraordinary power of cultural persistence; with American Indians, for instance, beliefs and values will persist even when the supporting economic and political structures have vanished. What holds for Indians holds as well for white Americans; the values they attached to westward expansion persist, in cheerful defiance of contrary evidence.[8]

We have not paid enough heed to those tenacious habits of thought, those ways of thinking that defy material reality, that stubbornly persist even when they are inconvenient or expensive or destructive. The persistence of the mentality of racial conquest, Limerick wrote, is the most important of those habits. It has survived even though the conquest has been something of a failure and racial minorities resist the white invaders. Like cowboys riding the range in Toyota pickups, denting their ten-gallon hats against the low cabin roofs, white westerners have not learned how to accept the multi-racial world as it is.

The search for regional identity becomes a little daunting when we try to follow Limerick all the way toward a multi-ethnic, anthropological perspective. We must learn, she urged, to write the cultural history of all the races and ethnicities that have struggled to find a place here, some of them arriving ten, twenty, forty thousand years ago, some only last week. If there is an identity to be found, it cannot be that of the white conquerors acting alone, superimposing their experience, their memories and beliefs, on everyone else. Above all, it is necessary to see that what has made the West distinctive is just this juxtaposition of radically unlike peoples, trying to understand one another or failing to do so—modern Asian-Americans confronting Euro-Americans confronting paleo-Asian-Americans to an extent unmatched anywhere else in the world. History in the West has been a conversation going on in several languages at once.

Undoubtedly, Limerick was on high moral ground when she urged us to approach regional history in this way. The collective experience of whites can no longer be taken as the only important experience in the past. Granting that argument, we are nonetheless left with a predicament. Do we end up finding a truly *common* experience, or do we instead have an experience that is so ethnically diverse, so fragmented, that it defeats the search for a collective regional identity?

The hard truth, it seems to me, is that, in terms of race, there has never been much of a collective western identity. Westerners have never really existed as multi-centered creatures. They have lived within the confines of their various ethnic groups, speaking different languages, expressing different beliefs and values, developing different identities one from another. Whites, for example, have never absorbed the worldview of the Indians, and Indians have never absorbed the worldview of the whites. It may be that someday a western type will emerge who will be the product of many groups interacting over time—who will have been transformed into something new by the experience of trying to penetrate another's point of view. But that composite westerner does not yet exist, nor has it ever appeared in the region's past.

On still another level, Limerick teaches us a useful lesson about approaching the mental history of the West, at least when we confine our analysis to whites only: there has been a tendency here to radically distance one's ideals from the external world to the point of innocence and naivete. Other historians, notably Henry Nash Smith, pointed out the same habit of mind, though more in regard to environmental than social realities.[9] Of course, the habit of mind is not altogether limited to the West, but there is something about this region that seems to intensify the tendency to live in one world while dreaming of or expecting another. The West is characteristically a country of daydreams and fantasies, of visions and nostalgia, where people seem constantly to want to escape from the life they have made for themselves and to enter a life more satisfying to the imagination. Sometimes it is a life in the future. Sometimes it is one receding quickly into the past: a vision of a valley farm in the Rockies; of a cattle drive north from Texas; of buffalo re-emerging from the earth and streaming once again across the prairie; of a boarded-up saloon where the piano still seems to be tinkling in the air. The western mind is full of such fleeting, jumbled bits of memory and romance. I believe an explanation lies in the fact that this has not been a region that grew slowly, organically, out of a long, continuous past; it has been a place of rapid change, repeated dislocation, surreal discontinuities, a place in which time has often seemed to break completely apart, leaving us not with a sense of the steady flow of experience but of vivid moments crashing along one after another. It has been a land in which the same man, as a boy, might have watched Billy the Kid ride through town on his way to a shootout and, as an old-timer, watched a radioactive mushroom cloud rise ominously on the horizon. No wonder that beliefs and dreams have often been so divorced from material reality. How could they possibly have kept pace? Things have moved too swiftly for that.

When we enter the realm of the western political imagination, the disjunction between fantasy and reality becomes especially sharp. We have not yet written a full history of the western political imagination; when we do, we will begin to appreciate just how sharp the disjunction has been and where and to what extent the westerner has diverged from the American mainstream. He has been eager to acquire a piece of land and to use it without any interference from any other individual, group, or institution. It is not a desire that the West altogether invented, for it existed in the white man's mind before Lewis and Clark, before the Constitution. We might call it the "Lockean imperative," for it is the notion described by John Locke in the early eighteenth century that a man defines himself primarily by laboring to acquire and develop a piece of property, taking it out of a state of wildness and into one of cultivation. It is the idea that what we own is solely the result of our personal efforts and has nothing of anyone else in it. It is the theory that all our freedoms and rights come from the ownership of property and that a free society is one in which men have been most free to acquire and use their property as they see fit. That kind of thinking reached a peak of influence during the middle and later nineteenth century, just as the American people were crossing the great rivers to cash in the biggest real estate bonanza ever. If we accept Louis Hartz's argument that new societies take their identity from whatever ideas happen to be ascendant at the time of their founding, then the western society was shaped indelibly by the idea of property acquisitiveness.[10] To paraphrase Hartz, westerners, unfurling the golden banner of Horatio Alger, marched into the Promised Land after the Civil War and never wanted to leave it. In the West, they hoped to acquire land and resources, exercise their entrepreneurial talents, rise to riches—and they needed no other end, no other principle of life.

But not long after the first waves of settlement and of statehood, the region began to have another set of values foisted on it by an eastern America that had not stood still but had gone on to explore new ideas and principles. Beginning in 1891, the federal government began to withdraw lands in the West from private entry and to set them aside, in perpetuity, as a great public commons. The first such move was the Forest Reserve Act, which in a few years had permitted the withdrawal of thirty-four million acres of forested lands, all in the West. The idea of forming such a commons out of the public domain came primarily from a group called the American Forestry Association, whose members were mainly easterners inspired by European ideas of socialized forestry and land use. They had begun to call for a revision of the old Lockean view, to demand that the land be put under collective ownership and supervision. With the presidency of Theodore Roosevelt, that new kind of thinking expanded, and it continued to expand as the federal government withdrew more and more lands from private entry and even began purchasing private lands to add to the commons. Today there are 740 million acres—one-third of the nation—under federal control. Some of those lands are forests, some parks, some grazing districts, and so forth. Overwhelmingly, they are in the western states and Alaska. Thirty-seven per cent of the state of Montana has been taken out of the reach of Horatio Alger and John Locke, along with 65 per cent of Idaho, 45 per cent of California, and 73 per cent of Arizona.

The implications for westerners in that course of events have been more profound than we have ever quite realized. It has put the region into a terrible ideological bind. Nowhere else on earth has the conflict between the old Lockean faith in free property as the guarantor of free men and the new faith in collective ownership as the promise of a secure society been so fiercely drawn.

It is instructive to compare this inter-regional conflict with that other, more famous one between the North and the South. The struggle that led to the Civil War was over the question of chattel slavery: Did one group of people have the right to own another as their property? The struggle between the West and the East has been over the question of privatization of the land: Did any set of individuals have the right to take control of all the land acquired by the nation as a whole? The South lost its struggle and, though more or less acknowledging its moral errors, has never quite forgiven the North. By now, of course, the West has lost its war, too; the public lands have become permanently public and they are going to remain so, more than likely in federal hands, for as far into the future as we can see. No sagebrush rebels have managed to reverse that outcome. But the wounds of defeat run deep, and resentments are never far from the surface. Many westerners are still fighting for their glorious lost cause.

The land has entered into western identity in more subtle and complicated ways than as property to be owned and fought over. In fact, it is to *all* of the influences of the land, especially to all of the peculiarities of the western landscape, that one must finally turn to understand the innermost history of the region—not only for its dominant white majority but for all of its peoples. In a sense, westerners have been conversing with the land as well as with each other, and their imaginations have been altered by that conversation beyond easy telling.

For almost everyone who has come into this country in modern times the land of the West has jolted the mind and tried the body. Very little of it has seemed designed for human ease. Even in these days of fast automobiles, the high plains are a trial of patience and a defiance to occupation. The mountains farther west are among the highest and most rugged on the planet—awesomely beautiful to contemplate but hellishly difficult to get over. And then there are the stark, hostile deserts of the interior, a landscape that people still find hard to love, one that has often drawn the angry, the misfitted, the rejected, the alienated. Everywhere in the region there is so much space—so much of an amplitude of rugged rock, soil, climate, and vista—that the landscape, like the gods of old, can leave men and women feeling humbled or diminished, threatened or exhilarated.

Many of the first white comers, men like William Swain, brought with them dreams of extravagant abundance—gold waiting to be plucked from the bottoms of streams. But the almost universal reality has been that the gold is an abundance that runs out fast, and then there follows an extreme privation that can be deadly. Unlike other regions, the lasting impact of encountering the western landscape has not been to encourage a sense of effortless abundance. On the contrary, this has been, in so many times and places, a land of scarcity, defying American expectations, American experience elsewhere.

Still, for all its difficult traits, the land has entered into people's identities and affections in ways that defy rational analysis or the tests of logic. Almost every western state, for example, has put some representation of the land, often a dramatic feature of its landscape or the products of its soil, on its automobile license plates—"Big Sky Country," "Land of Enchantment," the "Grand Canyon State"—or they show a potato, a mountain skyline, a shock of wheat. Some of those icons clearly indicate an attitude of human domination over nature, as in the case of Wyoming, where the license plate figure is of a cowboy trying to break the independent spirit of a wild horse, one of the West's favorite images of itself, repeated endlessly in the rituals of rodeo combat. Perhaps all of those badges of self-identification are similarly laden with a spirit of domination to some degree, like trophies carried home from battle, announcing to the world that an army has come to conquer and, despite the size of the foe, has succeeded. Perhaps there is also some darkly chauvinistic face of regionalism being uttered in those symbols, a claim that has all the belligerence and intolerance of nationalist or ethnocentric assertion elsewhere. But I think there is also something *accepting* in them—an embrace of the harshness, the grandeur, the numinous beauty of the land. More than they can quite express or know how to acknowledge, westerners have become attached to this place. They feel a part of it. They want to carry some totem of it with them wherever they travel.

You will seldom find this sense of attachment articulated in the halls of politics, for politicians, like businessmen or engineers or accountants, do not commonly deal in such matters. Writers, on the other hand, commonly do. They try to penetrate and express, through image, character, and narrative, the inner history of people; and because art requires experience, they write about the inner history of the people they know, the people they live with and among. When we turn to the art of the region's writers, we find a world of clues as to what the land means to westerners.

What I find expressed in western writing is, first, a strong sense of the embeddedness of human life in the cycles and patterns of nature and, second, a fascination with the distinctive psychological content of western landscapes. White or Indian, male or female, these writers do not generally describe a human condition that is deeply, decisively cultural, bound and limited by the cumulative experience of generation following generation. Instead, they tell us about humans trying to live in places where the scale of time is so far beyond recorded history as to seem timeless. They tell us about individuals going out to make a small impact on that timelessness, often failing and disappearing, abandoning their shacks and letting them fall into disrepair, leaving their cliff dwellings empty and silent, allowing their family bones to become jumbled and lost. Even now, in writings that deal more with cities, industry, and technology, human achievement seems ephemeral in the West, the cycles of nature utterly imposing. Outsiders as well as natives have come to that same conclusion of the futility of victory. Writer John McPhee of New Jersey, searching for the annals of a former world in Wyoming, quoted geologist David Love: "If there was one thing we learned, it was that you don't fight nature. You live with it. And you make the accommodations—because nature does not accommodate." [11]

My point is not that every westerner has actually learned that lesson of humility, for they have not. The point is that it has seemed to many to be *the* lesson to learn from dwelling in the West, a lesson taught by the dense abiding presence of the Cretaceous, the Permian, the Cambrian, by all the forces of rock and wind and dust, of mountain building and tearing down, of fires raging through a forest and drought searing the grasslands. This is a lesson the rest of America might come here to learn.

In the face of such natural power and persistence it seems quite illusory to insist on human domination over the earth. No modern writer has expressed that point better than Wallace Stegner in his famous letter on wilderness written almost thirty years ago:

While we were demonstrating ourselves the most efficient and ruthless environment-busters in history, and slashing and burning and cutting our way through a wilderness continent, the wilderness was working on us. It remains in us as surely as Indian names remain on the land. If the abstract dream of human liberty and human dignity became, in America, something more than an abstract dream, mark it down at least partially to the fact that we were in subtle ways subdued by what we conquered.[12]

Stegner was talking about all of America in that passage, but he was talking as a westerner, one already steeped for a half-century in the region, and he was looking at the American experience as a westerner is apt to do. For writers in Pittsburgh or Charleston, experience may look different. But to Stegner, as to so many western writers, the land has been and is of the first importance. It stands boldly, implacably in the foreground of experience, too wild really to tame, too old to change, too large to reduce to a mere human scale. Confronting the land, being subdued by it, westerners have found the beginnings of an identity.

Will the next hundred years produce in the Northern Tier states a different set of defining characteristics, making them more like places elsewhere in the world or less so, more distinctive or less, or distinctive in new ways? On the one hand, we are warned that the West may eventually disappear, as all regions may, into the homogenized, featureless world of the multinationals, the bureaucracies, the technocrats. On the other hand, we can see that people seem to be looking more intensely than ever for a sense of distinctiveness and rootedness, which regions like the West can satisfy. We will have to wait a while to see which tendency wins out. In the meantime, we have a deeper history to write than any of us has yet imagined.

Notes

1. The concept owes much to political economist Harold Innis. See, for example, his *The Fur Trade in Canada: An Introduction to Canadian Economic History* (New Haven, Conn.: Yale University Press, 1930); *The Cod Fisheries: The History of an International Economy* (New Haven, Conn.: Yale University Press, 1946). A good recent introduction is L. D. McCann, "Heartland and Hinterland: A

Framework for Regional Analysis," in *Heartland and Hinterland: A Geography of Canada*, ed. L. D. McCann (Scarborough, Ontario: Prentice-Hall Canada, 1982), 2–35. See also J. M. S. Careless, "Frontierism, Metropolitanism, and Canadian History," *Canadian Historical Review* 33 (March 1954): 1–21.

2. Robin Fisher, "Duff and George Go West: A Tale of Two Frontiers," *Canadian Historical Review* 68 (December 1987): 501–28; David H. Breen, "The Turner Thesis and the Canadian West: A Closer Look at the Ranching Frontier," in *Essays on Western History*, ed. Lewis H. Thomas (Edmonton: University of Alberta Press, 1976); Dough Owram, *Promise of Eden: The Canadian Expansionist Movement and the Idea of the West, 1856–1900* (Toronto: University of Toronto Press, 1980).

3. J. S. Holliday, *The World Rushed In: The California Gold Rush Experience* (New York: Simon and Schuster, 1981), 167.

4. G. M. Tobin, "Landscape, Region, and the Writing of History: Walter Prescott Webb in the 1920s," *American Studies International* 16 (Summer 1978): 10.

5. I made this point in terms of federal development of water resources in my book, *Rivers of Empire: Water, Aridity, and the Growth of the American West* (New York: Pantheon Books, 1985). Gerald D. Nash argued that it was military investment during World War II that was decisive; see his *The American West Transformed: The Impact of the Second World War* (Bloomington: Indiana University Press, 1985), chap. 2.

6. William Robbins, "The 'Plundered Province' Thesis and the Recent Historiography of the American West," *Pacific Historical Review* 55 (November 1986): 577–98.

7. Donald Worster, "New West, True West: Interpreting the Region's History," *Western Historical Quarterly* 18 (April 1987): 141–56.

8. Patricia Nelson Limerick, *The Legacy of Conquest: The Unbroken Past of the American West* (New York: W. W. Norton, 1987), 35–36.

9. Henry Nash Smith, *Virgin Land: The American West as Symbol and Myth* (Cambridge, Mass.: Harvard University Press, 1950), chaps. 11–19.

10. Louis Hartz, *The Liberal Tradition in America* (New York: Harcourt, Brace & World, 1955), esp. chaps. 1 and 8. Chapter 8 describes the evolution of liberal thought during the post-Civil War years, when the main influx of settlers came to the West and began to form its institutions and define its cultural norms.

11. John McPhee, *Rising from the Plains* (New York: Farrar, Straus, Giroux, 1986), 104.

12. Wallace Stegner, "Coda: Wilderness Letter," in *The Sound of Mountain Water* (Lincoln: University of Nebraska, 1980), 147–8.

Index

Contributors

LEONARD ARRINGTON is Lemuel Redd Professor of Western History Emeritus at Brigham Young University, Provo, Utah, and is a specialist in western economic history. He is the author of numerous books, including *Great Basin Kingdom: An Economic History of the Latter-Day Saints, 1830–1900* (1958) and *Brigham Young: American Moses* (1985).

CAROLE BARRETT is Assistant Professor of Indian Studies at the University of Mary in Bismarck, North Dakota. Barrett is a specialist in Indian education and is the recipient of several regional and state humanities awards.

ROLAND L. DE LORME is Professor of History and Assistant Vice-President for Academic Affairs at Western Washington University, Bellingham. DeLorme has written several articles on western legal and criminal history and is completing *Crime and Punishment on the American Frontier: A Research Guide* for Greenwood Press.

JOHN C. HUDSON is Professor of Geography at Northwestern University, Evanston, Illinois, and is the author of several studies of land use and railroads, including *Geographical Diffusion Theory* (1972) and *Plains Country Towns* (1985).

WILLIAM L. LANG is Director of the Center for Columbia River History for the Washington State Historical Society in Vancouver, Washington. Lang is co-author of *Montana: Our Land and People* with Rex Myers (1979) and *Montana: A History of Two Centuries* with Michael P. Malone and Richard B. Roeder (revised edition, 1991).

WILLIAM E. LASS is Professor of History and Director of the Southern Minnesota Historical Center at Mankato State University. Lass is the author of *Minnesota: A Bicentennial History* (1977), *A History of Steamboating on the Upper Missouri River* (1962), and *From the Missouri to the Great Salt Lake: An Account of Overland Freighting* (1972).

PAULA M. NELSON is Assistant Professor of History at Clarke College in Dubuque, Iowa. Nelson is the author of several cultural studies of the Midwest and of the W. Turrentine Jackson award-winning *After the West Was Won: Homesteaders and Townbuilders in Western South Dakota, 1900–1917* (1986).

FRANK POMMERSHEIM is Professor of Law at the University of South Dakota School of Law. Pommersheim serves as Associate Justice for the Cheyenne River Sioux Tribal Court of Appeals and is the author of *South Dakota Tribal Handbook* (1988).

DONALD READING is a private economic consultant on utility regulation in Boise, Idaho. Reading is the author of several articles on western economic history and is a former student of Leonard Arrington's at Brigham Young University.

KENT D. RICHARDS is Professor of History and Associate Dean of Graduate Studies and Research at Central Washington University, Ellensburg. Richards is a specialist in western political history and is the author of *Isaac I. Stevens: Young Man in a Hurry* (1979).

WILLIAM G. ROBBINS is Professor of History at Oregon State University and is the author of several books on western economic and environmental history, including *Hard Times in Paradise: Coos Bay, Oregon* (1988) and *Lumberjacks and Legislators: Political Economy of the Lumber Industry, 1890–1941* (1982).

W. THOMAS WHITE is Curator of the James J. Hill Papers at the James Jerome Hill Reference Library in St. Paul, Minnesota. White writes on railroad and labor history and is the editor of the *Great Northern Railway Company Papers* (1985), *James J. Hill Papers*, and *Northern Pacific Company Papers* (1985).

DONALD WORSTER is Professor of History at the University of Kansas, Lawrence, and is a specialist in environmental history. Worster's books include *Nature's Economy: A History of Ecological Ideas* (1967), *Dust Bowl: The Southern Plains in the 1930s* (1979), which won the Bancroft Prize, and *Rivers of Empire: Water, Aridity, and the Growth of the American West* (1985).

JOHN WUNDER is Professor of History and Director of the Center for Great Plains Studies at the University of Nebraska. Wunder has written extensively on constitutional and legal history and is the author of *Inferior Courts, Superior Justice: Justices of the Peace on the Northwest Frontier, 1853–1889* (1979), and *Historians of the American Frontier* (1988).